# Twin Souls

## A message of hope for the new millennium

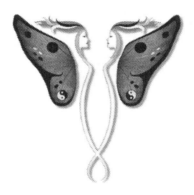

## ELIZABETH ANNE HILL

Cover Art by Kat Eaton

**Twin Souls—A Message of Hope for the New Millennium**
© 2007 Elizabeth Anne Hill
1st Edition

Page composition/typography and cover design: Lisa Bonnice
Cover art: Kat Eaton

Hill, Elizabeth A., 1965
ISBN: 978-0-9798628-0-9

1. Spiritual          2. Self-help          I. Title          II. Hill, Elizabeth Anne

Manufactured in the United States of America
10   9   8   7   6   5   4   3   2   1

**www.gateway4thegoldenage.com**
**www.catherinehillfoundation.org**

To John —
with lots of love!
Nadine

# Table of Contents

# Acknowledgements

I am eternally grateful for the love and guidance of my team in spirit: my twin sister, Catherine; my father, Howard; my mother, Gloria; and my guides, angels, and masters. I feel you all rooting for me every step of the way.

To my dear brother, Mike, who inspired me to begin writing *Twin Souls*, I say, "Fight on, brother." To my younger sister, Katy, who is far away at the moment, I say, "You are always in my heart." To Jack Didelot, I say, "You played your role like a pro. Thank you for being the yang to my yin."

I want to thank Midge Raymond, my brilliant editor, friend, and kindred spirit. Thank you to Lisa Bonnice, another kindred spirit, who helped me through the hurdles of self-publishing. Words cannot express the gratitude I feel for the amazing people who supported me when I needed it most and who encouraged me to follow my life's path. There are too many to mention here, but you will read about many of these special people in this book.

I want to thank the many mentors whose books inspired and guided me: Paramahansa Yogananda, Neale Donald Walsch, Wayne Dyer, Doreen Virtue, Nick Bunick, G.W. Hardin and Joseph Crane, Gary Zukav, Sanaya Roman, Marianne Williamson, Deepak Chopra, Michael Newton, Betty Eadie, Elizabeth Clare Prophet, Brian Weiss, Thom Hartmann, Gregg Braden, and many others.

I am blessed with many miracles in my life, and I thank God for each and every one of them.

Elizabeth Anne Hill

This book is dedicated to
Bubba, Lou, Josh, and all "Cathy's kids"

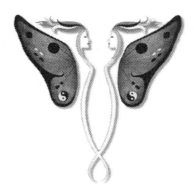

# Part One — The Story

"Why, God? What did I do wrong to deserve this?" I pleaded. My mind wandered backward in time to December 1986. At the age of twenty-one, I had lost my mother after her long, difficult battle with lung cancer. Now this. My twin sister, United States Border Patrol Agent Catherine Mary Hill, was dead at the age of thirty-seven, after her vehicle tumbled down a steep embankment.

I had always been the strong one in the family. I handled all things stoically and certainly never allowed myself to fall apart. But this—this was too much. I felt despair so deep that it was physically painful.

But somewhere in the back of my mind, a bell was ringing. Even in my desperation I felt a strange nagging sensation from the back of my consciousness. I thought about the days before my mother had died. She kept saying, "Look, don't you see them? They're so beautiful." We didn't know it then, but she was trying to tell us that she was seeing beings of light and angels coming to get her.

Now Cathy was gone, and I somehow felt that she too was trying to tell me something. She had been reading spiritual books before she died that had touched her deeply. She had begun working with homeless and troubled youth and felt she had found her purpose. Unlike her usual intense demeanor, she had seemed so happy and lighthearted in the days preceding her death. I knew that there was some point to all of it—but what was it?

As time passed, something remarkable began to emerge. My sister Cathy was there. She had not left me. I felt her and heard her talking to me, and I knew it was not my imagination.

Then the dreams began, and I realized that I was having very detailed conversations in my sleep. With whom, I wasn't sure. I woke up and saw blue lights near my bed and heard someone say, "There is a message."

I found the stacks of books she left behind and began reading them. I was stunned because I was learning firsthand that death does not exist. I was learning that life is much more than I thought it was.

Unlike most twins, Cathy and I had been opposites throughout our lives. We argued about everything, including politics, religion, spirituality, life, death, right and wrong, left and right. You name it—we fought about it. Now an unusual thing was happening. Across the supposed boundaries of life and death, we were coming together on these issues.

I suddenly felt exactly as my sister had at the end of her life. She wanted desperately to share her newfound wisdom with others, but most people would not listen, including me. But now I wanted more than anything for someone to see what I was seeing, and so I began to write.

Suddenly I felt a universal presence so immense that it took my breath away. Fueled by this unexpected source of energy, I read every spiritual book I could find, and I wrote down everything, including the words that I knew came directly from my sister. She did have a message for me and for the world, and I was the one to deliver it. Little did I know that over the next five years my twin sister

2

would lead me on an incredible journey full of wonder, wisdom, and astounding revelations.

Through the seemingly tragic death of my twin sister, I found my life's purpose. In fact, we found our combined life purpose. My question, "Why, God?" was answered with a resounding, "Bring the love back to the world." We brought the love back to our relationship by seeing the larger truths behind our opposing viewpoints, and our grandest vision is that the world will do the same.

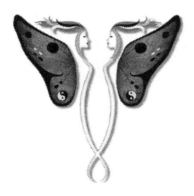

## Chapter One:
## Devastating News

October 25, 2002, started off like any other day. I got ready for work as a San Diego Police Department 911 dispatcher. I prepared my lunch, jumped in the shower, threw on some casual clothes, grabbed my ID badge, and headed downtown.

My shift was to begin at 2:30 p.m. I arrived thirty minutes early and began setting up my computer console. Paula, head administrator for police communications, appeared and asked me to follow her to the chief's office. I gulped. The chief's office. That was a highly unusual request. I couldn't imagine what the chief wanted to say to me.

As we rode the elevator, Paula seemed apprehensive, not her usual, authoritative self. I racked my brain. Maybe I had saved someone's life and I was going to get a commendation. Maybe I had caused someone's death by moving too slowly on a 911 call. But I knew that the chief would not handle these matters. As my thoughts raced, Paula asked if my husband was home. That was an odd question. My husband, Jack Didelot, a San Diego Police Sergeant, was home. He told me later that he was just getting ready to leave but for some reason he waited. Then he got my phone call.

By the time I made it to the chief's office, my knees were knocking. I could hardly breathe. The news I was about to receive would knock the wind out of me. I was told that the chief, David Bejarano, was at a meeting but was on his way back to see me. I watched Paula walk into Assistant Chief Gonzalez's office. He jumped to his feet. Both of them looked at me. I had an eerie feeling. It seemed as if everything was in slow motion. Every detail of the room passed before my eyes.

Then I saw the Chief of the Border Patrol for the San Diego sector, William T. Veal, his deputy chief, and another grim-faced member of Border Patrol brass walking toward me. What had Cathy done? Were they investigating her for something? Catherine Hill, Border Patrol Agent and my twin sister, was forever getting into trouble for some minor infraction like losing her binoculars and not reporting it quickly enough. But that wouldn't make sense. Why were they here waiting to talk to me in the office of the police chief? I remember looking down at my black sweats and white t-shirt. I thought I was underdressed to be in the chief's office.

Finally, I was ushered into a large conference room with a very long table. I still did not understand what was happening. Then time stopped. Border Patrol Chief Veal said the words that would forever change my life:  "There has been a tragic accident."

I couldn't believe what I was hearing. My vibrant, lively, and constantly-on-the-move twin sister was dead? This was impossible to comprehend. I had just seen her a week before. She was excited because she was going to start a master's degree program in counseling. Her newly found passion was to work with troubled kids.

By this time, Chief Bejarano had arrived. I sat in his corner office waiting for my husband to pick me up. My mind wandered to my mother. I couldn't decide what was worse, my mother's death to a long illness, or this sudden, crushing loss. I was vaguely aware that the people surrounding me represented the top level of law enforcement in San Diego. I didn't care. Frustrated, I asked why she had to die doing a thankless job no one really appreciated. They had no answers.

Chief Veal told me that the Border Patrol Peer Support Team would be stationed outside my house overnight in case I needed anything. My sister had been a Peer Support Team member.

Ironically, she had recently returned from the funeral of a fellow Border Patrol Agent from Florida who had died in an on-duty vehicle accident. She had received a commendation from U.S. Attorney General John Ashcroft for her role in helping the family of the fallen agent.

She told me about the agent's military-style funeral: the riderless horse, the bagpipes playing their mournful rendition of "Amazing Grace," the helicopter fly-by in "missing-man" formation, the 21-gun salute, the white-gloved honor guards carrying the flag-draped coffin, the haunting radio call that no one answered, and, finally, the seemingly endless procession of law enforcement vehicles, lights flashing, making their way to the gravesite.

Cathy loved the pomp and circumstance and the reverence of law enforcement funerals. She thought it was a good way to symbolize the deep loss agents feel when a fellow agent or officer is killed in the line of duty. She told me that if she died on the job, she wanted a send-off like that. Little did either of us know how soon I would be accommodating her wish.

Weeks later, at her funeral, the radio call hung in the air. "India 327, Agent Hill?" Silence. "India 327, Agent Hill?" Silence. "India 327, Agent Hill?" Silence. Then "All units, India 327 is 10-42." I-327 was Cathy's Border Patrol radio call sign. In police jargon "10-42" means "gone home." Catherine Hill had gone home. I had never heard silence sound so loud.

U.S. Border Patrol Honor Guard at the funeral of Catherine Hill

But in those few moments I looked out the window of the chief's office at the bright blue San Diego sky and wondered what God's plan was for her now. I felt great sorrow for my loss, but somehow I knew on a much deeper level that there was an important reason for her death. I know now that her death at the border barrier fence with Mexico is symbolic of the difficult issues facing our world.

My husband finally arrived and escorted me out of the chief's office to a line of people waiting to extend their condolences. As we drove away, I realized that my twin sister was gone, just like that, forever...or so I thought.

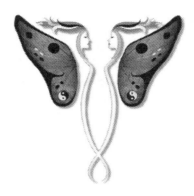

## Chapter Two:
## The Hill Family

### Growing Up

It was March 1965. My mother, Gloria, was pregnant with my sister and me. It seemed the battle had already begun. We were constantly kicking. My mother felt as though a rumble were going on inside her womb. I was supposed to be born first, but I got my arm stuck. My feisty twin had won by default and was born via C-section. I suspect she knew even then that she would leave the world ahead of me and managed to push her way out first.

We were born in the small town of Morehead, Kentucky, to Howard and Gloria Hill, both classical musicians. My father taught music at Morehead State College. We came into the world in a small Catholic hospital. We were the first twins ever born there and the smallest babies they had seen. We each weighed 2 pounds, 11 ounces. As the story goes, the people from the Kentucky hills came to the hospital on Saturday night to help pick names for the twins. I'm glad my parents didn't take the most popular suggestion: Molly and Polly.

The doctor told my parents that my sister and I were not expected to live. We were too small to sustain life.

One of the nuns suggested we be named after English queens in order to appear more elegant on our tombstones, hence the names Elizabeth Anne and Catherine Mary. The nuns kept a vigil at our bedsides twenty-four hours a day for several days. In the end, we survived. My mother said she thought this was how we became so ornery. We had to fight to survive. Eleven months later, we got a brother, Michael Andrew Albert. The English royalty idea had stuck.

In 1967 our father took a job at San Diego State College (now San Diego State University). We moved to San Diego and lived in a small rented house near the college. My mother taught music part-time at the college and was a violinist for the San Diego Symphony.

In 1969 we moved to a large house in La Mesa, a suburb of San Diego. My parents scraped together the money for the $40,000 purchase price. The house, built for a famous opera singer, was a historical landmark built on two acres of land in 1911. We found pictures stuffed in the bookcase that showed our house alone on the hill back when all of La Mesa was just dirt. There was a horse-drawn carriage parked in front.

The house was made of cherry wood and oak. A balcony overlooked the living room with a 20-foot ceiling. On one side of the room was a stage where my parents put a grand piano. On the other side was a hearth with a stone fireplace where we used to put our Christmas tree and hang our stockings.

It was a wonderful place to grow up, with a natural rock pool, a tree house, and a tire swing in our backyard. The property was full of hiding places. The man who owned the house before us had been in the military. We found an army helmet and a plane propeller in a room above the old stables. My brother, sister, cousin Mela, and I used to play for hours around the stables. We imagined an old man from World War II had built a bomb shelter somewhere in the yard and was still living there.

Mike, Betsy and Cathy

Our house had two basements. One day we were in the front basement looking for the underground tunnel when suddenly someone knocked on the wall. We screamed bloody murder and ran out of the basement. Later we found out my father was on the other side in the back basement. He heard us talking about a man living in a shelter and decided it would be funny to knock on the wall. We hadn't figured out the two basements were connected. My poor cousin Mela was always terrified after that. She was also afraid of my father, who was rather gruff at times.

My parents often went overboard at Christmastime. One year my mother decorated the entire house in the theme of an old-fashioned Christmas. Another year she made us go on a scavenger hunt on which we found three bikes under the house. Mike got the blue bike, Cathy got red, and I got green.

My mother loved to have parties. One of her extravagant Halloween parties featured a haunted house in the basement. She led us blindfolded to an assortment of nasty-feeling things like grapes for eyeballs and raw meat for brains. Then we were taken to the stables, where spooky music was playing. She hired college students from her music class to jump out and scare us. True to form, our cousin Mela got so scared she ran out of the stables sobbing.

I have many wonderful memories of our lives growing up in San Diego. My parents were both talented violinists and were often practicing, teaching students, or had classical music playing throughout the house.

My father used to cram all of us into his old Porsche and drive us to the beach and tennis club, where he played tennis while we ran around the park for hours. He took us to the beach and taught us to body surf in the ocean. Afterward he always took us out for burritos and ice cream.

Looking back, I realize why I don't have many early memories of my mother. She taught at the college during the day and played with the symphony nights and weekends. She was the kind of person who gave of herself and rarely got anything in return. She was known for her desire to help others. I believe my sister got her spirit of charity from my mother, who once took in two Vietnamese women who had fled their country during the Vietnam War. My mother allowed them to live in a small guest cottage on our property, originally a maid's quarters. Another time she took pity on a homeless teenager. Every day she came home from the Goodwill or Salvation Army store with more clothes for him. She paid him to do chores around our yard and fed him lunch and dinner.

The summer before my sister and I went into the eighth grade, my mother planned a trip to drive from San Diego to New York. This was a dream come true for her. She would get to spend time with her family and see the country. She hoped her three kids would learn something along the way.

We were not interested in an educational trip. All we wanted to do was go to the beach with our friends. The three of us complained and argued all the way across the country. My mother was so disappointed.

One problem was our mother's embarrassing behavior. We were horrified when we saw her walking down the street in New York City with her big bag of sweaters, maps, and a camera, waving her arms, yelling, "Yoo hoo, kids." She would stand in the middle of the sidewalk and open up her map while people pushed past her.

The Hill family at the Continental Divide

My brother Mike was a lot of fun but he was at that age where he gleeful enjoyed teasing me or my sister. The more annoyed we became by his antics, the more he would push our buttons. Cathy and I were famous all our lives for our constant bickering back and forth. My dad would yell at us in the back seat, "You two ladies sound like truck drivers," if we were talking too loudly and forcefully, which was often. My brother would imitate a truck driver with his hands on the wheel, driving down the road: "Bubabubaba."

In high school, our greatest concern was making the cheerleading team. I was traumatized during junior varsity cheer tryouts when I hurt my knee and did not make the squad. My sister did and I was devastated.

The heartache continued when Cathy made the varsity squad the next year, and I made junior varsity. I became the captain of the junior varsity squad, but people never seemed to tire of asking me why I didn't make varsity like my sister.

Elizabeth "Betsy" Hill

Catherine "Cathy" Hill

Finally in our senior year, we both made the varsity squad. I will never forget the high school dance at which the winners were announced. I was called second. It was down to the last name, and my sister's name hadn't been called. Now it was her turn to bawl her eyes out, and I was in great agony. But her name was called. The thrill of running out together in our beautiful blue-and-gold uniforms—under the lights, in front of the cheering crowd—was a feeling like no other.

14

After high school, Cathy and I attended San Diego State University. Cathy studied Business Management, and I majored in Communication. We became little sisters in a fraternity. Both of us were meandering through life without an inkling of our life purpose.

## The Death of Our Mother

One night in 1984, I came home from college and found my parents sitting in the den. I started chattering about my college health class, and I noticed my mother was acting rather strangely. I told her we had done a test to analyze our diet, and I had found out about some areas where I was lacking. She said in a quiet voice, "I hope I didn't cause you to be missing those things." That was odd. My mother was usually so upbeat, even silly at times.

Then my mother dropped a bomb on me. She told me she had lung cancer. My whole life changed at that moment. I went from being a happy-go-lucky person to one who had definite worries. I felt as if I were in the middle of a bad dream. The nightmare of my mother's illness went on for two years.

My mother had gone to the doctor complaining of shortness of breath. The radiologist told the doctor he saw something on the X-ray of my mother's lung, but the doctor insisted he didn't see it. Finally a CAT scan was ordered. My mother never followed up to find out if there was a problem. I think she was too afraid. No one contacted her to give her the results. Eighteen months later, she went in for a routine checkup. The doctor checked the CAT scan he had ordered more than a year before. He realized my mother did have something on her lung that appeared to be cancer. She was scheduled for immediate surgery.

My poor mother was so scared. She had no one to talk to; we were all so terrified we avoided the subject. My grandmother went with my mother to her doctor's appointments. After the surgery, the surgeon left the hospital without informing us of her prognosis.

I will never forget the scene we made in the hospital. My friend Martha, who had grown up across the street, had lost her mother to cancer. She screamed at the nurse to get the doctor on the phone. They didn't seem moved by our agony and desperation. Martha lashed out at one of the nurses, "How would you feel if your mother had cancer?"

Finally the doctor called and said, "Yes, it is malignant," and that was all. He hung up. I will never forget the sinking feeling that I had inside. I don't remember what my brother and sister were doing or how they found out, but I knew my mother was going to die.

My mother made the decision not to have chemotherapy or radiation. She had been reading about some alternative cures offered in Mexico. When I heard she was going to do the alternative, natural therapy, I got in the kitchen, cleaned out the refrigerator, and began making the food that was part of the special diet. My father took a second mortgage out on our house and took her to a clinic in Mexico. Apparently the treatment worked for some people, but it did not work for my mother. The idea was to cleanse the body of all toxins so it would fight back against the cancer. The patients were not allowed any painkiller except aspirin. She was in severe pain all the time.

My mother was the worrying type; she always expected the worst thing to happen. The worst thing did happen: She was not getting better. She was withering away. With nothing left to do, she came home. At this point, her treatment was outside the American medical system. She did not want to go back to the doctors who had treated her so badly.

The doctor who had treated her in Mexico sent her home with an IV in her hand and gave her some morphine. She had a bell by her chair in her room. In

16

middle of the night, she would ring the bell. I would jump out of bed and go down to give her the pain medication. She would be writhing in pain, and I would have to very slowly inject the morphine into the IV so as not to hurt her vein. She would sit back in her chair in relief when the morphine would finally hit her system and temporarily take away the pain.

One day she had a terrible allergic reaction to the painkillers and got hives all over her body. I didn't know what to do. I didn't want to take her back to her original doctor who had misdiagnosed her. I called my friend Martha, whose father was an anesthesiologist. He made a phone call and got her into the hospital where he worked. She was so horrified for anyone to see her as she was. She had lost so much weight that she was a skeleton compared to her former self. But she slowly got into the shower and got ready to go to the hospital. She knew it would be her last trip.

I couldn't imagine life without my mother. But I knew that was the reality. I was always the strong one in the family. I told my sister our mother was not going to live. She screamed at me, "You bitch! You are such a pessimist." I told her I wasn't a pessimist; I was a realist.

After a few days in the hospital, it seemed my mother's condition had improved. The allergic reaction was halted, and she received some better pain medication. But the doctor said that the cancer had metastasized.

She kept trying to tell us something. She would point to the end of the bed and say, "Look, don't you see them? They are so beautiful!" We thought she was hallucinating. As time passed, my mother was less and less lucid. She had a lot of pain, so the doctors continued to increase the pain medication to the point at which she was in a semi-coma. I was surprised when she suddenly sat up and asked if I would order her a hamburger. She was talking just like she used to. She told me she remembered how I had gotten in the kitchen to help her when I found out she was sick. She thanked me for being so strong. I fed her the hamburger.

That night, the phone call came. I heard my grandmother's voice on the phone as my father picked up the other line: "She's gone, Howard." I ran down the stairs and we all hugged. I said, "She is not in pain anymore." My father shook his head in agreement.

That was the extent of our conversation about my mother's death. We were not the model of a family dealing with death in a healthy way. My mother had been the glue that held our family together. Without her, we were just four separate individuals floundering around.

I know now that everything happens for a reason and is part of a bigger plan. Although my mother's difficult death propelled my sister and me into years of struggle and loneliness, it ultimately spurred my sister's spiritual quest for meaning. Later, it became my own spiritual journey and life purpose. I know now my mother was seeing angels and beings of light coming to help her make her transition. I have learned it is common for terminally ill people to be aware they are getting ready to die, and they often become quite lucid in the hours before death. Now I understand there is no "death." But I didn't know that then; none of us did. We just knew she was gone and we had to continue on with our lives.

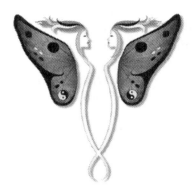

## Chapter Three:
## Twins' Story

### The Twin Connection

Many believe that every person has a twin soul somewhere in the universe. This counterpart is identical yet walks an individual path. It is said to be part of the yin and yang of creation. When brought together, these kindred spirits make up a powerful energy force that helps both souls access higher levels of consciousness and light.

Twins share an identical blueprint. They have the same genetic makeup and are greatly in tune with each other. Scientific studies have shown that twins have amazingly similar brain current activity.

In his book *Twin Telepathy: The Psychic Connection,* Guy Lyon Playfair has collected a large body of evidence that suggests that there is indeed a special connection between twins. For example: Two twins broke limbs at the exact same time while they were hundreds of miles apart. A man was shot in the chest; thirty miles away, his twin brother clutched his chest and slumped into a chair. A four-year-old girl burned her hand on an iron; her twin sister developed a blister of the same size and at the same location as her twin's burn. A woman in Australia was in a severe car accident in which the steering wheel crushed her chest. Her twin sister, who was many miles away, awoke with a loud scream, complaining of severe chest pain. Both women died in their respective ambulances on the way to the hospital.

Twin Souls have such a strong spiritual and physical connection that the relationship can sometimes be stormy. Jane Roberts' metaphysical book *Seth Speaks* discusses the energy between twin souls. She wrote that there is a huge amount of energy between twin souls and often the two can be influenced by the ego.

My relationship with my sister was a dichotomy. We felt a deep bond of love for each other. But at the same time, we had strong personalities and opinions, which led to much strife between us. A friend once commented, "The two of you are always arguing, but let someone else say something bad about one of you, and the other one becomes ferociously protective."

Looking back on our arguments, they seem comical. I see now that all people are products of their environment. The way a person is raised, his or her life experiences, the course of study one chooses, and occupational choices affect the way a person views the world. Even twins who have grown up together can have radically differing views of the world.

It is clear to me now that our differences were necessary. Ancient spiritual writings of the Sufis, a mystical dimension of Islam, state that for twin souls to complete each other, they must initially go their separate ways.

People often ask me if my sister and I finished each other's sentences or had the same thoughts. We did experience many of these types of twin phenomena, but the connection went much deeper. I felt her pain, joy, and sorrows, and she felt mine. I was incapable of happiness unless my sister was happy. My sister had many struggles and disappointments in the years before she died. I acutely felt each and every one of them. Even on the day I got married I was unable to feel complete happiness and peace because my sister was not at peace. I could feel her searching to understand her purpose. She wanted to know who she was and where she fit into the world.

## Cathy's Story

During my mother's illness, Cathy began to hyperventilate and have anxiety attacks. It happened while she was at school or work or at home in her small apartment near the college. Any time she thought about my mother's sickness and impending death, her heart would beat rapidly and she would feel a shortness of breath; panic overtook her. Later she hyperventilated in her sleep.

Shortly before Cathy died, she began corresponding with a friend named Tom on the Internet. Cathy described her sleep problem to Tom in an e-mail on October 8, 2002: "I have some sleep problems that began before my mom died of lung cancer in 1986. I guess you would call them panic attacks in my sleep. I wake up hyperventilating and gasping for air like I am suffocating. I also wake up screaming bloody murder, although I usually go right back to sleep. But the neighbors call the police because the screams are so loud and blood curdling. I would like to find out where this is coming from and stop it once and for all. I strongly believe it has something to do with an incident in a past life."

She experienced this sleep disorder from the time my mother died in 1986 until the day she died in 2002.

Although Cathy suffered greatly because of my mother's death, she was very tenacious and would not allow her struggles to stop her from finding meaning and purpose in life.

My sister was known for her strong personality. She was headstrong and often argumentative but had a heart of gold. She would do just about anything to help someone. Our mutual friend Amy told me after she died,

"I sure do miss that pushy, opinionated, pain-in-the-butt woman with her do-anything-for-you huge heart!"

I remember one instance when Amy was having problems with her boyfriend and wanted to leave him. Cathy drove a moving truck from San Diego to Los Angeles and helped her pack all of her belongings and drove the truck back to San Diego while Amy followed in her car. Although Cathy lived in a small studio apartment, she allowed Amy to live with her until she got on her feet.

Unfortunately, Cathy's intense personality caused her much heartache. She wanted to find her "Mr. Right" but couldn't seem to make the connection. I think she scared men away because she was a little too strong-willed. It didn't help that the soulmate she was searching for probably did not exist on earth. She was looking for Gandhi in a Navy SEAL's body. She never met anyone who fit the bill.

Although she often battled loneliness, she had a full and interesting life. I have heard that those who die young are adventurous and move through life in the fast lane. It is as if they know they have to cram life into a shorter time period. Cathy led her life this way.

Upon graduation from college in 1989, with a degree in business management, Cathy promptly decided a nine-to-five job was not for her. American Airlines hired her as a flight attendant. She relocated and was based out of the Washington Dulles Airport. Cathy enjoyed seeing the world. She met her friend Marcy, who became her travel companion to many remote and exotic places. She also met her friend and fellow flight attendant, Amy, with whom she flew to South America and the Virgin Islands.

Cathy joined a group called American Airlines Ambassadors. Their job was to facilitate international relations. She was sent to Istanbul, Turkey, in June of 1996, for a United Nations conference called "Conference on Human Settlements (Habitat II)." Years later I found her American Ambassador badge for the conference and looked it up on the Internet. I learned that the purpose of the conference was to address two issues of global importance: "adequate shelter for all" and "sustainable human settlements development in an urbanizing world." The premise of the UN conference was that every human being is entitled to a healthy and productive life in harmony with nature.

Cathy's job was to pick up an international dignitary from the airport and bring him to the conference. Cathy was assigned to chauffer a holy man from India.

She realized immediately that he was special. He was kind and gentle with a wonderful exuberance about him. It was her first encounter with an enlightened soul. He was an impish little man who was constantly giggling. Cathy was surprised by his joyful manner. She loved how excited he became when ice cream was served at the conference. Cathy questioned him about his cheerful attitude. The man counseled Cathy to look inward to find the happiness that had escaped her. Cathy was highly intrigued by the Eastern philosophies he spoke about.

Marcy and Amy met up with Cathy in Turkey. The three women had great adventures touring Istanbul. Then they went to the ancient biblical city of Ephesus, where they visited a Turkish bathhouse.

Cathy meets a psychic on the street

Amy recounted how Cathy ran into a psychic on the street in front of the bathhouse who said, "Your mother misses you. You should talk to her. She is with you and sees your struggles." These encounters in Turkey deeply affected Cathy and caused her to begin her search for answers to life's bigger questions.

23

Meanwhile my mind was on more earthy matters. I worked for Nextel Communications in Los Angeles and saw great potential in the start-up company. I decided to accept a position with the newly formed Chicago sales office. After visiting me several times, Cathy and Amy decided to join me in Chicago. They were granted a transfer from Washington Dulles Airport to Chicago's O'Hare Airport. Cathy was very excited about the move. She thought it would be her chance to build a new life for herself. I will never forget the day they drove into Chicago in a truck packed with all of their possessions. It was January 31. The temperature outside was ten degrees with a wind chill of twenty below zero. Amy and Cathy found two small studio apartments in the same old dilapidated building. We dragged all of their belongings up two flights of stairs.

The three of us enjoyed exploring the city. Most nights we gathered in one of our apartments and ate takeout food. Cathy's life did not improve dramatically as she had hoped. Neither Amy nor Cathy owned a car. They walked down the street in high-heeled shoes, pulling their suitcases in the bitter cold to the bus stop. They transferred to the El (Chicago's elevated train), finally arriving at O'Hare Airport an hour and half later. Cathy began to long for the sunny climate of San Diego. Her wish to return home would soon come true.

While in Chicago, she dated a man who was involved in federal law enforcement. This sparked a sudden interest in Cathy. She already knew that serving drinks with a smile was not her calling; the travel was beginning to wear on her. She told friends she was going to trade her dress, high heels, and nylon stockings for a gun, boots, and a badge.

She decided that a career in law enforcement would be a more suitable outlet for her intense personality. She felt it would be more meaningful and would bring her back to the West Coast. To be competitive in law enforcement in

California, Cathy knew she would have to learn to speak Spanish.

She took a leave of absence from American Airlines and flew to a Spanish school in Antigua, Guatemala. She spent many months there, where she fell in love with the people and culture. She talked often about their sense of family and togetherness.

Cathy with some Guatemalan friends

The indigenous people of South America were desperately poor by American standards, but she could see they were wealthier in their love and unity. The people she met were surprised by her situation. It was unheard of in their culture that a thirty-three-year-old woman would have very little family or support network. They could sense her loneliness.

She often came home to an empty house or an empty hotel room. Holidays were even worse for Cathy. She longed to be part of the joyful celebrations she saw in the Hispanic culture. For many years, my sister and I had the

Cathy in Buenos Aires

Cathy and Amy

With Marcy in Roatan, Honduras

Cathy and Lola

With Marcy, on horseback in Peru

feeling that everyone else had somewhere to go on special occasions. We didn't. We escaped this problem by working during most holidays.

In April of 1998, I got a job that relocated me back to San Diego. Cathy soon followed. She drove or flew to the American Airlines base in Los Angeles several times per week.

Finally Cathy's dream of becoming a federal law enforcement officer became a reality when she was accepted by the United States Border Patrol. She walked around telling everyone to watch out because she was a federal agent. She was told that the Border Patrol Academy was one of the most difficult in federal law enforcement, both in academics and physical fitness. She began studying immigration law and brushed up on her Spanish. She ran every day and lifted weights several times per week.

When she arrived at the Border Patrol Academy in Charleston, South Carolina, she was ready. From the beginning Cathy excelled in Spanish, federal law, and physical fitness. However, she had difficulty with the male-dominated environment and paramilitary aspect of the job. Here she was, a petite former high school cheerleader and flight attendant with a degree in business management in an agency in which they wore cowboy boots with their dress uniforms.

At thirty-five, Cathy was the oldest person in her class and one of only a few females. She toughed it out, and on March 17, 2000, she graduated from the 419th academy. She received the Federal Law Enforcement Training Center Fitness Award (FLETC), an award given for outstanding fitness for each Academy Class. Border Patrol Chief William T. Veal told me later that he never forgot the obvious pride he saw in both our eyes as I, wearing my own newly issued Sheriff's uniform, pinned the badge on her uniform during the swearing-in ceremony.

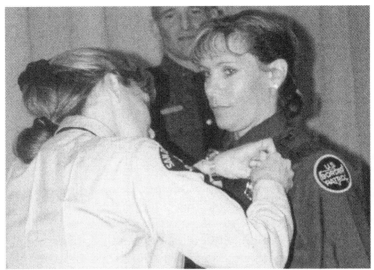
Sister pins sister

Cathy had many interesting assignments. She was sent to Idaho in the winter and Arizona in the summer. While on detail in Arizona, she walked through the desert in the middle of the night by herself, not knowing the terrain. She never knew what or whom she would encounter. Many people asked her if she was afraid. She just rolled her eyes. She was never afraid of anything. "I'm a gun-totin' mama," she told them.

One reason Cathy liked being a Border Patrol Agent was for the shock value. She liked pushing people's buttons. Cathy was cute and petite, and people did not expect her to be in law enforcement. One night when Cathy and Amy were out to dinner, Cathy struck up a conversation with a large, muscular guy with a military haircut. He asked Cathy and Amy if they were teachers or librarians. Amy said she worked in a law firm. Cathy was indignant by his assumption and announced that she was a Border Patrol Agent. The man was very surprised. Cathy loved to watch people's faces when she told them what she did for a living.

The stories she told were often hilarious. One evening she saw an overweight man swimming in the ocean around the barrier fence from Mexico into the United States. She ordered him over the loudspeaker, "*Regrese al sur*" ("turn back south"). But the man continued and soon was lying close to the shore. My sister ordered him to stand up. She could see he was out of breath but was exaggerating his inability to get up. He floundered around in the water for several minutes. His acting skills were so pitiful that she finally burst out laughing. She insisted the man swim back to the other side of the fence or face arrest and deportation. She watched as he swam back around the fence into Mexico.

Cathy was known for her great love of animals. Her fellow agents told a story about Cathy's rescue of two seal pups. She came across the seals while patrolling the beach and determined that their mother had abandoned them. She doggedly badgered Sea World until they finally agreed to send handlers to come get the seal pups. One of the seals was eventually named after Cathy.

Cathy (right) and friend
Marcy in the "Old West"

Her favorite part of the job was rescuing people. One night, while Cathy was assigned to a special detail along the Arizona border, an agent spotted some border bandits attempting to rob a family. Cathy grabbed her shotgun and ran toward the border with a crowd of other agents. She felt as if she were an Old West town marshal or one of Wyatt Earp's deputies as she ran toward the helpless family. She and the other agents scared the border bandits away, and the family returned to Mexico without further incident.

Soon Cathy's enthusiasm for the job began to wane. She thought it was vitally important to protect our borders from criminals and terrorists, but she felt great anguish for the women with children in tow, trying to come to America to make a better life for their families. At times she felt near tears, but she could never show her sorrow because it was her job to apprehend them and send them back.

A story she told really stuck with me. One night she arrested a smiling little Mexican man, who was wearing his best dress shoes. She felt great sadness for this man, who was obviously very optimistic and thought it appropriate to wear his best shoes while crossing the desert. She told me she could no longer stand to look into another pair of sad eyes. She kept saying, "This is not working. This is a negative solution to a negative problem."

Cathy continued to struggle with the idea of leaving the Border Patrol. She e-mailed her friend Tom on September 18, 2002, discussing her desire to find a new direction in her life: "After reading many spiritual books, law enforcement doesn't seem like a perfect place for me to be. I want to do something to help people and the planet." But she felt hesitant to leave. She knew there had to be some reason for her being there.

For the first time in her life, she was not scraping to pay her bills. She certainly wasn't rich, but compared to a flight attendant's salary, her job as a Border Patrol Agent paid quite well. She had always driven rickety old cars and lived in small, rented apartments. She was thrilled when she bought a brand-new Mitsubishi Eclipse and a condo in National City, a southern suburb of San Diego.

One day she was assigned to work with the Border Patrol's Explorer Scouts program, which helps teens with their career goals. As a Border Patrol Agent, Cathy worked fifty hours per week but still managed to find time to help her Explorers before or after work.

Cathy's Explorers hold hands at her funeral

She recruited me to teach essay writing. The class was held at Pizza Hut. She told the kids that they had better show up if they were serious about their futures. They showed up.

Many of Cathy's Explorers were mostly from poor Hispanic families. English was often their second language. If they didn't understand a concept in English, she explained it in Spanish. After Cathy died, they gave me a letter entitled "Agente Hill." They expressed their appreciation for her thoughtfulness and caring. They told me she made them do push-ups if they did not use proper grammar and gave them candy when they spoke in complete sentences.

Cathy's passion for helping young people led her to an organization called StandUp For Kids, for which she became an outreach counselor working with homeless teens. She walked the streets of San Diego finding homeless kids and asking them what she could do to help them.

This was a profoundly moving experience for Cathy. Her friends and family saw a marked change in her personality. To all who knew her, she seemed more calm and peaceful.

She told me she was going to a Halloween party at the StandUp For Kids center. She couldn't wait to see the kids' faces. She was also excited about her decision to get her master's degree in counseling so she could further assist underprivileged and troubled youth. She was scheduled to begin her master's program at the University of Phoenix on Monday, October 28, 2002. On Wednesday, October 23, she came to my house to pick up several bags of clothing to be donated to the kids. She seemed extremely happy that day, as if she had a glow of light around her. For some reason, we didn't engage in our usual bickering. My dog sensed something different in her also. She licked Cathy all over her face and refused to stop. That was the last time I saw her.

Early Friday morning, October 25, 2002, Cathy was killed in a vehicle accident while patrolling the international border. According to the investigation done by the San Diego Police Department, she was attempting to maneuver her Jeep Wrangler to get a better look at the border when she got too close to the edge. Her vehicle tumbled down the embankment into the Tijuana River Valley below. She was ejected from the vehicle and killed instantly.

Cathy's experiences with the poor and downtrodden shaped her view of the world. While in South America, she witnessed the abhorrent treatment of indigenous people. She saw how they were forced to give up their way of life. The only way they could survive was to work for large international corporations that wanted their farmland to raise cattle. She saw the beauty and the destruction of the rain forests and learned about its effect on the environment.

While working for American Airlines, she did not feel valued as an employee. She thought it was unfair that hundreds of flight attendants barely made enough money to survive, while those in upper management were making millions.

While working for the Border Patrol she realized that using force to keep people out of the country was a dead-end solution. While volunteering for StandUp For Kids, she saw homeless children forced into drugs, prostitution, and crime in order to survive. She was disillusioned by the fact that this could occur in America, the richest country in the world. These things shaped her perceptions and made Cathy who she was.

## My Life

The path I chose led me to sharply different conclusions about the world. In college I majored in Communication. I studied writing, public speaking, debate, and leadership skills. The professors who came from a variety of corporations to teach our classes impressed me.

After college I worked as a National Account Manager for several large telecommunication companies. I was involved in discussions about profit margins and saw how desperately companies struggled to produce profit and earnings for their shareholders. The focus of a successful company was sales for the quarter and how they compared to the previous quarter.

I called on small and medium-sized businesses. I heard the stories of business owners who were forced to lay off employees because of the heavy burden of government regulations. I saw how bids were lost because a business was not minority-owned.

I was impressed by stories of people who had started with nothing. Against all odds, they had created a successful business. I realized that many people were employed by these businesses. I saw how important it was for people to have ownership in their lives. It was clear to me that the less someone was given, the harder he or she worked to create something to be proud of.

As a salesperson in a large company, I was treated like royalty. Successful companies know their salespeople are the ones who generate revenue and treat them accordingly. I made more money than most people my age. I went on shopping sprees without even bothering to look at price tags.

After my move to Chicago, I met Patrick. He was quite a character. He spoke with a south-side-of-Chicago accent. We dated for four years. Pat was part of a family-run construction business. He lamented constantly about how the labor unions were killing his business. He listened to conservative talk radio shows all day. Soon he had me listening to Rush Limbaugh and reading the "National Review," a conservative magazine.

My sister was appalled. She liked Pat but was infuriated by his politics. But he was quick on his feet. She was no match for him. He was one of the most skilled debaters I have ever seen. Everywhere he went he converted people to his point of view. He never became angry but took great joy in calmly discussing the facts as he saw them. At times his political discussions would last until 3:00 or 4:00 in the morning. Pat was unflappable. He never belittled anyone. He always argued with a smile on his face. Cathy became so upset at Patrick while riding with us in the car one day that she got out and walked home in the snow.

Cathy and I began to argue more and more forcefully about our points of view. Poor Amy often got caught in the middle. She was usually on my side when it came to politics and later she agreed with Cathy on spiritual issues. But she was not about to endure the wrath of Cathy and me, so she kept her mouth shut. "Stop arguing, or I'm leaving!" was her usual mantra.

In 1998, my life took an unexpected turn. Strangely, I felt a strong pull toward law enforcement at the same time my sister did. Like Cathy, I was searching for something more fulfilling. I enrolled in a reserve police officers academy. It was remarkable that I made it through. I was traveling extensively and had to schedule my trips around my classes.

Betsy graduating from the Reserve Academy

I cared more about the reserve academy than I did about my sales job. I began volunteering for the San Diego Police Department's gang unit, hoping to be hired as a

Reserve Police Officer. Later I was hired as a Reserve Deputy Sheriff for the county of San Diego. I soon realized that brawling with criminals on the streets was not for me so I became a 911 dispatcher instead. However, my volunteer work in the gang unit led me to meet a police officer named Jack. When I met Jack, I felt an unusual sense of déjà vu. Something about his eyes seemed oddly familiar.

I was set up to do a ride-along with him. During the first hour in the car together, I had the strangest feeling that this was the person I was going to marry. All my life I had experienced a premonition that I would marry a man who was from a small town in the Midwest and was Catholic. I envisioned that he would be part of a strong, loving family. Bells must have been going off in my head. Jack fit this description in every way.

We chased gangsters all over the city that night. I followed Jack as he and another officer dragged an unwilling young male through a rundown apartment building. I tried not to scream as huge cockroaches scurried in our path. Later I stumbled through an open field trying to keep up with him as we searched for a suspect. It was an interesting first date, a night I would never forget.

For our second date, he took me to church with him. I was surprised by the contrast I saw in his personality. I was impressed with his deep religious faith. I had the feeling I was exactly where I belonged.

However, Jack told me he couldn't get married because he felt he was being called to become a priest. I was devastated. I was falling in love with him. I told him I would not see him again until he made his decision.

I kept myself busy. I went skiing, joined a boxing club, and went out to dinner with friends every night. This was the first time in my life that I noticed someone was sending me spiritual guidance. I was out jogging on the beach when I heard someone say very clearly, "You're doing the right thing; stick to your guns."

I had begun Catholic classes and continued to go even though they made me feel sad. One Sunday during Mass, the priest told a story about a police officer who was very disillusioned. The priest did a ride-along with the police officer and told the cop that he was doing God's work. The cop was renewed because he saw his job through the priest's eyes as one of helping others.

Later that day, a priest came to talk to our class about the priesthood and about marriage. What a coincidence— these were the issues I was wrestling with in my life. I burst into tears and told him my boyfriend wanted to become a priest. He just chuckled. He didn't seem too concerned about my predicament. The class instructor told me everyone in life has to discern what his or her calling is and that I shouldn't worry; the right thing would happen. When I told Jack these stories, I could see they had an effect on him.

A few weeks later, Jack came to my house to tell me he wanted to be married to me within a year. Some proposal. At first I didn't believe him and told him not to play around with something so important. But he was serious. A year later, we were married.

Jack is a product of his small-town upbringing. He grew up in historic Milan, Ohio, a town of 2,000 people. Like a picture postcard, the town has small businesses and a town hall with a clock tower and a quaint town square. Growing up in this environment gave Jack a down-to-earth personality with an old-fashioned, Midwestern work ethic. He is one of the most sentimental people I have ever met. He loves the holidays, especially Halloween and Christmas. He likes to drive around and look at Christmas lights or Halloween decorations. He would make me listen to Christmas music until I was sick. I had to take the Christmas tree down, or it would have stayed up all year.

Despite his small-town personality, he is also a tough-as-nails police officer. His mother told me that Jack has a "killer instinct." While riding with him, I could see what she meant. He would put his own life on the line to stop a crime or to save the life of another person. Before Jack was a police officer, he was a firefighter for the Milan Township Fire Department and the NASA Fire Department. One day after he became a San Diego Police Officer, he used his knowledge from his firefighting days to crawl through a burning building to save a man's life. During a SWAT incident, he threw himself onto a woman who was threatening to shoot her child. While working in the gang unit, he dealt with the most violent criminals in our society. These things shaped Jack's view of the world.

Jack takes his job as a police officer seriously, sometimes a little too seriously. One day when he was getting ready for work, I brought our neighbor's new puppy into the house. Jack was in the shower, but I decided to show him the puppy anyway. He got very upset and gave me a lecture: "When I am getting ready for work, I am going through a transformation. I have to concentrate on what I have to do tonight." I couldn't resist laughing at him.

"Who do you think you are, Clark Kent going through your transformation into Superman?" But it was true; his personality changed when he went to work. I think it had something to do with putting on the uniform.

Jack has seen many tragedies in his twenty-three-plus years of police work. He feels deeply for officers killed in the line of duty. But sometimes he takes his reverence to the extreme. My sister and I used to laugh at him mercilessly when he took us to the law enforcement memorial service in Balboa Park. Every year the services are held in May to honor fallen law enforcement officers.

Jack's attitude changed before we even got to the service. There was very little talking and no laughing allowed. When we got there, he would stand at attention with his sunglasses on and refuse to speak. If we were standing next to him, he would shoot us a dirty look if we cracked a joke. We thought his behavior was over the top. We used to stand there and giggle. My sister would say, "There's no laughing in law enforcement." Ironically we later went to the memorial service to honor my sister. I still felt her laughing at Jack for his overly serious demeanor.

They say opposites attract. Jack is meticulously neat and organized. Okay, he's anal. His co-workers in the gang unit called him "house mouse," which is a military term for someone who is always running around doing busy work so that everything is orderly and perfect. And I admit that I am often rather unorganized.

Jack grew up in a very structured environment. I grew up in a non-structured environment. He was taught to pay attention to every detail; I was not. He was taught that money was a luxury and that one should save as much money as possible. I don't remember money being discussed much while growing up. There always seemed to be enough.

Before my sister died, Jack's and my religious beliefs and worldviews were similar. However, after my sister died, our ideas about life grew increasingly different. Although he is deeply religious, he doesn't seem to have any sense of spirituality. He sees the world as a random place where things happen without rhyme or reason. On the other hand, I now believe all things happen for a reason and that nothing is random. Jack believes we do not have control over what happens in our lives; we simply have to react to whatever comes our way. I believe we create everything that happens to us. Jack is a very logical, linear, and left-brain thinker, while I am an intuitive, right-brain type of person who sees things on a larger, global level.

Jack and I bickered at times because he became upset when things were not as orderly as he would prefer. I have read that perfectionism is a curse because it causes people to focus so intently on every detail that they miss the bigger picture. On the other hand, Zen Buddhism teaches that in order to stay in the moment, we must pay attention to details. I asked myself what we could learn from our situation. I believe that every problem is created to teach us a symbolic lesson about life.

"A-ha," I said to my husband. "I get the lesson. Your way may very well be more efficient than mine, but does that make it the right way?"

Like the relationship I had with my sister, Jack and I share a strong bond but often have opposing ideas. It seems the unity of opposites is a theme that will follow me throughout my life.

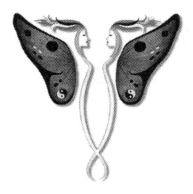

## Chapter Four:
## Unusual Happenings

When I arrived home after receiving the news of my sister's death, the anguish was unbearable. I was grieving for all the things she didn't get to do. My husband kept telling me, "She will get to have all of those things now." Would she? I wasn't so sure. Not only did I feel a deep personal loss, but I was also consumed with overwhelming fear and confusion about death. I wondered where my sister was and what she was doing. I hoped that somehow I would receive a sign that she was okay.

### "Your Sister Cathy Is Fine"

Three days after my sister died, I was preparing to meet with the Border Patrol to plan her funeral. Suddenly I became overwhelmed with the enormity of what I was about to do. I fell to my knees sobbing. I prayed for understanding. Then something happened that stopped me in my tracks. I heard a clear voice say, "Your sister Cathy is fine. Remember what she was doing and reading before she died." A feeling of calm washed over me. At that moment I realized that her death had meaning. Those words are etched in my memory forever.

My grief lessened after that. In an odd way I knew that my lifelong prayers for her had been answered. I knew there was no greater love I could show her than to let her go and know she was where she was supposed to be. I understood I would only miss her in the physical sense. "She is my twin," I thought, "of course she will not leave me." I was right.

## E-mails and Books

I heard my husband calling me excitedly from the computer room. "Your sister sent out an e-mail the night before she died." I felt a shiver run up my spine as I read her message; it was St. Theresa's prayer: "May today there be peace within. May you trust in God you are exactly where you are meant to be. May you not forget the infinite possibilities that are born of faith. May you use those gifts you have received and pass on the love that has been given to you. May you be content knowing you are a child of God. Let this presence settle into your bones and allow your soul the freedom to sing and dance. It is there for each and every one of you."

Several people called and e-mailed me about Cathy's message. She had sent it to everyone she knew.

Later that week we received an e-mail from "animallover1." It was Cathy's e-mail moniker. Nothing was written in the e-mail. I thought it was strange but brushed it off as some kind of fluke.

A few days later another e-mail incident occurred. I had been trying for several months to reach a friend who had moved away to Wisconsin. I didn't have her phone number or e-mail address. After Cathy died, she called me. When I told her what had happened, she immediately recommended I read one of James Van Praagh's books. She told me that he was a famous medium who was also Catholic. After I hung up with her, I realized I still didn't have her e-mail address. But a few days later, I received an e-mail from her.

"I got your e-mail but there was nothing there," she wrote. I was baffled. I told her that I hadn't sent her an e-mail and that I didn't even have her e-mail address. But I looked in my e-mail address folder and there it was. I had no idea how it got there.

Even though I was skeptical about mediums, I ran to the store to buy James Van Praagh's book *Healing Grief*. I was intrigued when I read a story about a boy who died and was communicating to his mother through James Van Praagh. He wanted James to tell his mother that he had knocked over a flowerpot at his funeral so she would know he was there.

A large flowerpot had been knocked over at Cathy's funeral. A few people told me that they felt it was Cathy letting us know she was there. I ran to call our mutual friend Amy in Virginia to tell her to buy the book. She became very flustered.

"I just read *Healing Grief*," she said. "I was about to call you and tell you to read about the flowerpot!"

## Medium

After reading Van Praagh's book, I felt a strong impulse to visit a medium. I had always been fearful of psychics and mediums because I had somehow gotten the idea that they used evil powers to get their information or that they were frauds.

I remembered an encounter I had with a psychic a few years earlier. A friend had hired her to give readings at her bachelorette party. I was terrified to talk to her. My friends literally pushed me into the room, where I was relieved to see that she was a normal person. In fact, she was very kind and reassured me there was nothing sinister about her abilities. She explained that all people have the gift of intuition but some have a heightened sixth sense. She had spent many years developing her ability so she could help others.

I asked her whether she saw my husband and me having a happy marriage. "I see a lot of love there. You are together for a specific purpose."

"Will my sister find love and happiness soon?" I asked.

She was silent for a few minutes. "She will find all she has been seeking, but not for two years."

Exactly two years had passed since the reading. My sister had died a few months earlier. I decided it was time for another visit to a medium. A friend referred me to Kim. When I met her I was assured by her businesslike manner. She explained she was clairvoyant (able to see those in spirit) and clairaudient (able to hear those in spirit).

She began by telling me she could see a man who wanted to tell me something. She laughed. "He really has a great sense of humor. He's showing me charades. He traced a 'B' in the air." I wanted to hear from my sister, but the man wouldn't go away. He told Kim he was an old friend of my family.

"He says you are asking many questions," Kim said. "He is bringing you the answers by guiding you to certain books."

It dawned on me who the man was. It was Ben, a friend of our family who had been highly educated and had traveled extensively. He had been especially well read on the subject of religion and had even gone with my sister and me to our world religions class in college. He had been almost eighty years old at that time and passed away soon after. Kim's description of his sense of humor fit. I was thrilled. Ben was the perfect person to help me find answers to my questions.

Finally we moved on to Cathy. Kim was having some trouble reaching her because she was still processing her death. "I can see her; she is a little fuzzy to me. Did she die suddenly? I can see you look very much alike." I hadn't told her the circumstances of Cathy's death or that we were twins.

"Your sister is holding on to earthly things. She needs to let go of them before she can continue her transition." I laughed. That sounded like Cathy. I asked if the contact we were making would help her. At first Kim said our contact would not help Cathy, but she changed her mind. "Your sister is saying, 'No, no, that isn't true.' It is important you came today. Cathy can feel your grief. It is making it more difficult for her to move on."

"Let go, Cathy," I said. "I know you are okay." I watched as Kim's expression changed.

"I see her. She's starting to become clearer. She is making her transition!"

I was filled with joy at hearing this and became even more elated when Kim described a woman who was among a group of people waiting for Cathy. "I believe it is your mother." I hadn't told her that my mother had died. Her description of my mother was breathtakingly accurate.

"Your mother has a message for you. She is saying that she and your sister had to leave so you could shine as an individual. You have an important purpose on earth." My mother continued, "I know you are feeling grief, but someday soon you will realize that time is not what you think it is." She told Kim that I needed to learn to be quiet. "What does that mean? Is she talking about meditation?"

"Yes, it is a meditation. Your mother also advises you to continue to read and write down your experiences. The information will become important in the future. You will help others with your writing. I see you working with hospice, but it is much bigger than hospice. You will help people understand death better." I was amazed by this information because I had already thought about volunteering at a hospice.

We touched on several other areas of my life, and as the reading drew to a close, I asked Kim if there was anything else my sister wanted to tell us. "She says she loves you all. When she is around you, you will see blue wings. She is showing them to me. They look like butterfly or angel wings. I am getting huge affirmations on this."

The reading was over. I sat in stunned silence. I was ecstatic about the information I had just received. I knew it was real because the electricity in the air was palpable; I could even smell electricity, as if there had just been a thunderstorm. My sister and mother had been in the room with me. I could still feel their presence as I drove away.

## Blue Angel and Blue Butterfly Sightings

I asked my sister to show me where I would see these blue angel and butterfly wings. I had a very distinct thought I would see them on the t-shirt of a little girl and an old woman. In my mind's eye, I also saw greeting cards and backs of cars. I envisioned the airport as another place where I would see these symbols. This made sense because Cathy had spent many years in airports as a flight attendant. I didn't have to wait long to see my first blue butterfly. It was our birthday, March 19, 2003. I was in the airport preparing to meet Cathy's friends for a birthday celebration in Cathy's favorite town, Bisbee, Arizona.

I thought, "It's our birthday. If you are with me, please show me a blue butterfly." No sooner had I sent that thought out than I turned around to see a little girl with a large butterfly in blue sequins on her t-shirt.

Cathy's friend Marcy experienced a similar incident while waiting in the airport. While standing in a card shop, she asked Cathy to send her some kind of sign. Her eyes landed on a blue greeting card. The most beautiful blue angel covered the entire card. Marcy had several other encounters with butterfly and angel cards. She sends me a copy of each one.

Another day I was at the airport with my husband. We were getting ready to leave for a trip to visit his parents in Ohio. We were arguing about something silly. In a gloomy

46

mood I headed toward the gift shop to buy a drink for the plane ride. As I walked in I was drawn toward the card section. I saw a Hallmark card with a blue butterfly on the front. I bought my drink and the card and raced back to my gate to board the airplane.

After we took off, I pulled out the card. My eyes welled up with tears when I saw what was written inside: "This heavenly blue butterfly will fly high in the sky, higher and higher. The sunlight will touch the blue on its wings until it seems to disappear. We think it is gone because the blue of the butterfly is the exact same blue of the sky. We think it is gone, because our eyes are too weak to see and it is difficult to believe what we cannot see. But the blue butterfly is not gone. It is still flying, higher and higher, nearer the sun. Blue against blue. For now and forever." I heard my sister's implicit message: "You think I am gone because you can't see me, but I am never gone. I am always with you. Except now, I am free of life's burdens. I fly like a butterfly as high as you can imagine."

My dog Ernie (short for Ernestine) loved Cathy. I think she sensed Cathy's love for dogs. Whenever I was in my sister's condo after her death and Ernie was with me, she would begin to whine. I could see she sensed my sister's presence.

Marcy came to visit me on my second birthday after Cathy had died. We decided to have a picnic at Cathy's gravesite. Ernie went with us. As we were driving into the cemetery, she started whining. Marcy and I looked at each other.

"Do you think Cathy is here?" Marcy said. We went into the flower shop to pick out a bouquet for both my mother's and sister's graves. Strangely, I didn't feel any sadness. I was compelled to look at the cards. A picture of a blue butterfly flew gracefully on the front cover of one of the cards. I understood why I was not sad. She was there.

I wondered if I would ever see a real blue butterfly. They are fairly rare in North America. One night I dreamed I saw one. I remember calling Marcy to tell her I had seen a real blue butterfly. The dream proved to be prophetic.

For some reason, I felt compelled to go to the San Diego Wild Animal Park. When my husband and I entered the park, I saw from the corner of my eye something blue. It was a picture of a blue butterfly.

"There's a butterfly exhibit here," I said emphatically. I raced around the park frantically looking for the exhibit. My husband thought I was acting crazy, but I ignored him. I ran up to a park employee, who confirmed there was a butterfly exhibit and gave us directions. When we arrived, there was a long line of people waiting to go in.

"Maybe we should come back later," I said. But my husband suggested we wait. He had finally caught on to the fact that there really was something amazing going on. When we went inside, we were stunned. It was a mock South American rain forest. I burst into tears; the place was filled with hundreds of blue butterflies.

When I called Marcy to tell her of my amazing experience, she said that she had seen a blue butterfly in her yard earlier in the day.

Amy often complained that she didn't have as many blue butterfly sightings as Marcy and I did. I kept telling her that Cathy was probably saying, "Do I have to hit you over the head, Amy? Pay attention."

One day she was out in the woods near her house walking her dog when a blue butterfly appeared. It started following close behind her. "Hello, Cathy," Amy said awkwardly to the butterfly. She hoped no one was watching her. I knew Cathy was with Amy when she described what happened next: "The butterfly started hitting me in the head!"

I had become a volunteer for San Diego Hospice and had been visiting "Lois," a ninety-one-year-old patient, weekly. At first I had difficulty finding ways to connect with her because of her severe dementia. I began pushing her in her wheelchair down the halls of the nursing facility. She really enjoyed looking at the pictures on the wall. She especially liked the country scenes. This became a ritual for us. She talked about how much her grandmother would like the pictures. For Christmas I bought her a book of Thomas Kincaid paintings, and on Christmas Eve, I surprised her with the book, some Martinelli's sparkling cider, and two champagne glasses. We toasted Christmas, and I set up a small tree that lit up in the corner. It was so wonderful to see the happy look on her face. She loved the book of paintings. If we came to a painting she especially liked, I told her, "This is what heaven looks like."

She told me, "Oh, I am too old for Heaven."

I laughed. "No one is too old for Heaven, silly."

I suddenly thought she needed an angel on her tree. I read that angels come to meet people when they die, and I wanted her to be reminded of what the angel would look like.

We went out on our usual stroll. An elderly lady came out of nowhere and insisted we follow her to her room. She said she wanted to show us something. When we got there, I was shocked. She wanted to show us her angel collection. She had angels all over her room including a few blue angels. The woman gave Lois an angel to take back to her room.

Another day I was scheduled to visit Lois, but I was asked to work two extra hours at work and was exhausted from my twelve-hour shift. I didn't think I could muster the energy to visit her. But something was pushing me to go. Reluctantly I drove to the nursing facility. As I walked in I spotted Lois in her wheelchair in her usual spot. On the front of her blue sweatshirt was a huge blue butterfly.

## The Meaning Behind the Blue Butterflies

Butterflies are often used to symbolize death and the freedom the soul feels as it is released from the body. Elisabeth Kübler-Ross, the famous author and hospice doctor, used the image of the butterfly to describe death to her young patients.

She explained that all our lives we are like caterpillars walking on the earth. When it is our time to leave, we go into our cocoon, and at the moment of death our spirit emerges, free like a butterfly to soar away from its once heavy, earth-bound body.

I didn't realize immediately that there was a more specific meaning behind the blue butterflies until Marcy came to dog-sit for me. She brought several pictures of herself and Cathy in Chile and Argentina. It was evident from looking at the pictures that Cathy was most happy while traveling in South America.

When I returned from my vacation, Marcy was excited to tell me about a trip she had taken with Ernie to a dog beach in Coronado, a peninsula off the coast of San Diego. This had been one of Cathy's favorite places.

"Suddenly I felt Cathy's presence," Marcy recalled. "I could tell she was trying to communicate with me. I couldn't believe it took me so long to figure it out. It dawned on me why Cathy had chosen the blue butterflies."

A scene had flashed in her head of a trip she and Cathy had taken to Foz de Iguazu, Argentina, one of the world's tallest waterfalls. Thousands of blue butterflies swarmed everywhere. Cathy kept saying in Spanish, "*No hay palabras*," which meant "there are no words," to describe the beauty of the blue butterflies.

While on Coronado that day, Marcy froze in place as an overpowering thought hit her. She realized that Cathy has been trying to tell us, "There are no words to describe the beauty of where I am."

Marcy and Cathy at Foz De Iguazu, Argentina where Cathy first saw the blue butterflies and had no words to describe their beauty.

## Cathy and Betsy Go to Washington

In May of 2003, the Border Patrol invited our entire family to Washington, D.C., for the annual Law Enforcement Memorial Service. I had begun to feel Cathy's presence around me on a regular basis. I spoke to her often. Many times I felt as if she spoke back to me. I knew she wouldn't want me to miss a trip to Washington, the center of politics. I was thrilled because we were told we might have an opportunity to meet the President.

"Okay, Cathy," I said. "I know you didn't agree with his politics, but you know how happy it would make me to meet him." I felt so sure my sister would help me meet the President that I began telling everyone about my upcoming trip to Washington to meet President Bush.

The Border Patrol treated us like royalty. An agent who had been a friend of Cathy's escorted us on the plane. When we arrived, we were surprised to find two columns of agents lined up in dress uniform, standing at attention. As we walked through the airport, people stared at our entourage of olive-green-and-gold uniforms moving toward the baggage claim. A couple of agents were almost fighting over who was going to carry our bags.

I asked Cathy to please give me some kind of outward sign to show me she was there. She did. The first event was a candlelight vigil for all the families from around the country who had lost a family member in the line of duty. The keynote speaker was U.S. Attorney General John Ashcroft. After every single name had been read, the entire crowd of 1,000 people lit candles and held them up. I asked Cathy to please blow out my candle. A few minutes later a slight gust of wind came out of nowhere. Only my candle went out.

Finally the day came when we were to go to the Capitol for the main ceremony. The keynote speaker was President Bush. Approximately 160 families had lost loved ones in 2002. We waited in the hotel conference room. As they called our names, each of us was searched then put on a bus bound for the Capitol.

I thought about how many people in the world lose family members without any of the fanfare we were receiving. I thanked Cathy for choosing to die the way she did. I don't think I could have handled it if she had driven off the road while driving down the highway, another anonymous death.

As we pulled up in front of the Capitol building, the sight was incredible. Police officers from all over the country lined up in columns. They snaked around the Capitol lawn for at least a mile. The band was playing a patriotic tune. I was shocked that this was all for us. I knew Cathy was enjoying herself immensely. She loved the ceremonial aspects of law enforcement. As we marched toward our chairs in front of the podium, I knew Cathy was marching right next to me.

I waited breathlessly to see the President. Finally he came up to the podium to speak. I don't remember anything he said because I was nervously waiting for the time when I would get to meet him. He stopped the ceremony to come down onto the lawn where we were sitting. The crowd surged forward. To the chagrin of the Secret Service, he stayed there for more than an hour. I watched as he hugged and kissed tearful person after tearful person.

I began to think there were too many people around him. But my husband got in front of me and pushed his way to the front of the crowd, and my determination kicked in. I followed him toward the President. I think he noticed my husband in uniform moving his way. Suddenly the crowd parted. He was right in front of us. I reached out and grabbed his arm. "Mr. President, I lost my twin sister. I know you can identify with that because you have twins."

He grabbed me by my shoulders and put his face so close to mine I could see into his eyes. I saw the compassion in his face. He hugged me and said, "Your twin sister? I bet that is painful for you. Where did this happen?"

Betsy and Jack meet President George W. Bush

I told him she was a Border Patrol Agent in San Diego. He still had a vise grip on me. I finally got the

53

courage to ask for a picture. The President said, "Of course." My husband handed the camera to a Secret Service Agent who snapped the picture. I walked away elated. I was dying to talk to my sister about meeting the President. I thought back to all the times we argued over politics. I asked her, "So who was right?" To my surprise an answer came, although not the one I was expecting. "There is no greater fallacy than to believe one way is right and another is wrong."

## Cathy's Encounter with an Old Friend

I knew that Cathy had been corresponding over the Internet with someone named Tom. They had struck up a friendship but had never met in person. After Cathy died, I found Tom's e-mail address in Cathy's computer and contacted him. I was amazed when he sent me forty pages of e-mails he and Cathy had exchanged. For some reason, I did not read through them carefully until I had completed the first draft of this book. I was floored when I realized that many of the things she wrote were identical to the things I had written about in *Twin Souls*.

"I believe there is a message for you in these e-mails," Tom told me. That was not the first or last time that someone mentioned a message that Cathy was trying to relay to me.

The day Cathy died, Tom wrote an anguished e-mail to one of Cathy's good friends who shared it with me: "It seems so unreal. We have been communicating by e-mail since September 15. We discussed a myriad of subjects including the environment and world politics. But we spent most of our time discussing death and the hereafter...Cathy had come to a strong realization of her spirituality over the past few years. She was actively pursuing knowledge and truth and had come to great peace and understanding with her beliefs.

"We had many long talks over the phone and via e-mail about her discoveries. I am deeply saddened that I never met her in person to see her smile or laugh. She was a very beautiful woman in body, mind, and spirit. I am grateful that she was able to find the peace that most people search a lifetime for and never find.

"The great thing about Cathy is that she was trying to spread the word about the things she had discovered to anyone who would listen. She wanted to make a difference, even if it was one person at a time. Amazingly, I knew her exactly 40 days. I feel as though I have known her for an eternity."

I could see Tom was experiencing grief over Cathy's death. At first I thought it was somewhat odd for someone who had never even met my sister. But he told me a story that gave me a better understanding of his connection with her. "On March 19, 1983, I had a very vivid dream." He remembered the date because it was his son's birthday. It is also Cathy's and my birthday. "I was told in the dream that I would meet someone I had known before in a past life as a Native American, but I would only know her for a short time because she would die in a car accident."

I couldn't believe the synchronicity. My sister had become very intrigued with Native Americans when she traveled to Arizona with the Border Patrol.

I could see that her meeting Tom was not a coincidence. He helped me start the Catherine Hill Foundation. He played a significant role in the planning of two successful fund-raisers benefiting StandUp For Kids: the Blue Angel Gala and the Blue Angel Gala II.

## The Writing of Twin Souls Begins

I knew my sister was with me each time I experienced an unusual occurrence in my life. I tried to share the information with my father, brother, and some of Cathy's friends, but I couldn't seem to reach them. I knew that Cathy had probably tried to make her presence known to them, too, but they were not open to it. I was frustrated. If they knew what I knew and experienced what I had, they would understand that she was not dead but the same feisty Cathy. I remembered my mother's advice to write down my experiences and began to fill the pages of many notebooks with thoughts, feelings, and spiritual experiences. *Twin Souls* by Elizabeth Anne Hill with Catherine Mary Hill had begun to take shape.

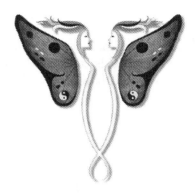

## Chapter Five:
## Catherine Hill Foundation

### Cathy's Kids

In her book *Spiritual Growth*, Sanaya Roman channeled a gentle spirit named Orin, who described a wave of light moving through our universe. Orin said that the light makes any positive action more influential than a negative action. My sister found this to be true while helping her Explorers and homeless teens. I saw a profound change in her as she discovered this unexpected source of light. Helping the less fortunate brought meaning and purpose to her life.

Cathy wrote to Tom on September 18, 2002, "I have been doing volunteer work with an organization called StandUp For Kids. They work with homeless and street kids to try to help them survive and eventually get off the street.

"We have a huge population of street kids here, which I never knew. I have found this kind of work very rewarding and meaningful."

I remembered the message I had received after my sister died: "Your sister Cathy is fine. Remember what she was doing and reading before she died." I thought about what she had been doing, and I knew I had to find a way to continue her legacy.

A week after my sister died, I called Rick Koca, the founder of StandUp For Kids, and asked if I could pay a visit to the StandUp For Kids center where my sister had spent many of her last days.

My father, husband, and I walked into the brightly painted room. Kids were sprawled everywhere. My father saw a group of sullen, angry teenagers. My husband saw the criminals he dealt with on a daily basis. I saw vulnerable, scared children, trying to look tough. I remembered my sister telling me that acting surly and indifferent helped them survive.

I noticed a dark-haired kid staring at me incredulously as if he had seen a ghost. I realized he had seen a ghost. He didn't know that Cathy was a twin. I introduced myself and he calmed down a little. He told me his name was Lou. I remembered Cathy talking about him. "There's this kid Lou. I think I'm really reaching him."

Lou and I walked outside. I could see he was in pain and on the verge of tears. "I finally found someone who cared about me, and now she's gone." He sobbed. The depth of his feelings surprised me.

"She is still with you, Lou. I know that may sound strange to you, but she is with me. I can feel her. I know she wouldn't leave you either. If you need her, just talk to her."

I told him how often Cathy had spoken about him. He was thrilled. He asked me over and over again to tell him exactly what she had said. "She said you were smart and had a lot of potential. She was hopeful that you would get off the streets." I could see the obvious pride in his eyes. But the pride soon turned to despair. He told me, "I am doing things that I never thought I would do. I'm on the edge. I will either get off the streets or become a criminal."

I reached into my pocket and pulled out Cathy's American flag pin. "Cathy loved this flag pin and wore it on her uniform. You can have it." Again I was amazed by how touched he was by such a small gesture. His eyes brightened. "Are you one hundred percent sure she actually wore this on her uniform?"

"Yes, she did, Lou. She wore it over her heart."

He ran off with his new prized possession.

Rick called me inside to meet two other young men, Josh and Bubba. Josh grinned at me with rotting, yellow teeth. Bubba's head was shaved into a mohawk. They told me how much Cathy had meant to them. Both Josh and Bubba were in the process of joining the military at Cathy's coaxing. I remembered her telling me she had persuaded some of the kids to join the military because she believed this would give them a sense of pride and discipline.

Bubba pulled me aside. "I have to tell you something. On Halloween night I rode the bus to Cathy's grave so I could bring her a carved pumpkin I made. I lit a candle inside the pumpkin and I read from my Bible. I left it in a tree above Cathy's grave." At this point he lowered his voice to a whisper. "I lay down on the grass and fell asleep. When I woke up, I saw it had rained. But I wasn't wet, and the candle was still burning."

I bit back tears as I heard this incredible story. Although Bubba towered over me, I threw my arms around his scrawny, six-foot-three frame and hugged him tightly. I thanked him for the beautiful story. I handed him my sister's Border Patrol pin. He thanked me profusely, as if I had given him a precious stone. A month later, I visited my sister's grave and saw the Bible in a plastic bag, hanging from the tree over her grave.

As we left the center, I felt I had gained a new perspective on my sister. A strong thought came to me: She was not a religious person, yet at the end of her short life, she had embodied the highest Christ-like ideals. It was evident in the faces of the homeless kids she had cared so deeply about. They were society's throwaways, but she saw beauty and hope in them. To her they were diamonds in the rough.

The strangest sensation moved through me, as if I were experiencing the pure joy Cathy felt while helping others. She had transcended the realm of the mundane because she had aspired to something larger than herself.

What could I do to keep her incredible spirit alive? I felt an idea coming to me. In my head I heard, "The Catherine Hill Foundation." I would start a foundation in her name and raise money to benefit her kids and other causes that were close to her heart.

### The Blue Angel Gala

A month later, the first meeting of the Catherine Hill Foundation was called to order. A group of six people sat in a small conference room discussing fund-raising ideas. We came up with the name for our first event: the Blue Angel Gala, benefiting StandUp For Kids. Immediately I felt the spiritual force of light I had read about propelling the foundation. Each person who became involved added something that was needed.

Bill was a classmate from high school who offered the services of his law firm. He set up the foundation as a non-profit, California corporation.

Martha and Diana, two lifelong friends, began collecting auction items and soliciting corporate donations. Another friend, Karen, agreed to store and catalog the auction items at her house.

Tom worked in law enforcement but also ran an Internet company. He persuaded his business partner to design and host a Web site for the foundation.

Jack, another high school friend, worked for a local news station in San Diego. He asked his former colleague Kimberly Hunt, a popular newscaster, to host the Gala. He and a co-worker put together a touching video tribute for the event.

60

John ran a large security company that handled sporting events. He rounded up autographed sports memorabilia and wrote the foundation a check to get things up and running.

Debbie was a good friend of Cathy's for many years. The three of us attended classes together at San Diego State University. Her degree in accounting became vitally important. She did the books for the foundation and successfully filed paperwork with the IRS for our 501(c)(3), non-profit status.

Claudia, a friend with a creative flair, stepped in to coordinate the event. She negotiated a substantial discount with the Sheraton Hotel. She came up with the theme "Old Hollywood Casino" and began searching theater companies for authentic decorations and props.

Marcy is a talented artist. She designed a perfect blue angel logo for the foundation.

Anne seemed to come out of the woodwork. She was a veteran fund-raiser and jumped in with both feet to help. She recruited her friend Barbara, an auction coordinator, to handle our silent auction for a minimal fee.

I was excited about our steady progress, but I noticed when I told people about the Gala, often their first response was to point out why I would not be successful. My husband was the chief naysayer. He is very uncomfortable with anything that resembles chaos. He likes things to be planned and executed flawlessly, and a volunteer organization doesn't always run that smoothly. He put great effort into passing out flyers, soliciting auction items, and recruiting people to come to the Gala, but he kept reminding me that many other organizations were trying to raise money and that I shouldn't be surprised if I was turned down for donations or if not many people came to the event. I knew his intent was not to discourage me; he was afraid the Gala wouldn't be successful, and he didn't want me to be disappointed.

As the day of the event approached, I received e-mails from committee members asking me to solve multiple problems. I began to panic. What if the whole thing fell apart? What if no one came? I became so worried I couldn't sleep.

One week before the Gala, we had only received a few RSVPs. I lay in bed at night, crying. I just wanted it to be over. Finally I heard someone say, "Trust and patience—it will come together."

The day of the big event, the other committee members told me not to help set up but just to show up at 7:00 p.m. My husband and I got dressed in our hotel room. Neither of us spoke. Our nerves were on edge.

We took the elevator down to the first floor and walked down a long hall toward the ballroom. As the doors came into view, I was overjoyed. People were lining up. The room was brightly lit and already full of festive

KUSI News Anchor Kimberly Hunt MCs for the Blue Angel Gala.

partygoers. Everything seemed to sparkle. Women in long gowns and tiaras were handing out white boas to the women and top hats to the men. As we entered the room, white-gloved waiters passed out champagne. Guests were happily bidding on silent auction items, gambling at the casino tables, eating, and drinking.

The crowd cheered as Kimberly Hunt took the stage and introduced me. I gave an emotional speech. After I had finished, Bubba came to the podium wearing his Army dress uniform. The crowd was deeply moved as he spoke eloquently about his life on the streets, the help he received from StandUp For Kids, and his encounters with Cathy.

He told a story I had heard Lou and several other kids tell. The last night they had seen Cathy they had stolen her shoe and were playing catch with it. She was feigning anger and trying to get it back. "Even though she was only about five feet tall, she was tough. We all knew she would take on anyone in the room!" Bubba laughed. "So we didn't mess with her for very long. But she was a good sport about it."

The video was shown, and it brought the entire room to tears. After the video people rushed to the auction tables to raise their bids and then flooded the dance floor.

As the evening came to an end, I felt overwhelming relief. We had pulled it off.

Betsy and Friends at the Blue Angel Gala

## The Blue Angel Gala II

Many people approached me and insisted I should have another event. I told them emphatically, "No." I couldn't imagine enduring that kind of stress again. But Tom told me, "This is only the beginning."

After the Gala, it was my job to track down people who won auction items but hadn't purchased them. I went to collect from a woman who had the winning bid on some jewelry. I was escorted into her office. As I waited for her to bring me a check, my eyes landed on a statue of a butterfly. Then my eyes moved to the center of one of the plants. A blue butterfly was propped up inside the plant. The more I looked around the room, the more blue butterflies I saw. I was holding back laughter by the time the woman came back to hand me her check. I knew I would be planning another gala.

I wondered where we would have the event. My friend Claudia kept mentioning the Westgate, a quaint, European style hotel in downtown San Diego. Her husband, Dirk, had stayed there a few times and knew the manger. Claudia asked Dirk to e-mail him to see if he could help us. Dirk e-mailed the manager, and I followed up with a phone call. I did not hear back from him right away.

Anne had agreed to take over the coordination of the event from Claudia. One day I was driving to meet Anne at a theater company to get ideas for a new theme when I noticed a car with a blue butterfly on the back windshield. When we entered the theater company, I saw a stack of stationery with blue butterflies on the front. I thought, "Something is going to go right today."

I discussed with Anne the possibility of having the event at the Westgate Hotel. She suggested that after we were done with the props, we drive directly downtown to take a look at it. As we were driving, the manager of the Westgate called. I had a tingling feeling all over. I knew the Gala would be held there. Sure enough, the manager was very accommodating, and we made the decision to have the second Gala at the Westgate.

I thought about Bubba. I knew he was deployed with the Army in Afghanistan, and I hadn't heard from him. I wanted to find a way to involve him again. I told Cathy, "I really need to talk to Bubba." A week later, not only did Bubba contact me, but I discovered he was on leave in San Diego for a week.

Anne found a videographer named Joe who was willing to put together a new video for a fee of only $100. We met Bubba at the StandUp For Kids center. Again we were surprised at how well Bubba spoke off the cuff about his experiences as a homeless teen, his new life in the Army, and how meeting Cathy, a StandUp For Kids counselor, had changed his life.

Things appeared to fall into place. Several new volunteers stepped forward and began working diligently, collecting cash and silent auction items. A printer agreed to print 2,000 invitations free of charge.

I needed a graphic artist to design the invitations and the auction booklets. I received e-mails from two women whom I did not know. One offered to do the invitation; the other offered to do the auction booklet. I was somewhat baffled. I was not sure how they had come to me. When I questioned them, their responses were rather vague. One of the graphic artists instructed me to go to her Web site to look at her work. I smiled. The home page showed the image of an angel.

Another day, I received a call from a woman whose name I did not recognize. We played phone tag for a few days. She was very persistent so I continued to try to reach her. When I finally spoke to her, she told me she had heard about our Gala and wanted to help. She explained that she had been an abused child and wanted to find a way to help troubled teens.

She was a creative person and offered to be in charge of the decorations. This was just the skill I needed at the moment. She also volunteered to print and hand-decorate 300 auction booklets to be handed out at the Gala. I was mystified. It seemed as though a solution presented itself for every problem that would arise.

The theme of the event was going to be the "Enchanted Evening." I wanted to find a ball gown that would promote the fairytale atmosphere. I pictured an elegant, purple gown with a hint of sequins.

In my mind, I saw a small dress shop on Fifth Avenue. I had never been inside but had walked by many times. I entered the shop and saw the purple dress, just as I had envisioned it. It was my size. I purchased the dress and thanked my sister for guiding me to it.

Amy,
Betsy
and
Deb

Betsy with blue butterfly

Amy
and
Marcy

Betsy and friends at Gala II

66

A month before the Gala, problems and obstacles began to emerge. The auction committee called me in a panic. They didn't think we had enough silent auction items. The fund-raising committee was concerned that not enough cash was being collected. Three days before the event, our Master of Ceremonies canceled. We were having difficulty pulling everything together. I began to feel frazzled again.

The day of the Gala arrived with a new problem. We had too many auction items and not enough room to display them or people to set up the room. Everyone was tense and looking to me for answers. I felt on the verge of a nervous breakdown when I heard someone say, "Without adversity, there is no triumph."

I thanked whoever had delivered the message and left for my scheduled hair appointment. I said a prayer that everything would come together.

When I made my entrance at 7:00 p.m. I marveled at how smoothly things were going. A piano player greeted guests as they stepped into the lobby. The hotel had been transformed into the land of enchantment. Teenagers wearing butterfly, fairy, hobbit, and wizard costumes guided the partygoers through a check in line and up a sweeping staircase. I followed the crowd up the stairs and found festively decorated auction tables displaying a wide variety of items such as jewelry, wine, and airline tickets.

I smiled to myself as I thought about all we had accomplished. We had started with six people in a room talking about fund-raising ideas. In a two-year period, we received our non-profit status and established a Web site and sponsor list. We had two successful fund-raisers and donated more than $40,000 to StandUp For Kids. My sister had told friends that she wanted to get a large group of people together in the community to do something good. Her wish had come true.

The struggle had been worth it. It was clear that Cathy was working through me so that she could continue helping the kids she cared so much about. My life's spiritual journey was being revealed. The successful creation of the Catherine Hill Foundation gave me a glimpse of what my sister and I would accomplish together. Tom was right. It was only the beginning.

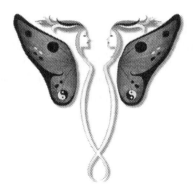

## Chapter Six:
## The Message Is Within the Books

After my sister died, I met several spiritually gifted people who told me that there was a message my sister wanted me to share with the world. I also dreamed that someone was trying to give me a message. What was the message?

I sat contemplating this when I surprised myself by writing: "The message is within the books." It was an obvious conclusion but one that had escaped me until I wrote down the words. Cathy had left stacks of books behind for me to read, and I was told by Kim, a spiritual medium, that Ben, a wise old family friend, was also bringing answers to my questions by guiding me to certain books. Each book taught me something unexpected and opened a door to a new understanding.

### There Is Life after Death

The first thing I had to accept was that there is life after death. Without that knowledge, I could not understand any other truths. A friend recommended that I read about near-death experiences.

I bought a copy of *Embraced by the Light*, which describes one of the most detailed near-death experiences ever recorded. Betty J. Eadie died during complications from surgery. The story of her journey to a place of love and light is awe-inspiring. As I read, a feeling of peace spread through me that I hadn't felt in a long time.

One of Cathy's main criticisms of religion was that it actually promotes fear instead of love. I had begun to see that in many cases this was true. One Sunday I was sitting in Mass when a question came to me: "Why are religious people so fearful, especially about death?" A line in the Mass caught my attention. I had heard it many times, but that day I heard the message behind it. "We pray for those who have gone to their rest in the hope of rising again." I thought, "What a terrible image, 'resting' in a dark, cold grave 'hoping' you will be found worthy to rise again."

During her journey, Eadie, who had been Catholic most of her life, had a wonderful encounter with Jesus and was able to ask him many questions. I was astonished when I realized that she was concerned about the very same line in the Mass that I had questioned a week earlier. Jesus explained that the grave is for the body, not the spirit. With that simple explanation, her fears about death dissipated.

### After-Death Communication

It seemed that Cathy was doing everything she could to let me know she was still a part of my life. I wondered if other people had similar experiences. One day I was searching the recommended reading list of one of the authors I had recently read. One book title jumped out at me, *Hello from Heaven: A New Field of Research—After-Death Communication—Confirms that Life and Love Are Eternal* by Bill and Judy Guggenheim. I ordered it immediately.

When the book arrived, I knew it was significant because the cover was blue with butterflies on the front. In their research, the Guggenheims spoke to people around the world who had similar experiences after the death of a loved one. Clearly, family members who die want us to know that they are still with us in spirit and that they are happy.

To learn more, I went to see a live appearance of medium James Van Praagh. Van Praagh said that one of the ways our loved ones reach out to us is through electricity. He asked the audience, "How many of you have had your garage door go up and down by itself or seen lights flickering?" Seventy-five percent of the people in the room raised their hands. I was one of them.

Another way our loved ones reach us is through what some would call telepathy. In *Hello from Heaven* it was described as "hearing" something in your head or having thoughts that seemed to be coming from an outside source. People described how they could hear family members' voices. I was glad to learn about this because I felt as though my sister and others were communicating with me this way.

Many people described vivid dreams in which their loved ones spoke to them. Several people described scenes in which someone stood next to them, showing them a scene of their deceased family member happily engaged in some activity.

A few people have even answered their telephones to find their deceased loved ones on the other end. The messages were always very short: "I'm okay" or "I'm very happy; don't worry about me."

One night I was thinking about the fact that Cathy hadn't gotten to meet her "Mr. Right." She had always wanted to meet a guy who drove a Jeep. It was one of the things that made me feel very sad. A few days later, I had a dream that someone was standing next to me, showing me something. It seemed as if I were watching a movie. I felt as if I were being allowed to look into another world. I saw two people riding in what looked like a convertible Jeep Wrangler. Even in my sleep I was stunned. It was Cathy, with a good-looking guy, driving along a road in beautiful colorful desert. Cathy loved the desert. She turned her head and smiled at me.

The next day I told Cathy that I appreciated the dream, but I wanted to hear from her own mouth that she was okay. I prayed for her to find a way to talk to me directly. A few days later, I dreamed that I was at work as a 911 dispatcher when I felt a strong energy came through my telephone headset. I heard someone talking, and I realized it was Cathy.

At first her voice was very high-pitched, almost whiney, with a lot of static. I realized that this was how many mediums described the voices of people who have "crossed over." The first thing I understood was "It's not scary at all" and then "It is so beautiful here. I am so happy. I'm in my favorite place." Then her voice faded away. I thought about Marcy's vision of what Cathy had been trying to tell us through the blue butterflies—"there are no words to describe the beauty of where I am."

Before I woke up I heard someone say, "That is why she wanted you to read that book." I woke up with tears streaming down my face. There was no doubt in my mind that it really was Cathy, and she was reassuring me that she was okay and not to fear death.

In another dream I went to see a medium to try to make contact with Cathy, but the medium was not able to make the connection. As I walked away, I heard Cathy's voice calling me: "Beeeeeetsy," she screamed in an exasperated tone. I looked across the street and there she was, plain as day. She said, "I was there the whole time." I said, "I know."

I continued to have dreams in which I saw Cathy, and she told me that she was always around me. Once I dreamed I was trying on clothes, and she said, "I tried that on, too." I said, "Well, it was probably too big then." She was always smaller than me, which annoyed me. I know now that these were more than dreams and that it really was my sister.

## A New Understanding

I have always had questions about religion. After my sister died, these questions became more urgent. Once I had a clear understanding about life after death, I began thinking about life's bigger questions. How could one group of people claim to be God's chosen people? Although I had recently become Catholic, I had a sudden interest in Eastern philosophies, as Cathy had. The books I had been reading allowed me to see the ancient truths behind these teachings. This led me to ask, "Who really was Jesus and how did he fit into other religious teachings?"

I came across a book that answered many of these questions. Cathy's friends and I took a trip to Bisbee, a quirky little town in the high desert of Arizona. Cathy had fallen in love with it when she was sent there on special detail with the Border Patrol. In the basement of an old antique store was an area that could only be described as "Cathy's book corner." All the books were there, the ones that she had read and many more like them. Our mutual friend Amy knew which books Cathy had read, and she had read many of them herself.

She was handing me stacks of books when she came across one called *The Messengers: A True Story of Angelic Presence and the Return to the Age of Miracles.* She said, "You have to read this!" But when she saw I already had an enormous stack of books, she put *The Messengers* back. Yet with a title like that, I had to have it. I grabbed it and ran upstairs to pay for it.

The book tells the true story of a successful Portland, Oregon, businessman named Nick Bunick. Bunick had never been a religious man, but he had an overwhelming interest in Jesus. He had had many unusual spiritual experiences that he could not explain and he had a strange feeling that he had experienced something extraordinary but couldn't remember it. He was persuaded to see several spiritual mediums and they all said the same thing: "Oh, my God! You walked with the Master!" Bunick had no idea who "the Master" was. To his surprise, he was told that in a past life he had been the Apostle Paul of Tarsus and that he had walked alongside Jesus.

Finally Bunick agreed to see Julia Ingram, a past-life regression therapist. Under deep hypnosis, he told the story of his life as Paul, then called Saul, and his relationship with Jesus, called Jeshua. I felt a tingling sensation all over when I read this. I feel this surge of energy whenever I come across profound spiritual information.

The book showed that the original teachings of Jesus are harmonious with Eastern philosophies. It also maintained that Jesus did not come to give the world one particular religion or to be worshipped but to spread love and brotherhood to all of humanity by his incredible example.

Bunick was reluctant to share this information. But angels prevailed upon him to tell his story. After Julia Ingram and G.W. Hardin recorded Bunick's amazing story in *The Messengers*, Bunick went on to write *In God's Truth*, a poignant account of the lessons he had learned from Jeshua (Jesus).

An interesting phenomenon began to happen. Bunick, his friends, and his colleagues began to be awakened at 4:44 a.m. He discovered that in Aramaic the word "angel" means "messenger." He learned that the number 444 is a message from the angels to remind us of God's love in the world. According to Doreen Virtue, Ph.D., and Lynnette Brown in *Angel Numbers*, 444 means that thousands of angels are surrounding and guiding us.

Other people who have read *The Messengers* have experienced the 444 phenomenon. The number 444 has become a significant symbol in my life. My husband even noticed it. One Sunday we were running late for church, which was common. He glanced at the clock on the VCR.

"Look, it says 4:44; maybe the angels are trying to tell us to hurry and not be late for church."

I often saw this numeric symbol at work. We had a map screen that divided every section of the city of San Diego into three-number districts called "beats." Each time a new address was entered on the computer terminal, the map screen changed to show the proper location and beat number. One day I saw that my map screen showed beat 444. I had loaned *The Messengers* to my co-worker Bethany to read so I showed her the 444.

Later that day I received a phone call from a young man who was outside the police station using a pay phone. He said he was from Norway and he had lost his wallet. He had no money and did not know what to do. He asked me for help. I felt heartbroken. I was tired of telling people that there was nothing I could do for them. I decided that I was going to give him some money. I sent a message to my co-workers asking if anyone else wanted to donate money. A few people did.

One co-worker, "Sara," seemed extremely hostile toward the idea. She began loudly ridiculing me for being gullible and allowing myself to be scammed. I ignored her and during my lunch break went to talk to him. I gave him some food and money I had collected. I also looked up the numbers for the Norwegian consulates in Washington, D.C., and San Francisco and let him use my cellular phone to call Norway.

When I got back to my desk, I continued to receive angry messages from Sara. She demanded to know if I was going to tell the people who had donated money that they had been scammed. Then she complained that I was late coming back from lunch. Even our supervisor got involved.

I was stunned. I couldn't imagine my co-worker getting angry over something as simple as my reaching out and helping someone. I couldn't help but think there was something symbolic about the situation.

I glanced at my map again. I felt a chill go up my spine when I realized that my screen was still stuck on beat 444. I asked Bethany, "Isn't the map supposed to change every time I enter a new address?" She confirmed that it was. Bethany could see how upset I was about my co-worker's anger. She reminded me of the 444 on my screen. My map was stuck on beat 444 for the rest of the day.

I woke up in the middle of the night thinking about the incident. Even though I had to get up at 4:00 a.m., I couldn't go back to sleep. I began to worry that maybe it had been some kind of scam. I would feel bad for taking other people's money if it was a scam, not to mention that I was probably going to get written up for being late from my lunch break.

Finally I heard someone say, "So what if it was a scam? Does that make a difference?" And I heard, "What is the book *The Messengers* about?" I had been receiving this type of communication ever since my sister died.

"Well," I thought, "*The Messengers* is about Jesus. And I had done what Jesus would have done, hadn't I?" I felt relieved and went back to sleep. The next day at work I sat at a different computer console than the day before. My map screen was stuck on beat 444 the entire day.

I was upset with Sara for several weeks and did not speak to her. But one day I heard someone say, "She was just playing her role." I realized that all the people in our lives are simply playing roles in a great heavenly play. Once we see our lives from this new perspective, our view of the world will change forever.

A month later I was sitting at my workstation reading something that brought my attention back to the young Norwegian. It said that random acts of kindness are more powerful than we know and understand. It also said that Jesus is still among us in spirit and that we will know him because he will disguise himself as someone in need. Something compelled me to look at my map screen. The beat was 444. The time was 4:44 p.m.

While reading *The Messengers* I realized that my Christian viewpoint was merging with my sister's preference for Eastern philosophies. It felt liberating. It made me feel as though I saw a much larger picture of life. I began to ponder what would happen if the entire world followed this trend. What a powerful and positive shift this would be.

## Divine Inspiration

I discussed with a friend my interest in Eastern philosophies and my desire to understand the parallels between Eastern and Western religions. He recommended *Man's Eternal Quest* and *Autobiography of a Yogi* by Paramahansa Yogananda.

I learned that Yogananda's mission was to come to the United States from India to educate Westerners about Eastern philosophies. His desire was to bring Eastern and Western religions together. Yogananda was a Hindu originally, but his love and understanding for Christ and his teachings was beyond anything the West had ever seen. Yogananda's insightful writing stunned me.

### The Saint

For twenty years Daya Mata was Yogananda's assistant and is currently his successor. She said that she had never once seen him deviate from his Christ-like behavior. He always showed the highest ideals of love, forgiveness, and compassion—the hallmarks of Jesus' life on earth. Mata said that Yogananda truly was a saint.

I learned that the bodies of saints often do not decompose after death. For example, Saint Francis Xavier's body was exhumed many times over a period of several years. Each time his body showed no signs of decay. The intact bodies of six saints can be seen behind the altar in a church in Vodnjan, Croatia.

Paramahansa Yogananda died in 1952. According to those closest to Yogananda, his body showed no signs of physical disintegration for an entire month before he was buried.

## The Hermitage

Yogananda started a non-profit organization called the Self-Realization Fellowship with several temples and ashram centers around the world. I learned that one of them was in Encinitas, just north of San Diego. I wondered when I would get the chance to see it. I didn't have to wait long. One day my husband, Jack, and I drove to Los Angeles. On the way back, we decided to get off the freeway and drive down the coast. This was not something we would normally have done. What possessed my husband to do it that day, I don't know. All of a sudden we came upon a beautiful white, blue, and gold Eastern-looking building. "What is that?" I asked. It was the Self-Realization Fellowship Temple. I had been led right to it.

Later that week a friend agreed to go with me to see the Encinitas Hermitage. The place was beautiful. We walked through meditation gardens and saw a glorious view of the ocean. We went inside a small cottage. Huge portraits of Paramahansa Yogananda, Jesus, Krishna, and other spiritual figures hung on the walls. A line of people waited to see one particular room. We asked what was in the room. A woman told us that at the end of his life, Paramahansa Yogananda had lived there. Reportedly, several times while Yogananda was in deep meditation, Jesus had appeared to him. The woman said that he had written a book called *The Second Coming of Christ*, based on his contact with Jesus. I asked how I could get the book. She explained that Yogananda's foundation had not released it yet.

The woman told us that the spiritual energy in the room was so strong that we would be able to feel it. When I got close, I could feel a tingling all over my body, especially in my hands. I could imagine an elderly

Yogananda sitting in a deep and blissful trance conversing with his beloved Jesus. I had never before felt the peace that pervaded my whole being while I stood near Yogananda's small room facing the Pacific Ocean.

## Jesus' True Message

Later I received word that Yogananda's long-awaited book was going to be released. I immediately ordered it and couldn't wait for it to arrive.

When I received the 1,600-page, two-volume series, I felt as though I were holding a rare jewel. The reading was difficult and intricate, but the insights into original Christianity and the comparisons between the teachings of Christ and those of Bhagavan Krishna and other Eastern philosophers were absolutely brilliant.

With Jesus as his guide, Yogananda analyzed the New Testament verse by verse and uncovered Christ's true intended meanings. In many cases, a misinterpretation or an incorrect translation of a single word changed the meaning of an entire verse. These simple misinterpretations caused centuries of bigotry, intolerance, and fighting among the world's great religions.

Even Yogananda was surprised to learn the true meanings behind the words. "Many of Jesus' sayings and parables, which have undergone transformations due to mistranslation from the Aramaic, I did not understand at a first reading," he wrote. "But as I prayed and attuned myself with Him, I received the meaning directly from Him. Revelations that I never expected have been given to me; little did I dream what wealth of truth lay concealed." Yogananda compared the salient messages of the Bible and Hindu scriptures, and found only harmonious unity between them.

I knew Yogananda's message was important for *Twin Souls* after having several dreams in which I heard someone say his name. While coming out of one the dreams I also heard: "Jesus did not come to the world so that his teachings would be twisted into messages of fear."

Yogananda believed that Jesus came in a very dark and unenlightened time. The people were ill-equipped to understand his complex spiritual messages. His teachings were meant for a later time. In fact, a passage from the New Testament confirms that Jesus himself believed this:

"Jesus was sitting with his disciples teaching when Simon said to him, 'Master, you tell these truths, yet how is it they fall on so many deaf ears? The people gather to listen, and know not what you speak.' Jesus told him, 'My teachings are not for this age but for the next.'" Many believe, as I do, that his message was meant for the twenty-first century, a new era of enlightenment.

I came to the sudden realization that the purpose of Cathy's death was to propel me to help spread this new enlightenment by writing *Twin Souls*. And I knew there would be many other books to follow.

### A Conversation With God

Cathy wrote to Tom on October 6, 2002, "I have been reading a series of books called "Conversations with God" by Neale Donald Walsch. The books have been translated into 27 languages and have caused a revolution all over the world. In these books is the kind of thinking that is going to save this planet. Of course they are not popular with the organized religions because they have unconventional ideas about God. They have ruffled some feathers and that is good. In my opinion, it is time for a shake up in every aspect of our lives."

No book about the life of Catherine Hill would be complete without a discussion of *Conversations with God*. Cathy was so enthralled with Walsch's work that I had quotes from *Conversations with God* read at her funeral.

My sister had begged me to read the *Conversations with God* books, but I was stubborn and refused. After she died, I tried several times to read them, but I couldn't seem to connect with them. Finally, three years and dozens of books later, I read *Conversations with God* again.

I was flabbergasted when, on my third try, the books came to life for me. I believe it was necessary to read the other books in order to lay the groundwork for my understanding and acceptance of the information. It was a perfect example of the saying, "When the student is ready, the teacher will come."

Neale Donald Walsch is an ordinary man who had an extraordinary conversation with God. I had a difficult time believing this at first. I believed that people could communicate with those in spirit, but God? I couldn't comprehend that. But as I began reading the profound spiritual messages within the pages of the *Conversations with God* books, my viewpoint changed and I learned that everyone communicates with God all the time.

On Easter Sunday, 1992, the conversation begun. Like Yogananda, Walsch acknowledges that he is not the author of the books, although he did help guide the direction of each book through his questions. He was a channel through which God could speak to all of humanity in the contemporary language or our time.

Life had been difficult for Walsch. He could not find happiness in relationships. He barely had enough money to make ends meet and was even homeless for a year. On that Easter morning, he felt especially frustrated and thought he would go right to the source of all his problems, God.

He wrote a passionate letter to God, full of bitter questions. To his surprise, as he wrote the last of his questions, his hand remained poised over the paper. Suddenly, the pen began moving by itself. He wrote, "Do you really want an answer to all these questions or are you just venting?" Walsch answered, "Both. I am venting, sure, but if these questions have answers, I'd sure as hell like to hear them!" God responded, "You are 'sure as hell' about a lot of things. But wouldn't it be nice to be 'sure as Heaven'?"

Thus began a humorous, awe-inspiring, and uncommon dialogue. As I read, I felt the now-familiar tingling from head to toe. It was as if I were remembering something I had forgotten. This is one of the themes of the *Conversations with God* series: We have forgotten who we are and why we are here.

I never would have believed any of this information if it hadn't come to me in the manner that it did. But it did come to me, and it took me several years of reading and writing to understand why the information was so important.

The *Conversations with God* books have turned my worldview on its ear. It doesn't matter what viewpoint, culture, or background you come from; there is something for everyone to learn in these remarkable books.

Three revelations in *Conversations with God* really struck me. I knew instinctively that these things were the essence of what Cathy was trying to tell me.

First, we are on the verge of destroying our planet in a number of different ways. I would have scoffed at this idea a few years ago, but now I believe it is not an exaggeration. Humanity has discovered a variety of insidious ways to murder one another, and wars are being waged around the world. Sadly, many of these things are being done in the name of God.

Walsch was told in *Conversations with God* that our current level of technology far exceeds our level of spiritual evolution, and this is extremely dangerous. This is not the first time in our planet's history that civilization reached great technical heights. Atlantis was one of many societies that reached a level of advancement far above what exists now. But technology was their God. They destroyed themselves and almost everything else. Surprisingly, Walsch learned that it is our religions, governments, and other institutions that are helping to fuel these problems by promoting the idea of separation instead of unity.

The second revelation is that we must take another look at our most sacred beliefs about ourselves and God. This time in history has been predicted for thousands of years. Science and spirituality are coming together in recognition that human beings are much more powerful than we thought. We have just begun what is known as the *golden age* when people will understand what Jesus meant when he said, "Isn't it written that ye are gods?" Cathy and I believe that we will re-examine our views about God and we will come to the conclusion that God is everywhere and in everything. There is no place that God is not. Walsch learned that we must transcend religious dogma and reject the idea that God is jealous, angry, and punitive. We should realize that God is the divine spark that gives everything life and that we are all inter-connected.

The third revelation is that our thoughts are extraordinarily powerful. The greatest changes begin at the level of belief. My sister was always talking about critical mass. This principle of quantum physics states that if a certain number of people think a certain way about something, a chain reaction will occur and it will manifest itself into reality. Hitler was a negative example of this, and Jesus was a positive example.

Cathy told Tom that she had great concerns for the planet. She wrote, "The world is at a critical juncture." This is why she was pushing me so hard to read all of her books. She wanted me to see the significant problems the world is facing, and she wanted me to see that there are solutions to these problems.

Cathy wrote to Tom on October 6, 2002, "The main premise of the book I am reading—*The New Revelations*, by Neale Donald Walsch—is that in order to change our behavior we will first have to change our views about life, God, our relationships with other people, politics, the environment, and many other things. Whatever we have been doing hasn't worked for us for a very long time."

I thought about what Yogananda had written back in the 1930s, '40s, and '50s, and I realized that there were significant similarities between what Yogananda wrote and what Neale Donald Walsch wrote.

Yogananda had a discussion with Christ, and Neale Donald Walsch had a dialogue with God. I was thinking about these synchronicities when I heard my sister chime in, "Can you get any more reliable sources?" She had a point there.

## Chapter Seven:
## Life's Road Signs

In Cathy's favorite book, *Journey of Souls*, Michael Newton assembled amazing stories of his clients' lives in the spiritual realm. Newton developed a hypnosis technique that allows people to "see" their lives while in spirit. They were able to explain, in detail, how they chose their lives on earth.

Newton learned that we give ourselves what I call "road signs" to direct us down the right path. A road sign comes in many forms. It could be something that seems to be a coincidence but is really synchronicity. It could be someone with whom we feel a great spiritual connection. These people come into our lives at just the right moments. We might only meet these messengers once, or we might know them for a lifetime.

### Synchronicity

All my life I felt a strong pull to become Catholic. When I met and married my husband, Jack, I converted to Catholicism. Because of our work schedules, my husband and I often attended a Sunday afternoon youth Mass. It was uplifting to see hundreds of young people swaying to the sounds of a teen-led band with guitars, drums, and a saxophone.

The church was gorgeous. It was a perfectly round building with a huge skylight. The architecture was such that parishioners could see sky, grass, and waterfalls that surround the church. The style was modern yet somehow classic.

Cathy was very critical of organized religion. She wrote to Tom, "People are searching for answers and organized religion is no longer providing them. I don't think they ever did, but that is just my opinion."

Many of her criticisms I now share, so I wondered why I had felt compelled to become Catholic. One day I asked, "Why was I led to become Catholic?" I got a clear answer: "You would not have been able to discuss religion without experiencing first-hand, one of the world's largest religions." I believe many people are beginning to shift their focus from religious dogma to the unity and universal truths behind all religion.

Despite her criticisms of religion, I felt my sister's presence when I attended that particular church service. Every Sunday my eyes were pulled to the right of me and I was compelled to look for blue wings. Each time I saw at least one or two girls wearing something with blue butterflies or angels.

These wings weren't only blue; they often had a sparkling quality to them. I felt that Cathy had a special connection because of the young people who made up the late Sunday afternoon Mass. She showed me blue butterflies to let me know I was exactly where I was supposed to be in order to fulfill my life's purpose.

### Computer Lock-Up

At one point I sat down and wrote a thirty-page letter to my brother, Mike. I wanted to describe for him the amazing things happening to me. He had a terrible time with my mother's death and was having a difficult time with Cathy's death. I wanted him to realize, as I did, that there was a purpose for her death. In fact, that very letter grew into the book you are now reading.

During the planning of the Catherine Hill Foundation's Blue Angel Gala, I decided to send a copy of Mike's letter to everyone working on the Gala. I tried to send it via e-mail but my computer locked up. I couldn't send it no matter what I did. I tried a few more times then gave up. I said out loud, "What? You don't want me to send it?" I guess the answer was no. I couldn't figure out why. I called my sister's good friend Jackie, who was helping with the Gala. I told her what had happened. She said, "Some people may not be ready to hear this kind of information, and you don't want to jeopardize the Gala. You can't force spiritual information on people."

I started laughing. "You mean you don't want me to try the Cathy Hill shove-it-down-their-throats method?" My sister used to get so excited about what she read that sometimes she would try to force people to listen to her, which never worked.

I know now that the timing was not right—that the letter needed to be turned into this book. Sending it to a huge group of people would have been disastrous on many levels. Cathy was not going to let that happen.

Another time I found documents on my sister's computer that she had written about problems she was having at the Border Patrol. She felt as though someone in a supervisory position was unfairly targeting or blackballing her. A few of her supervisors and trainers had taken a dislike to her. I am sure that some of it had to do with the fact that she had a hard time keeping her opinions to herself, an unacceptable thing in a paramilitary organization.

Cathy wrote to Tom on October 13, 2002, "Sexism is alive and well in law enforcement. The Border Patrol is no exception. Women have to do things differently because of our size and physical strength but I believe we have a place in law enforcement. I found out that many people can't accept that, and they find subtle, and not so subtle ways of showing their dislike and disrespect for women. I really didn't expect it to happen to me. I am not sure why. I guess it is because I had never really felt discrimination before and just thought it was being exaggerated."

I thought the details of her struggles were important, but every time I tried to print what she had written, the printer would spit out a blank page. I tried a number of times. Finally, I asked her, "You don't want this to be part of the story?" I heard quite clearly, "It doesn't matter." That was that. I was happy that I was getting clear direction as to what information was important for our story. My computer has locked up on multiple occasions, and each time I realize it is the hand of those in Spirit stopping me from jeopardizing important messages.

## Spiritual Connections
### Carol

A week before I began training for my volunteer job at San Diego Hospice, my husband and I were walking downtown when we came across a bookstore. I felt compelled to go inside to the section on death. I bought several books by Elisabeth Kübler-Ross. Kübler-Ross was a hospice doctor for twenty years. Her insights about death and dying touched me deeply and prepared me to become a hospice volunteer.

The first night in the training class, I realized I was in a room filled with people on the same page as I was. I seemed to connect in particular with a woman named Carol. She said she had read all of Elisabeth Kübler-Ross' books.

Later in the training we were asked to write down and then share with the group whom we would invite to a dinner party if we had the chance. We could invite anyone, alive or dead. The exercise was designed to help group members get acquainted. I wrote Paramahansa

Yogananda. Carol had also chosen Paramahansa Yogananda. This would not be the first or last time Paramahansa Yogananda would be a road sign for me.

During a break, I heard Carol say she had psychic abilities. I kept thinking that I should approach her to discuss my book. The night before the last training, I had difficulty falling asleep. There seemed to be a lot of "noise" in my head. I felt as if I were being pushed to print a copy of my manuscript and show it to Carol.

"I felt you might be interested in this," I told her.

She only had time to read a few paragraphs, but she said she was very taken by the story. I told her about some of the remarkable things that had been happening to me. Carol stood for several minutes, seemingly deep in thought.

"Wow, I can really sense that you have a lot spiritual guidance around you. I think that you are definitely going to be a successful writer. I see that people who would not normally read this information will read it. Somehow I see people who are shut-ins reading what you have written. I also feel like someone has a message they have been trying to give you." There it was again, the suggestion of a message.

I felt strong electricity in the air while talking to Carol. I called my friend Amy to tell her about what Carol had said. Amy's response was prophetic. "Sometimes people come into your life for just a very short time to encourage you or deliver a message. You may never see her again." I didn't see Carol again, but I was encouraged, and her message was delivered.

Almost a year later, I was out walking my dog when I became curious about Carol's comment about shut-ins. Then the answer came to me. By shut-ins she didn't mean physical shut-ins; she meant people who have shut themselves in psychologically. I pictured people who have lived their lives in fear, paralyzed by misinformation. I thought especially of people who are afraid of death. I was thrilled. I thought, "I can give these people a second chance to release the fear and live their lives to the fullest!"

### Portia

In October 2004, I was frustrated beyond words. I was tearing my hair out over the planning of the Catherine Hill Foundation's Blue Angel Gala II. It seemed that everything that could go wrong did. My life was so hectic I couldn't think straight. I was taking a difficult, upper level Spanish class with an instructor who prided herself on losing half the class the first day of school. It was the last class I needed to finish my degree. I was on graveyard shift at work and getting very little sleep. Every minute of the day was crammed with some activity: work, school, or the Gala. My husband was unhappy because I didn't have any time to spend with him.

I felt as if my life were completely out of control. I was ready to throw in the towel. I wanted to quit working on the Gala or quit my class. Something had to give. One night I grudgingly agreed to go with my husband to a baseball game downtown. The last thing I had time to do was go to a baseball game, but I felt sorry for my husband, so I went. Even though we were late for the game, my husband insisted on stopping at his favorite pizza place on Fifth Avenue near the ballpark. I, of course, was on a diet in preparation for the Gala so I stood outside looking in the window of a small storefront that read, "psychic readings."

A man dressed in business attire walked up to me and said, "You must go see her; she is very good. I go to her on a regular basis." At first I brushed it off, making some excuse about waiting for my husband. But the man was insistent. I told myself that if the place was still open when I got back from the ball game, I would go in and get a reading.

I thought about what had happened during the entire game. I had an ongoing dialogue in my head with my sister and my other guides. "If you people want me to go for a reading, then it needs to be open when we leave the game." It hit me that this was not some chance event and I had better get back over to the reading room as fast as I could. My husband was enjoying the game and was not about to leave early. I waited impatiently for the game to be over. When we walked back to the small shop, it was nearly 11:00 p.m. The shop was still open.

Inside waited Portia, a small woman with a thick Russian accent. She had incense, candles, and crystals everywhere. It all seemed clichéd to me, and I wanted to leave. But something stopped me.

Portia began, "I see that you have done much for others, but others have not done many things for you. Your karma is moving toward you in this lifetime. You are doing a very good job with your karma, and you will have great rewards."

She told me many things that were extremely accurate. I knew they were designed to let me know she was for real. She discerned that I had fallen in love in 1999. I met my husband in 1999. "You are not soulmates but you have come to go through something together."

Portia told me she could see I lost my mother and that it had made a huge impact on my life. She felt I had also lost someone else very close to me in the past two years. "I see that you have had some kind of spiritual vision or connection with this person who has crossed over." I told her I felt a strong connection to my sister and felt she had been talking to me. Portia sat in silence for a while.

"Yes, I want you to know that you have had and will continue to have very strong communication with your sister. It is very important that you understand what your sister is telling you."

Portia was insistent that she saw some kind of depression or negative energy around me. I told her I didn't really feel I was depressed but I did have spells of anxiety because of all the things I was working on at the moment. After the reading Portia asked me what I did for a living. I told her I was a 911 dispatcher. "Ah, that explains it. You are carrying that negative energy with you. You must find a way to let go of it. I don't think you are getting enough sleep, either." She was right; I had been working the graveyard shift for months. "But what you do really makes a difference in the world; I want you to know that. This job is difficult for you because you are sensitive to the energy of others. You do get exasperated with your callers at times, but you make a big effort to help people and be kind to people, and that is very good."

She told me that I was a generally healthy person but she saw that I would have some kind of breathing problem. She was right; later, a problem with my breathing did develop.

Finally Portia told me what I believe I was there to hear. She said that she saw many obstacles around me, but she could see that I was going to be successful and told me not to be discouraged. "Not only now but also in the future you will have great financial success. You will be well known and will travel overseas. You have a strong spiritual gift, which you have tried very hard to develop. It has been difficult for you, but do not give up." This was certainly true. I had tried to meditate for months, but meditation does not come easily for me. I have a hard time shutting off my thoughts to quiet my mind.

"You will see a change within three days," she said. I wondered what that meant. Sure enough, in about three days I began receiving e-mail messages from people who had collected cash and auction items for the Gala. One of the auction committee's biggest complaints was that we did not have enough jewelry or sports memorabilia. Those had been big sellers the year before.

At our final auction meeting before the Gala, I noticed that a majority of the items brought to the meeting were autographed sports memorabilia or jewelry. Other people noticed it, too, and were thrilled with our good luck. I, on

92

the other hand, knew it was not luck at all. The Gala was an overwhelming success despite the obstacles.

## Helle

One day an announcement came across my computer from The Learning Annex that Dr. Brian Weiss, the author of *Many Lives, Many Masters*, was coming to San Diego. *Many Lives, Many Masters* was one of the first books I read after my sister's death. Our friend Amy had persuaded me to read it. It had a great impact on me. His book has helped to change the way many people view reincarnation. I immediately knew that there was an important reason for me to go and I knew it had nothing to do with past-life information.

I paid extra for my husband and me to attend a reception before the main event. The fact that my husband was going at all was unusual. I had somehow convinced him to read Dr. Weiss's book. It was one of the few he agreed to read.

When we arrived Dr. Weiss was answering questions from a small group of people. I heard a woman with a strong accent asking a question about dreams she had been having. She mentioned she had been writing a book about her dreams that was similar to Dr. Weiss's book. He encouraged her to continue writing and he said her being there that night might change the direction of her life.

A while later I was standing next to the woman. She was tall and elegant with gray/blonde hair and startlingly blue eyes. She was very friendly. She said her name was Helle and she was from Denmark. I asked her about her book and told her I was writing a book, too. We chatted and she showed great interest in my book. We exchanged e-mail addresses. The rest of the seminar was interesting, but I did not have a past-life experience because I was unable to relax sufficiently to reach a hypnotic state. The important reason for coming to the seminar, I realized, was to meet my new friend Helle.

Dr. Weiss gave us an intriguing exercise to show that everyone has intuitive abilities. We were instructed to take a small item from a partner, a person we did not know. I partnered with a man in front of me and Jack partnered with the man's wife. I held the man's car keys to see what information I could come up with. I had a persistent thought that the man was proud of his son for following in his footsteps. I thought that he also had a daughter. My partner was impressed. He did have a son and he felt great pride in his son's choice to follow him into the software industry. He had just two children, a son and a daughter.

Jack's partner said she saw he was outdoors a lot, drove around in a car for a living, and that he liked to play practical jokes. All of this was true. Even Jack did well, and he was quite skeptical. He said he saw railroad tracks in a downtown area of a city near water. The woman told Jack that her son lived in San Francisco and that the tracks might have been trolley tracks near his house. Many people in the room recounted accurate information about complete strangers.

The next day I felt compelled to e-mail my manuscript to Helle. I didn't hear back from her right away. When she responded I was brought to tears. She loved the book. She gushed on and on about how good she thought it was and how well written it was. She insisted that I needed to get it published right away. "Your message must get out," she said. At that time I had stopped writing, but her enthusiasm pushed me to start again.

Helle and I felt a strong connection and became good friends. She asked if I would introduce her to Yogananda's Self-Realization Center in Encinitas. She lived nearby and had been meaning to go but felt uncomfortable going by herself. I jumped at the opportunity to meet her there. My husband, Mr. Cautious Cop, warned me to be careful and told me I should only meet her in a public place. He was concerned because I didn't know her well. I couldn't believe he didn't see the light I saw around her and in her eyes. "You can spot a criminal from two hundred yards away, but you can't spot an angel when she's standing in front of you," I told him. He wanted to know how I knew she was an angel. "I just know," I said. It is almost impossible to explain to a born skeptic how I could know something on such a deep level, but I knew Helle was sent to help me, and I would not be deterred from meeting her.

We met at the Self-Realization Fellowship Center and walked through its beautiful meditation gardens. I was so happy to be back there. We sat on a bench overlooking the ocean. Every time I had been in that spot the sun seemed to be shining off the water. It made the ocean look like a giant sparkling sapphire.

We sat and talked for hours. It was as if we had known each other for a long time. When I looked at her face, I saw the light in her eyes again. She told me she had lived all around the world but had recently moved to Carlsbad, in northern San Diego County. She loved the view of the Pacific Ocean from her bedroom and she never wanted to move again.

Helle explained that she is a "lightworker," someone who spreads light in the world by helping others lose their fear. To my surprise, she said that I was a lightworker too.

Helle told me about her array of spiritual friends around the world. She knew she had strong spiritual intuition. Like me, she was struggling to develop her sixth sense.

As the sun set we continued our conversation at a quaint yellow coffee house up the road. She was such a good listener. I told her all about my family, my sister's death, and about all the amazing things that were happening to me. She took my hands and told me she sensed I had not completely grieved for my sister. She said I had worried about my sister her whole life, like a parent. I was surprised by her insight. I had always worried about my sister. And when she died I had not allowed myself to grieve for more than a few days because I had to plan her public funeral and deal with burial arrangements. I had cleaned out her condo and returned her car to the dealership from which she leased it. I had met with the Border Patrol regarding her benefits and sent out death certificates to all her creditors. I had spent days rounding up her medical records for the life insurance company. Even though I had been given great understanding regarding her death, I had not really grieved the loss of her presence in my life. Helle could see all this in me.

Helle told me about her friend Lisa, an angel therapist. She said an angel therapist works directly with the angelic realm to bring messages of help and healing to others. Helle had already spoken to her friend about me. Lisa told Helle that her purpose is to be a teacher to others and that she would help me talk to Cathy. Chills went up my spine when she told me that. Our meeting was very significant.

Two weeks later, Helle and I got together again at her house. We decided to try the psychic experiment that we learned at the Brian Weiss seminar. We exchanged rings. I sat holding her ring in my hand with my eyes closed. Calm washed over me. I felt a high vibration around the ring. I could sense Helle was an enlightened soul and we were destined to meet.

Helle sat with her eyes closed for many minutes. When she finally opened them I could see she was trying to find the words to describe what she saw. Finally she asked, "Did your sister have a very forceful personality?" I almost fell out of my chair laughing. Did she ever! Helle said that at first she thought she wasn't getting anything but then she realized she saw an object coming towards her but it was so large she didn't know what it was. She realized it was a huge butterfly. She could feel Cathy's spirit. She was coming through strongly. Helle said it was the most forceful energy she had ever felt. "It was as if she was saying, 'I am here. I want my presence known!' Your sister is definitely protecting you. She feels indebted to you for all you have done for her. Wow! She is opinionated, isn't she?" When I told Cathy's friends what Helle had said, they laughed hysterically, too. Like me, they had no doubt that Cathy had come through.

Helle was new at being a medium so she wasn't sure how to interpret the message. "Maybe you should let go of Cathy so she can do what she needs to do and you can move on with your life." That did not resonate with me, but I was thrilled that Cathy had come through to Helle.

Four days later, I got a panicked e-mail message from Helle saying she needed to speak to me right away. I agreed to meet her at her house that week. When I arrived, Helle was very excited. She told me she had made a really big mistake about Cathy. She had been experiencing the most excruciating migraine headache the past four days and she concluded that she had said something wrong, Cathy was trying to get her attention. Helle called her angel therapist friend Lisa in Florida for answers. "Lisa, I think I have angered Betsy's twin sister, Cathy."

Lisa laughed. "Rookie mistake, Helle. Just pass the information on; don't try to interpret it." Helle had given me incorrect information and Cathy was trying to let her know. Lisa told Helle that Cathy is with me because she has chosen to become one of my spirit guides and that she is a big part of my life and would not be going away for all of eternity.

Lisa went on to tell Helle that *Twin Souls* would be a great success. She also said something that I had already suspected: "Her sister's death seemed like an accident to the world, but it was not an accident at all. Cathy's death was part of a much bigger plan, as all things are. Her sister died so that Betsy would do exactly what she is doing now." Wow! That was exciting.

Helle's headache went away immediately. Helle and I laughed about her introduction to the spirit world. "I believe you when you say your sister is feisty! I think she is even more opinionated and pushy in spirit than she was in life. The two of you working together will be a force to be reckoned with."

My sister and I have been accused of speaking our minds quite forcefully when we have something to say. Sugarcoating things was never Cathy's forte or mine. When reading what I had written, Helle was always trying to point out gentler ways to something. I think it is a comical balance between my feisty twin sister and my calm and sensible friend Helle. I realized that I was always pushing to make bigger, bolder statements, and poor Helle was always trying to slow down the freight train of my sister and me coming at the world.

### Sonia

A few weeks later, Helle had a party. She invited another friend she had met at the Brian Weiss seminar named Sonia who was from Spain. I was excited to meet her because Helle said she was a great masseuse and a gifted psychic. When I met her she reminded me of a Spanish version of Cathy, feisty and petite. Right off the bat we got into a political discussion. I felt as if I were arguing with my sister all over again. Sonia, who speaks with a strong Spanish accent, substituted Spanish words when she didn't know the words she wanted in English. Both of us are passionate people, so the discussion did not go well. I became angry and stubborn and decided I was going to refuse to get a massage or a reading. Then I felt compelled to change my mind. I'm glad I did.

As Sonia prepared to start the reading, an item in the corner fell over. She said, "We have other people in the room with us, but don't worry about it. They will settle down."

I could see right from the start that Sonia is good at what she does. She gave me several pieces of information that she couldn't have known. She mentioned that my mother-in-law had just broken her right arm and the doctors were discussing surgery and that she did not want to have surgery. This was exactly right. Sonia mentioned that we had just bought a house and warned we should be careful renting it out. She said there was going to be a problem. We had just bought a house for investment purposes in Coeur d'Alene, Idaho. Later we did have problems renting it because of a trailer park adjacent to the property. With Sonia's words in mind we sold it instead and made a decent profit.

Sonia also mentioned my family and asked why we were so separate from one another. This was an accurate description. My immediate family consisted of my father and my brother. We weren't good about staying in contact. She said that the spirits were reminding me to keep in touch, with my brother in particular.

Sonia could see my sister's energy all around me. "Your sister is with you forever. She sure wants you to be financially successful." She laughed.

Then Sonia told me what I had waiting to hear: "This book that you and your sister are writing—it is your destiny. That was an expensive price to pay for your destiny, no?" Sonia added.

I was confused by her accent. "What do you mean?" I said.

"The loss of your sister was an expensive price to pay in order to fulfill your destiny." That was certainly true. But I understood so clearly what we are doing together that the excitement replaced the grief.

Sonia and I became friends. She came to my house often to give me a massage. She is amazingly psychic and gave me advice throughout the massage. "Do not stop writing this book; it is going to break things wide open. Do not slow down, and do not stop. This is a very good time for this information to come out. The world needs it. You are going to be very famous."

One day she asked me, "What does the word 'duty' mean in English?" I told her what it meant. She said, "You have the word 'duty' scratched on your back." She thought for a while. "Your back represents your past. I think this means that your book is a duty you have been given and it is something that you must fulfill in this lifetime." After a while the word faded away.

## Lena

One afternoon Helle and I went to a bookstore. We both had books we wanted to purchase. As we looked through the spiritual section, we noticed a thin, dark-haired woman sitting on the floor looking through a stack of books. I saw her glance up at Helle several times. Finally she said, "I know this is going to sound strange, but I feel I must meet you. I see light around you and I feel you have a message for me."

"Here we go again," I thought.

The woman's name was Lena. She was originally from Hungary. She told us that she was experiencing severe kidney failure. She had begun meditation and was reading about self-healing techniques. She said she had been intuitive all her life but since she had started meditating she was becoming good at channeling messages from the other side.

"Oh, Cathy, you are so obvious!" I thought. I knew she had a hand in this encounter. This was not the first time she worked through Helle to get information to me. Sure enough, I began to tell Lena about Cathy and *Twin Souls*. "Oh! I just had chills all over when you started talking about your sister and your book! Your sister is here now, you know, and she's poking me!"

"Of course, she is," I thought. I felt the familiar flush and tingling sensations.

"Boy, she has a very strong personality, doesn't she? She is kind of tough and a little cynical, with a dry sense of humor but with a soft heart."

"Yep, that's her," I said.

Helle, Lena, and I went for coffee to talk. I got out one of my sister's old tattered Border Patrol notebook that

100

I carry around to take notes. These things happened so often that I had to write them down before I forgot. I also receive sudden strong thoughts, which I know come from my sister or some other higher consciousness.

"Your sister likes it when you write things down like that," Lena said. "You will continue to have 'lightning bolt' thoughts that you should write down."

Lena is another gifted spiritual medium. Everything she said made perfect sense. "I want to tell you something I see about you. It has to do with your health. You are not in poor health, but I see blackness around you. What do you do for a living?"

I told her. "Oh, of course," she said. "You must get out of there. You are carrying around the negative energy of your callers."

I had a déjà vu moment when she said, "But I just got a strong feeling that you are making many ripples in the world. Anything you do in the world makes a ripple that goes farther than you can imagine. When you help just one person, it makes a huge difference. When you help multiple people, the ripples go forever. You are there for a purpose but should get out soon." This was almost identical to what Portia had said about my job.

After my sister died, I had wondered many times why we had held such opposing views on everything. For several weeks before I met Lena, I saw the yin and yang symbol in my head. I figured we were opposite yet the same in many ways, and that was why we represented yin and yang.

Lena confirmed this when she suddenly blurted, "You two represent the yin and yang of the world, the opposing forces in the universe." I couldn't believe it. We continued to talk, and every so often she would get a piece of information and relay it to me.

"Oh, wow! Your sister and you made a pact before you came to this life to write this book! It's your purpose.

Your sister wants you to know that. It's going to be very important. I see you going on shows. Maybe talk shows."

I had always had a feeling about Oprah so I asked Lena about it.

"I got a chorus of yes's on that," she laughed. Sonia had said the same thing about Oprah. A few minutes later, she said, "The way your sister died and where she died will become important."

Later that week, Helle's husband David asked if I could show him the fence along the border that everyone was arguing about in Congress. I called the Border Patrol to see if they could tell me where the fence was. I spoke to David Brown the Patrol Agent In Charge (PAIC) at the Imperial Beach station where my sister had worked. "Sure, I can show you where the fence is. It is the exact spot where your sister died." My thoughts jumped to what Lena had said about my sister's death. "Damn that woman if she didn't choose to die right in the center of controversy," I thought.

**Neale Donald Walsch**

Neale Donald Walsch, the author of *Conversations with God*, started a non-profit foundation called Humanity's Team. Helle sent me an e-mail message to let me know that Humanity's Team was sponsoring a seminar called "Seeds of Transformation: Toward a Spiritual Renaissance in a Time of Fundamental Change" at Bard College in New York. I was intrigued, but I thought it would be impossible to get off work, and I would have to change vacation plans, plus my husband was not big on the idea. He thought it was extravagant that I wanted to fly all the way to New York for a three-day conference and asked if I couldn't just wait until Walsch came to the West Coast.

I didn't feel like fighting with my husband about it so I decided to forget about going. But every time I opened my e-mail I was reminded of the conference. I felt as if I were being pushed to enroll. Suddenly I knew I was going. I didn't have approval to take the time off work, but I booked the conference and my flights anyway and figured my husband would just have to get over his reservations.

No sooner had I booked my flights than a friend forwarded an e-mail message. It was St. Theresa's Prayer, the prayer that Cathy sent out the night before she died. I was stunned. I asked my friend if she knew the story behind the prayer. She didn't. I knew this was not a coincidence. It was as if my sister were saying, "Yes, yes, yes. Go to the conference!"

A few weeks later, another e-mail message arrived, this one advertising a workshop with Neale Donald Walsch to take place after the conference. It sounded interesting, but again I hesitated. I would have to change all my travel plans and get my shifts covered at work and argue with my husband because the workshop was quite expensive.

I felt I was being pushed once again. I asked Lena and Sonia about it. Both said it was important that I attend. So I paid all the change fees and rearranged my travel plans so that I could stay two extra days for the seminar.

Before I left for the conference, I asked my sister if she would do something that would bring Walsch's attention to me and our book. She did. On the second day of the conference, I attended a session on comparative religion moderated by Walsch. At the end of the session he told the group that he had published a new pamphlet called "Part of the Change." He held up the pamphlet. My heart almost stopped. On the front cover was a large blue butterfly. When I met Walsch and showed him my book cover he was amazed by the symbolism of the blue butterfly and the synchronicity with his pamphlet cover.

Each person at the workshop was asked to say why he or she was there. As I told the group about my story, the room fell silent. I had everyone's attention. Neale jumped in and told them about the coincidence with the blue butterfly.

Walsch is known to be very intuitive. He told me that my sister had sent me to the seminar and he saw that I would be writing a section in my book about death and dying. He told me that he was also writing a book about dying and he thought it was important to understand that death is simply a change from physical form to spirit. Walsch was excited to share with the world that death is not a tragedy but the most glorious moment of our lives. It is the time we have chosen to go home.

I was thrilled. Once again I felt electricity run through my body. I felt the hand of my sister guiding me to the right people and places that would help me accomplish our combined life purpose. It was as if the pieces of a very large puzzle were falling into place.

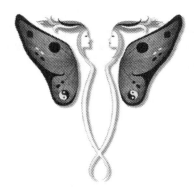

# Part Two — The Message

I spent more than three years reading the books my sister had left behind, and I felt that I had been guided to many others. I could plainly see the underlying messages that ran throughout all of them. I had made many inquiries about life's bigger questions and felt that I was receiving many answers. I was given "road signs" that showed me my intuitions were correct. Yet I was still hesitant. I often woke up in the middle of the night tossing and turning, thinking about the purpose of this book.

I learned that humanity is at a critical turning point in history. I discovered that the world's institutions, from our religions to our political systems, are failing us. And I was thrilled to hear about a refreshing new spirituality that had already begun to transform the world. I wondered how I would deliver such a monumental message.

Although I clearly understood the urgency of the message, I was afraid to speak the truth. I told my friend Helle that I had decided to delete the controversial subjects from *Twin Souls* and simply write about Cathy's contact with me. She told me in no uncertain terms that my book was *not* just a sweet story about twin sisters but that it was much more. She insisted I deliver the message that Cathy wanted me to relay.

The next day I was out jogging when I heard Cathy's indignant voice: "Do you want this to be a fluff piece? You can't change the world while worrying about offending people." Who was I to argue with that?

## More Help from the Medium

Almost three years after Cathy died I decided it was time to pay Kim, the medium I had seen before, another visit. As Portia had predicted, I had developed a strange breathing problem, and I wanted to discuss it with her. Even though I was in constant communication with Cathy and many others in spirit, I knew it would help to have someone who was more adept at receiving spiritual messages bring me more clarity and confirmation on the book's purpose.

Immediately Cathy came through as if nothing had changed in the past three years. "I see your sister sits above you and in front of you, so she can talk directly at you."

"That sounds like her." I laughed. I wanted to know if Cathy really was one of my spirit guides.

"Only in regard to your books, not as a guide for your life. Your sister is saying, 'You don't want me guiding your life.'"

"Well, no kidding, yours wasn't all that satisfying for you," I countered.

I told Kim how Cathy had had a difficult time sustaining lasting relationships because she was always pushing the envelope and arguing with people about her opinions.

Kim laughed. "That was her purpose. She did exactly what she was supposed to do. The image I see is her with a pin poking and prodding people."

"Well, she did a good job of that. She even does it in spirit." I remembered Lena in the bookstore saying, "Your sister is here now, and she's poking me!"

106

I was thinking of a joke I had with Helle that Cathy and I are "gonna shake 'em up." Cathy had written to Tom that she believed it was time for a shake-up in every aspect of our lives.

Kim started laughing. "Your sister says, 'We're gonna shake 'em up!'" I had no doubt that Cathy was in the room at that point.

Kim continued, "This is huge. What you and your sister are doing is very important. I am getting enormous physical affirmations on that. This won't be significant to you, but when I do readings, ninety-eight percent of the information I tell people has to do with the way they have been living their lives and the consequences of those actions. About two percent of the time, I deal with destiny. Destiny is when someone is doing what he or she came to do and may involve several lifetimes. Whenever I encounter destiny, I get chills all over my body. I have been sitting here 'rushing' for the past ten minutes. This is really important stuff we're talking about."

I remembered Sonia's similar words: "This book is your destiny" and "That was an expensive price to pay for your destiny," meaning the loss of my sister.

I told Kim that I had been putting a lot of pressure on myself to finish the book.

"This is not meant to be stressful," she said. "You are being led down a very narrow path. Everything is happening perfectly. What I am hearing is, 'Timing is everything, and that is out of your hands.'"

Kim asked me how many chapters the book would be when completed. I told her that I had written a chapter outline with sixteen chapters.

"No, I'm hearing twenty-four chapters. Your sister says the book will be twenty-four chapters." Twenty-four chapters sounded like an eternity of writing. I wondered what the twenty-four chapters were going to be.

I asked Kim to find out if I was leaving anything out of the book that was supposed to be included. Cathy told

Kim that I had been given ideas that I had discounted and asked me to stop doing that. She also said I had been attracting a lot of "doubting Thomases" and naysayers who had made me feel discouraged.

"It's important to include these experiences in the book to show that these things happen when you are trying to accomplish something like this. And it will show that you have stayed true to your life purpose, despite others' well-meaning attempts to steer you in other directions."

## My Doubting Thomases

It seemed that everywhere I turned someone was giving me advice about the book. People told me that they felt what I was trying to do was too ambitious and that I should limit it to something more conventional. Other people said that I was writing about too many different subjects. A friend told me that when you write about everything, you write about nothing. Our mutual friend Jackie warned me not to criticize organized religion because she thought that would turn people off. My father-in-law warned me not to criticize the Catholic Church. He thought I should forget about the problems in religion and focus on the declining morals in America.

Helle loved the story and wanted me to discuss religion and spirituality but told me I should avoid discussing politics. She believed the subject was too polarizing and that people would think I was trying to push my own political agenda. I knew my feisty twin would never let me get away with that.

### Some Changes are Necessary

I excitedly told my friend who had recommended Yogananda's books about the changes that were going to take place in the world and how I was writing a book that would help facilitate the changes. I was surprised when he answered, "Each person has to work through his or her own issues. If mankind is doomed on this planet, then that is what is meant to happen, and people will just have to go live somewhere else."

I tried to explain to him that some changes are meant to happen and some people come to earth to promote these changes. I told him that if our planet is doomed and we do not make every effort to save it, then we as human beings have not fulfilled our purpose to be the highest version of ourselves. I felt strongly that a transformation was already taking place in the world. But many more people are needed to spread the word.

### Writers' Club

Helle started a writers' club and invited several friends who were either aspiring writers or people who were already published authors. Helle asked me if she could give a copy of my manuscript to "Karen," a friend who wrote a column in the newspaper. I agreed and waited to see what her comments were. I didn't hear anything back. I finally asked Helle what Karen thought about the manuscript.

"Well, Karen is Jewish, and she doesn't like all the details about Jesus. She thinks you should attempt to talk about religion without focusing on Christianity."

I pondered how I could re-write the story without the references to Jesus. But somehow I knew the information about Jesus was very important, and I remembered what I had been told about being Catholic: "You would not have been able to discuss religion without experiencing firsthand one of the world's largest religions."

The day of the writers' club meeting I printed out one of my chapters. I was nervous and became very embarrassed when I was suddenly overwhelmed with emotion as I explained my story and attempted to read the chapter.

When I was finished, Karen said, "Are you going to be able to let go of this story? You are very emotionally attached to it." She also told me she wasn't clear on the purpose of the book.

I went home feeling very confused and dejected. That night I asked my sister, "What is the purpose of the book?"

"We are advocates for change," she answered.

### "You Are Not a Writer!"

A friend suggested I work with a freelance editor and recommended "Jill," a very tough, no-nonsense person who I noticed was very non-spiritual. I thought working with her would give me an opportunity to explain to someone with no spiritual background what the book was about.

One day I arrived at work and realized I had forgotten my backpack full of books. I was upset with myself because I normally spent time reading and gathering information in between 911 calls. I randomly picked up a magazine and read an article about a famous author who had wanted to write a book but many people had tried to discourage her. One co-worker even told her, "You are not a writer." But she persevered and became a best-selling author. The article gave several other examples of people who had followed their dreams even though other people told them it couldn't be done.

This was inspiring because I was feeling somewhat overwhelmed and was having increasing difficulty communicating with Jill. A few days later, she called me and bawled me out. "You are a difficult client. You're not listening to what I am telling you to do. You have an interesting story, but you should get a ghost writer to finish it. You are not a writer!"

I was stunned. I felt complete inner turmoil. Wasn't my life purpose to write this book with my sister? Why did she say I was not a writer? Later I realized that she was just playing her role.

110

Needless to say, I moved on to a new editor. Helle had discovered Midge while taking a writing course. I did not meet Midge in person right away but I had a strange feeling that we had a spiritual connection. She liked my writing style and was fascinated by my story. She told me later that she had, for some reason, been interested in twins all her life and had even done research about what happens when one twin loses the other.

Within a few weeks, Midge unexpectedly received some blue butterfly stickers in the mail. I received the exact same stickers a few days later. Midge was floored when another batch of blue butterfly stickers showed up in the mail when I sent her another one of my chapters.

### "I Don't Believe You"

I worked with a woman named "Cynthia." At any hour of the day or night she could be heard laughing and joking with everyone around her. She was constantly being reprimanded for stirring up trouble so I was suspicious when she asked me to tell her about my book. I began to explain about Cathy and the blue butterflies and how I had begun to receive messages from her. Cynthia stopped me in mid-sentence and loudly pronounced, "No offense, but I don't believe you!" Cathy told me my job was not to persuade people so I simply said, "That's okay. Someday you will."

### Outside the Mainstream

I was initially inspired to write *Twin Souls* because I could not seem to reach my father, brother, and some of Cathy's friends. They could only see a horrendous tragedy and loss in her death. I wrote a long letter to my brother about the things that had been happening to me. I included some of my insights regarding the unity that I believed was possible between the religions and how I felt that the East and West could come together if they just discovered the common truths within their religions.

I e-mailed a copy to Tom. I figured that he would encourage me. After all, he had spent hours e-mailing my sister discussing spiritual subjects. I was stunned when he e-mailed me back, "While I agree with your heartfelt words and ideas, they are not views held by the mainstream. I would not recommend showing them to anyone."

I knew that Tom was a little disappointed that the Catherine Hill Foundation had not continued to organize more galas. I kept telling him that when the book was completed there would be plenty of money for the Catherine Hill Foundation to pursue its goals.

Tom e-mailed me back with some discouraging facts about book sales: "In 2004 195,000 new books were published. This generated $28.6 billion in revenue from the sale of the books. This translates that the average book had sales of $146,667, which comes to approximately 7,000 books. 50,000 books will make a book a million dollar seller. Those who publish their own book sell an average of 77 books (50 are usually bought up by family and friends)."

### "Why Would Someone Read This?"

I refused to be deterred by these figures. I spent many hours working on the book and was thrilled when I had completed the first section, *The Story*. I decided to print a copy and give it to my father.

I was anxious to hear what he had to say. A week later he called me. "Have you shown this to someone who has written a book before? Maybe you should do that. I am just not sure why someone would want to read this."

I was crushed and very angry with him. For several days I stewed over his insensitive behavior. But I felt as though someone was telling me, "Don't worry about him; he is being blocked intentionally." Finally I got over his criticism. I knew that somehow he was not seeing the whole picture and that he, too, was playing his role.

Kim confirmed this. "The rejection you are experiencing is intended and is part of the process. These people are playing devil's advocate so that when you receive criticism in the future it won't bother you. Your father in particular came to this life to challenge your beliefs. From the time you were a teenager he played this role. I see an image of him poking you with a pin." (I guess the pin thing runs in the family.)

"Part of your personal life journey is for you to learn that all things have a purpose and happen exactly as they are supposed to. You must learn acceptance before you can change things. There will come a time when you are in the spotlight when you will have to walk your talk. That is what these people are forcing you to do."

Later I realized that I have always had difficulty accepting things at face value. If someone had a problem, it was my job to fix it, and I worried about everything. Cathy was the same way. But I was confused by this apparent contradiction. How could I learn acceptance and promote change at the same time?

Cathy said, "You have evolved, and that is the most powerful tool for change. Others will follow your lead."

She reminded me of something Yogananda said: "Change yourself, and you will change thousands."

Kim continued, "That is why you have encountered these obstacles, so that you will get the rejection out of the way. And you will learn to differentiate between what you want and what others want for you."

## Breathing Problems

It all made sense. But I still had questions. "Why am I having these breathing problems?"

"Well, the first thing I see is a man in your life who is putting immense pressure on you."

"Yes, my husband has been putting a lot of pressure on me ever since I started working on the galas and writing the book," I told Kim.

"The pressure you feel from your husband as well as the pressure you have put on yourself has caused this problem. I see an image of a balloon being imploded from all angles."

I felt frustrated because my husband's ideas of success and mine were very different. He deemed a person successful if he or she picked a career and stayed until retirement. From his perspective, my jumping from job to job was an indication that I was not on the correct path, and he didn't hesitate to share this belief with me. But I knew that nothing was further from the truth. I could see how each thing I had done in my life led to the writing of the book. But because there was no paycheck at the end of the month, he was having a difficult time seeing the value of my writing.

I decided to become a part-time employee so that I could spend the majority of my time writing. My husband wanted to be supportive but couldn't get over the fact that I had given up a secure job with benefits for something that was not a sure thing.

I tried to tell him my book was a sure thing. I was receiving daily signals that let me know I was doing exactly what I was supposed to be doing.

But my husband didn't see the signals or the huge spiritual force I felt while writing. He did not understand the enormous undertaking I had agreed to take on.

I tried to discuss the topics of the book with him, but he just brushed them off or ridiculed them. At first I was angry, but then I heard Cathy say, "Well, he is more open to the information than you were when I tried to tell you."

Kim explained, "Your husband is along for the ride for a reason, and make no mistake—you are on a ride. I am being shown this big slab of granite that both of you are standing on. The piece of granite is just flying through the air. It's as if you are moving through life very quickly. This will be a time of great growth for your husband. He is actually a very receptive soul, but he often allows himself to be immersed in fear."

"But what is his purpose? I think he is a very good leader."

"He is a good leader, but first he must learn to be a good follower. Part of his purpose right now is to keep you grounded on the earth because you have to be able to function in the realm of the living as well as the realm of the spirit. You are like a helium balloon, and he is holding onto the string. He is putting pressure on you because instinctively he knows that someday he will have to let go of the balloon string. You will both have your dreams, but they will not play out as you think."

## Cathy's Message

I told Kim I felt a strong spiritual presence around me, especially while writing. "That is not your imagination. You have a tremendous amount of spiritual support. I am being shown a strand of light that is threaded through your consciousness, almost like an I.V. As you are writing, different spiritual entities are connecting to the stream of light, and their consciousness becomes one with yours. Then, that spirit disconnects and another is connected. That is the role your sister plays, connecting up the different essences at the proper time."

As the reading came to a close, Cathy gave a magnificent explanation of our relationship and our job together: "As time has gone on since my death, we have progressed in our ability to communicate with each other. What we've done is synchronized the frequency of our thoughts so that we have a direct link back and forth.

"We are able to do this because we have been together for so long and will be together forever. We can communicate in this way because we have such a deep connection and affinity at the soul level.

"All our lives we argued and sometimes we still do, spirit to person, because we are so close. When we are separated, our views and understandings are limited. But together we are able to see all sides. We can see the whole picture. We have taken on this huge task and so it is important that we combine our wisdom. It is important that the world combines the wisdom it has been given in order to bring love back."

Kim agreed that the purpose of *Twin Souls* is to bring about the return of universal love to the world. She explained that it has always been there but is buried under a lot of anger, hatred, and confusion. She also confirmed that the unity of opposites is a central theme of our task together.

"I am being shown an image of a bunch of little dots around the world converging and interfacing with each other to become one single unit. I am hearing, 'When you come into communion with your opposite, you become one.'"

### Let the Light In

One night after the reading, I had a dream in which I was looking down on a group of large buildings. I saw that some of them were churches and some were nondescript rectangles. Then I saw windows and doors being flung open and sunlight was streaming in. Somehow I knew that this was the first time in centuries that light had been let in. I realized these buildings symbolized our world's religions, governments, educational systems, and other broken institutions. The message was clear: It is a new day, an era of renewal and hope, and a time to let the light back in.

### Holistic Treatment for the Planet's Ailments

I was researching holistic remedies for a minor health problem I was experiencing. A friend gave me a book called *Beyond Flat Earth Medicine* by Timothy R. Dooley, N.D., M.D.

The book gives a brilliant analogy that describes the state of one of the world's broken institutions— conventional medicine.

In the past, people believed that the earth was flat. Science and religion supported this perspective. When people began saying that the earth was round, this suggested that everything the "flat-earth people" believed was inaccurate. So they clung to their beliefs for as long as they could until the weight of evidence was overwhelming. Things were resolved when it was understood that the flat-earth view was part of a more comprehensive spherical view.

A similar conflict has existed in medicine for hundreds of years. A German physician, Samuel Hahnemann, developed a theory that disease is a process that affects the patient as a whole. Conventional medicine continues to take the older approach by treating the disease and its symptoms, not the patient.

I experienced this firsthand when I developed the problem with my breathing. I went to see my doctor, who told me there was nothing that could be done, that I should eat smaller meals and sleep at an incline. She gave me some antacids and sent me away.

A few years earlier I had attended a class on pranic healing, a method of using and manipulating light and energy around and within the body to cause the body to heal itself. Prana is the life-force energy that sustains the human body. I watched as the instructor cured a woman of severe, chronic back pain in thirty minutes. She learned that the cause of her back pain was mainly emotional. The instructor said that most ailments are spiritually and emotionally based. The woman cried for several minutes as the instructor manipulated and released the trapped, negative energy in her aura. She walked away pain free.

One night I was terrified when my lungs felt as though they were being squeezed so tight that no air could get in at all. Kim had informed me that the pressure was coming mainly from an emotional source, so I attempted pranic healing on myself and found that there was a glut of energy trapped in my midsection. I had learned that the body has seven energy centers known as "chakras." I knew that the solar plexus chakra has to do with power and control.

The next day I visited my chiropractor, Dr. Magos, who is a specialist in Applied Kinesiology. This system was developed in the 1960s by Dr. George Goodheart of Detroit Michigan. Goodheart discovered that during a chiropractic exam, normal and abnormal body function could be accomplished by using muscle tests. Since that time, the system has been broadened to include evaluation of nutrition, acupuncture, cerebrospinal fluid function, nervous, vascular, and lymphatic systems.

She also used a special diagnostic tool called Neuro-Emotional Technique. This technique addresses the mind-body connection between wellness and our emotional state. Feelings such as fear, anger, and grief can negatively affect a person long after the original event that caused them. If we do not fully resolve emotions they become "stuck" and can seriously impact our health.

She went through a series of tests to see which emotions I was feeling and then made adjustments with the corresponding pressure points and body organs. We discovered that I was experiencing stress because of the pressure my husband was putting on me and I had taken on his feelings of fear, loss of control over our financial situation, and the insecurity he felt over the change in our roles. Within minutes the tight feeling was gone. I could take a full, deep breath for the first time in several weeks.

I asked Dr. Magos if she had some information regarding the Neuro-Emotional Technique. When she handed me the flyer, I burst out laughing. The front cover was a picture of a woman's hand releasing a blue butterfly.

I saw clearly that conventional medicine is "flat-earth" medicine. And I realized that the analogy of "flat-earth medicine" could be taken one step further. Every problem that I will present in this book is inter-related and is a symptom of a much larger disease. Currently the disease is being treated with "flat-earth medicine." Instead, the illness must be cured holistically, by addressing its root cause: humanity's lack of spiritual understanding.

## Astrology Reading

I had finished writing *Twin Souls* in July of 2006 and sent it to Midge for editing. I began to think about how I would get it published. By February of 2007 I still hadn't found a publisher, and I felt that perhaps something was missing from the book that needed to be added. I was still feeling ambivalent about how people would receive the information, which I knew might be hindering me from attracting the right publisher.

I searched the Internet one day and saw an offer for a free astrological reading. I had never put much stock in astrology but thought it would be fun to see what it was about. I requested a free reading. I received an answer back from a woman named Jenna who said that she was an astrologer and a psychic that she sensed tremendous energy around me, and that she saw the enormous changes I had been going through. She said that I was moving into a time of great growth in my life, and she wanted me to send her all of my information so that she could do a more detailed reading. I was hesitant to send out my information over the Internet, so I decided not to answer her Email. But she continued to send me messages and was insistent that if I did not get a reading from her, I should get one from someone else.

Finally I contacted a woman whom a friend had recommended. Eleanor was in her sixties and had been doing astrology readings since 1976. She specialized in providing in-depth psychological-spiritual counseling. Earlier in her life she spent time doing humanitarian work in India and other places around the world. I learned that she had degrees in both physiology and pharmacology and had taught nurses and other health-care professionals.

I gave Eleanor the time, date, and location of my birth, and she formulated an astrological chart, which she sent me ahead of my reading. The chart looked very interesting. It was full of blue and red lines, symbols, and numbers. I was interested in finding out what each one meant.

When the reading began, Eleanor told me that she had looked at my Web site (www.catherinehillfoundation.org) and had read the introduction to *Twin Souls*. She found our story to be very unique and powerful, and she said that she was honored to help me in any way she could.

Eleanor explained that most people believe that astrology has to do with reading their horoscopes in the newspaper. But in reality, astrology is an ancient science that, when used correctly, can accurately predict a person's personality traits, character, struggles, talents, life purpose, career aspirations, relationships, and economic outlook.

Astrologers realize that free will plays a large role in the outcome of a person's life but an astrological chart will help people understand the things that have occurred in their life and it can also help with the timing of events.

I learned that astrology is the study of the correlation between the positions of each planet, the stars, and the constellations of the zodiac at the time of birth. When the planets, signs, houses, and angels are charted, a very complex and detailed profile is formulated.

Eleanor said that what I was really looking at was a dynamic energy diagram, and that my sister's would have been almost identical to mine.

I discovered that I was born under triple water signs, Pisces, Scorpio, and Scorpio rising, which means that I am extraordinarily intuitive and connected to spirit. She also explained that a large part of my energy shows up in the "house of selfless service."

"You have all the signs of a humanitarian, and so you must make choices day by day and moment by moment to

120

serve others or suffer. Your natural talents are for writing and communicating. But you must use your talents on behalf of others or you will be thwarted along the way."

Eleanor directed me to a mass of blue lines going back and forth across my chart.

"Those lines show that you have a tremendous amount of oppositions in your life. You have this major push-pull that often involves other people. It's as if you feel you need to fight for what you believe is right or you feel disempowered.

"Oppositions are very strong teachings to take your power back. Because of all the water signs in your chart, you are very intuitive, but you are looking outside yourself for permission to speak your truth instead of using your authentic power, which comes from a higher source. The only authority you need is your own inner guidance."

I couldn't believe how accurate Eleanor was in her description of the oppositions in my life. And it certainly explained the problem I had in my solar plexus chakra. I realized that I was making the mistake of waiting to get other people's approval before speaking out. All I really needed to do was trust my intuition and my connection to spirit.

Eleanor explained that all people born in 1965 have the same strong desire to change the outdated social structures of the world in some way. She said that many of us feel extremely restless and are often seen as revolutionaries. We want to see changes in science, religion, medicine, and the environment. Our group purpose is to move mankind forward. Eleanor said that Cathy and I would feel this even more strongly than most because of our energy configuration.

"You and Catherine in particular have a Mars/Pluto combination, which brings out strong passion and intensity in your personalities. Impatience would be the least of your challenges. You have immense warrior energy. It is the same energy that is seen in the charts of most generals, soldiers, and warriors.

"When I saw pictures of you and your sister in

uniform on your Web site I said to myself, 'That's Mars/Pluto.' You both have the character traits of people who want to protect and defend others. But beyond that, you have the energy of the spiritual healer and leader. It is a very fiery combination. In a man it could bring out violence and rage, but at its highest, it is the energy of the sacred warrior. It's such an intense configuration of energy that it is almost like the 'charge of the Light Brigade.'

Twins in uniform

"This powerful energy needs to be harnessed and used in the service to all humankind. You and your sister both came in with this gift. It will seem like harnessing wild horses but just know that you have tremendous capabilities, and you have all that you need to move out into the world. You and your sister are powerful change agents. That's why you're here."

I knew intuitively that the healing of oppositions was not only my lesson. The entire world is struggling with duality: good versus evil, right versus wrong, left versus right, my way versus your way.

By coming together in partnership with one another we can heal the power struggles that humanity has created. I remembered the message Kim received during our reading: "When you come into communion with your opposite, you become one."

Twins turn 21

Betsy plays queen for a day as Cathy looks on skeptically

Can you pick out Cathy?

Cathy    Betsy

The Catherine M. Hill, dedicated by the Border Patrol, Spokane sector. Agents patrol the Columbia River between the United States and Canada.

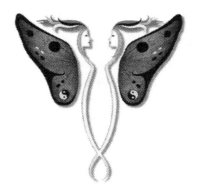

## Chapter Eight:
## Unity and Universal Truth

Throughout the writing of *Twin Souls*, I felt as though I was receiving strong guidance, especially while writing about spiritual subjects. I knew that many of the issues my sister and I had pondered regarding life's bigger questions were being answered in a way that I could relay to our readers.

Cathy and I had spent many hours heatedly discussing spirituality and religion. I had become Catholic just before getting married and argued with the conviction of a convert. My sister wanted me to see that spirituality was much more than one particular sect or set of beliefs. After Cathy died, I felt as though we came together on these issues. She conveyed to me that there are many paths to God. None are wrong. I pictured an ocean and many rivers leading to the ocean, and I understood that God was the ocean and that the rivers were the many paths leading to God. I felt as if Cathy were saying to me, "If the world would just embrace the differences, an unexpected unity would occur."

During my hospice volunteer training, a chaplain came to speak to us. She was a heavy-set woman with graying hair. I was a skeptical at first and wondered if she was going to deliver a sermon. But I was impressed when she opened with a short meditation. What she said next surprised me. It was as if she had read my mind and expressed my thoughts: "The Dalai Lama tells us that ninety-five percent of the world's religions are essentially the same. It is the other five percent that we argue over." Later we asked her what religion she belonged to. She was a Catholic nun.

I was elated. Here was a Catholic nun quoting the Dalai Lama and echoing my own realization that there is a golden thread of universal truth that runs throughout the world's great religions. In his book *Forgotten Truth*, Huston Smith wrote that we merely need to look more closely at the universe to see a remarkable pattern emerge before our eyes. Underneath the differences, we would find common ground.

It is difficult, with the fractured state of religion today, to see the oneness. There are many reasons why we cannot see the commonalities behind the teachings of the world's religions.

Much of what has been passed down through the ages has come from ancient texts, which seem archaic to us. Many of the great insights shared with the world have been misinterpreted and misunderstood. Cathy and I believe it is time for all of humanity to take a second look at the original intent and wisdom within all religious philosophies. It is important to understand that throughout all time and across all races and genders, great souls have walked the earth to enlighten and teach the world.

In *Tomorrow's God*, Neale Donald Walsch learned that all of the world's scriptures taken separately are incomplete. However, if the messages within all the sacred texts were combined, the truth would emerge. This reminded me of Cathy's statement, "When we are separated, our views and understandings are limited. But together we are able to see all sides. We can see the whole picture...It is important that the world combines the wisdom it has been given in order to bring love back."

When we grasp the similarities behind religion, the philosophies will blend together to form a beautiful mosaic.

## Common Principles

Every major religion recognizes a Supreme Being or Creator who is eternal and unchanging. Many call this ultimate reality God. All religions hold the belief that God is omnipresent and all-powerful. All religions call for faith in something larger than the self, something that is unseen.

Even religions which are considered to be polytheistic recognize only one Absolute. For example, Hindus believe that the attributes of God (Brahman) are manifested in many gods, just as Christians believe that God is manifested in Jesus. Native Americans see God in everything, including nature. Whether God is seen as personal or impersonal, the One Source is the Eternal Truth.

Another common principle is love. It is imperative to love God above all things and to love all of God's creatures, including human beings, animals, and nature.

All religions instruct their members to follow the golden rule. For example, in Islam it is said, "No one of you is a believer until he desires for his brother that which he desires for himself." Buddhism's version is "Hurt not others in ways that you yourself would find hurtful." Judaism teaches, "What is hateful to you, do not do to your fellow man." Christians are told, "All things whatsoever ye would that men should do to you, do ye so to them; for this is the law of the prophets..." Hinduism says, "This is the sum of duty; do naught onto others what you would not have them do unto you."

Every religion incorporates morals and ethics and has teachings analogous to the Ten Commandments. Most religions encourage brotherhood and charity for the less fortunate.

## Meditation

All religions promote prayer or meditation. Meditation is also called "yoga" from the Sanskrit "yuj" meaning "union." Eastern philosophers believe that yoga is the merging of the individual soul with Spirit. It is the act of quieting the mind and looking inward to make conscious contact with God. Many people believe that meditation is simply a system of breathing and relaxation techniques and they do not realize that prayer and meditation accomplish the same things, just in different ways. Prayer is talking to God while meditation is communing with God through silence. It is through stillness and silence that God can talk to us. Inner stillness is often spoken about in the Bible: "Be still and know that I am God" (Psalm 46:10). Readers of the Bible are told to listen to the "still, small voice within."

I remembered my mother's advice to learn to be quiet. For several months, I routinely attempted to sit without moving, clearing my mind of all thoughts. I waited for something to happen, but nothing did. I felt relaxed afterward but I wondered what the big deal was.

One day Helle and I met for lunch and a walk on the beach. Helle waited for me as I went back to my car to get my jacket. When I returned, she told me my sister had paid her a visit.

"It was as if she was hitting me on the arm, saying, 'Tell my sister to go meditate!' I think she wants you to go up to the Self-Realization Center after you leave here."

I told myself that I didn't have time but something compelled me to go anyway. I walked through the meditation gardens and allowed myself to relax as I looked at the flowers and waterfalls. I realized that meditation comes in many forms. As long as the mind is calm and centered in the present moment, a meditative state can be reached. I discovered that I was able to remain in a state of stillness around anything of beauty, especially nature.

I found a quiet spot near the ocean, closed my eyes, and felt the warmth of the sun beating down on me. I listened to the sounds of the birds and the waves hitting the beach below. For the first time, I glimpsed a round, indigo-blue light behind my eyelids and experienced a brief flash of oneness with all things, which many describe during meditation.

The light behind my eyes alternated between indigo-blue, white, and gold. I asked Yogananda to come and help me meditate. I felt as if his spirit was there, surrounding me, giving me a feeling of complete calmness. I sat like that for what seemed like a few minutes, but in reality was over an hour.

The peaceful effects of the meditation stayed with me for the entire day. I was ecstatic that I had finally seen the spiritual eye, which prophets have spoken about for millennia.

## The Spiritual Eye and the Christ Consciousness

The spiritual eye, also known as the third eye chakra, is located on the forehead between the eyebrows. In *The Second Coming of Christ* Yogananda called it the entryway into the state of divine consciousness. It is said that by focusing on the spiritual eye during meditation, one can perceive the Christ Consciousness, which is the infinite intelligence and light of God that is present within all creation. Jesus spoke about the spiritual eye when he said: "If therefore thine eye be single, thy whole body shall be full of light" (Matthew 6:22). Almost identical words appear again in Luke 11:34-35: "When thine eye is single, thy body also is full of light...Take heed therefore that the light which is in thee be not darkness." Yogananda believed that in the Christian scriptures, the Christ Consciousness is the "only begotten son," the only pure reflection of God the Father. Jesus, Moses, Krishna,

Buddha, Mohammad, Yogananda, and all other great masters who have walked the earth became one with the Christ Consciousness.

Yogananda compared ordinary human consciousness to a small cup, which cannot hold the ocean that is the universal Christ Consciousness. It is only through prayer and meditative techniques known to sages, saints, and yogis throughout the ages that one can attain this level of expanded consciousness that Buddhists call enlightenment. Many say that Jesus taught morality to the masses, but to his closest disciples, he taught the science of meditation and self-realization.

## Self-Realization

Walsch learned in *Conversations with God* that self-realization is a process of complete dedication of the body, mind, and soul to the creation of the self in the image and likeness of God. In the West this has been called "salvation."

Yogananda gave an almost identical definition: self-realization is a knowing in the body, mind, and soul that we are one with God.

The Bhagavad-Gita teaches that self-realization is the awareness that this world is false and only the soul is real. In his book *The Second Coming of Christ* Yogananda showed that although many religions have strayed from the idea of self-realization, the original teachings of all religions included an inner, intuitive connection with God.

## Reincarnation — The Science of the Soul

Cathy wrote to Tom on October 8, 2002, "I am glad to hear that you believe in life after death and reincarnation. I just don't understand how people can continue to deny that these things exist, despite all the evidence that they do."

During my first reading with Kim, I asked her about my past lives. I wasn't quite sure if I believed in reincarnation at that time, but I knew Cathy had, so I decided it wouldn't hurt to inquire. To my surprise, Kim was able to see and describe many of my past lives.

She said my brother, Mike, was my son in a past life. He had died when he was eight years old. In that life I was devastated and agreed to come into this life as his sister to help try to raise him up to the next spiritual level. This sounded amazingly accurate. I was always worrying about him. It seemed as though he was frequently facing some challenge or obstacle in his life. Kim said that things would "lighten up" for him over time if he followed his intuition and released negativity. My only job was to encourage him.

She saw my husband and me together in several lifetimes. The first one she saw took place in ancient Rome. We worked in a pottery shop. He was the owner of the shop, and I was his employee. He was always telling me what to do and advising me to be careful with the pottery. I was always rolling my eyes and muttering under my breath. I laughed hysterically. I explained to Kim that this dynamic was still in place between us and had caused the most problems for us.

My husband possesses what Cathy called "cop-like paranoia" and is always warning me to be careful of this and to watch out for that. I am always rolling my eyes and telling him to stop giving me advice and to mind his own business. I told Kim about an ongoing joke I had with my husband about our past-life history: "I told you a thousand years ago to mind your own business!"

In another life, she saw my husband as my grandfather with a long gray beard. She described how he loved to sit for hours telling me stories. I burst into laughter again. I explained to her that Jack is known for his love of conversation and storytelling. A friend of my husband's told me, "Jack could stand on the street corner all day, striking up conversations with complete strangers."

Cathy found his storytelling very comical and told me to stop interrupting him while he was telling a story. But his love of detail and my impatience drove me crazy: "Can we have the Reader's Digest version of this story, please!"

Kim described another lifetime approximately one hundred years after the time of Christ. She saw that my husband worked several jobs so that he could scrape up enough money to provide for his wife and three children.

Suddenly she put her hand over her mouth and started giggling. "I see your sister. She was a belly dancer or harem girl. You were her friend and secretly gave her money so that she wouldn't have to make a living that way. She was very grateful for your help. Your husband was always upset because money kept disappearing."

That at least partially explained my husband's fixation with having enough money in our current life. We both had good jobs, zero debt, no kids, and money in savings, but he still was always fearful we would not have enough.

I asked Kim if she saw Cathy and me in any other lifetimes together. She sat for a minute with her eyes closed, as if she were watching a movie in her head.

"Yes, I do see you and your sister together a lot. One lifetime took place during the time of the Druids, and the two of you worked with herbs and healing potions. I am being shown intertwined souls, so I believe you were twins in that lifetime also."

She described another lifetime in which Cathy was a Native American in the high desert plains.

"She belonged to one of the ancient tribes, which completely disappeared. It was a very peaceful life for her. I see that she was very wise, like a shaman. She used her mind to materialize things."

I was floored by this information. I remembered what Tom told me about his dream of meeting someone from a Native American lifetime. It also explained my sister's love of the desert, her interest in Native Americans, and her fascination with the abilities of the human mind.

132

Later I sat thinking about the fact that I must have had a life somewhere in the East because I was suddenly so drawn to anything having to do with the orient, especially India. As soon as I thought about a former life in India, I felt the hair on my arms and legs stand up and chills were rushing through my body for at least two minutes. "Wow," I thought, "I did live in India before." That explained my desire to bring the East and West together.

As Kim told me about each lifetime the information resonated deeply, and I knew that it was accurate. I felt as though my ideas about life had expanded beyond anything I could have imagined. I knew that the idea of reincarnation is extraordinarily important for humanity's understanding of our purpose on earth.

Physicist Amit Goswami, Ph.D., calls reincarnation "the science of the soul." In his book *Physics of the Soul: The Quantum Book of Living, Dying, Reincarnation, and Immortality*, he showed that the concept of reincarnation has been subject to much scientific review. University of Virginia psychiatrist Ian Stevenson has accumulated 2,000 cases of children who have had past-life memories. Every case was subject to intense scrutiny and each detail verified. Stevenson even accompanied several children to the villages of their past lives. In each case, the child had never been to the village before but could point out landmarks and knew the way to the house in which he or she lived. Many even knew the names of their previous family members, which were later verified.

There have been several famous cases of past-life recall in children. One involved young twins whose parents found them speaking to each other in a foreign language. They learned later that the twins were speaking Aramaic, a language that is all but extinct in today's world.

In his groundbreaking book *Many Lives, Many Masters*, Dr. Brian Weiss recounted his amazing encounter with the past lives of his twenty-six-year-old patient Catherine. She had been experiencing severe phobias and was virtually paralyzed by fear. He spent eighteen months treating her with conventional therapy methods, but none were effective. Dr. Weiss tried hypnosis, but to no avail. Then one day during a hypnosis session, he gave her an open-ended command to go back to the time in her life that was causing her problems. Suddenly Catherine was describing scenes from a life in 1863 B.C. A flood or tidal wave had devastated her village. She drowned along with her infant child.

As the sessions progressed, Catherine revealed knowledge of many lifetimes. In the space between lives, she channeled Dr. Weiss's deceased loved ones and master spirits, who encouraged Dr. Weiss to continue his work with past-life regression.

Catherine was immediately cured of her symptoms, and Dr. Weiss brought to light the truth of reincarnation for readers in the West.

According to Yogananda in *The Second Coming of Christ*, all the religions of the world have incorporated reincarnation as a basic tenet. During the time that Jesus was alive, Jews held reincarnation as an absolute truth. It was the cornerstone of the Jewish faith until approximately 1800, when they decided to "modernize" their beliefs. Teachers of the Kabbalah, the mystical path within Judaism, have embraced reincarnation for thousands of years. The Gnostics, Essenes, and numerous early Christian theologians such as Clement of Alexandria, Origen, St. Jerome, and St. Gregory accepted the doctrine of reincarnation as truth.

Yogananda pointed out several passages from the Bible in which Jesus referred directly to the principle of reincarnation. For example, the Book of Revelation states, "Him that overcometh will I make a pillar in the temple of my God, and he shall go no more out" (3:12). This meant that when a soul overcomes his mortal desires, he becomes a pillar of immortality in the mansion of Christ

Consciousness and will no longer feel the desire to be reborn on earth.

Jesus alluded to reincarnation when he said, "Verily, verily, I say unto thee, except a man be born again, he cannot see the kingdom of God" (John 3:3-4).

Yogananda said that Jesus' choice of words in this passage show his belief in rebirth. He meant that the soul has to be born repeatedly in various bodies until it reawakens to the realization of its perfect union with God.

Although reincarnation is not currently accepted in mainstream Islam, the Sufis, who were originally an integrated part of Islam, believe in rebirth.

The doctrine of reincarnation was removed from Christian theology and declared heresy in 553 A.D. by the Second Council of Constantinople. It was at this ecumenical council that the infamous anathemas were passed (*anathema* is a Latin word meaning "curse upon you.") The first anathema was that if anyone continued to teach the doctrine of rebirth of the soul, he would be excommunicated from the Church. In some cases, people were executed for their belief in reincarnation. The Church was afraid that the idea of prior lives would weaken its growing power. It was believed that reincarnation gave people too much freedom and therefore would not encourage them to seek immediate salvation within the Church. The scribes were ordered to remove references to reincarnation from the Bible. It took twenty-five years to remove most of them, although at least eleven references still exist.

I believe that reincarnation is the ultimate justice. What you are not in this lifetime, you have been or will be in other lives. For example, a man in Sri Lanka was raised as a Christian, but as a child, he was able to recite Buddhist chants. His parents took him to a Buddhist monastery. The child remembered living in an almost identical setting in a past life. As he recited, the Buddhist monks realized that his chants were quite different from contemporary Buddhist chants. The child was recalling prayers from an ancient Buddhist lifetime.

In his book *Through Time Into Healing*, Dr. Brian Weiss described a Jewish woman who, during a past-life regression, repeated the entire Catholic Act of Contrition, a prayer that Catholics use to atone for their sins. After the session, the woman was mystified; she had never even heard the Catholic Act of Contrition.

As Yogananda pointed out in *The Second Coming of Christ*, truths that are suppressed lead to a host of errors. The millions who have been taught to disregard reincarnation have not used their "one life" to seek God and help others, but to enjoy the world with no concept of life purpose or karma.

The ramifications of a religious doctrine that teaches only one lifetime without the balance of karma were the two hundred years of torture and killing of the Christian Crusades, all done under the guise of religious righteousness. These ungodly atrocities have re-emerged again with the misguided Islamic Jihad (holy war).

Yogananda explained that ordinary souls are compelled to reincarnate because of their earthbound desires and the law of cause and effect of past action (karma). The transmigration of the soul is the system of eternal life we are all part of. Cathy wrote to Tom, "I think it was Eleanor Roosevelt who said, 'It is no stranger to believe that our soul showed up in our body in this life than it is to believe that our soul has inhabited other bodies in other lifetimes.'"

## Coming Together

I believe the world's religions will unite. Yogananda believed this also. *In Man's Eternal Quest* he wrote that he did not see people as Jews, Christians or Hindus. He felt that all humans were his brothers and sisters. He worshiped in all temples because he believed that each one was erected to honor the one Father. He predicted that in the future unity would prevail and that a church of all religions would one day be a reality.

In his book *The Power of Now*, Eckhart Tolle wrote that there is only one true spiritual teaching. This teaching is the essence of all religion but has, in most cases, been lost.

Tolle says that enlightenment is not a superhuman accomplishment meant only for the Buddha or Jesus but is merely the state of oneness with something that is infinite and indestructible. It is, paradoxically, within the self but is also much larger than the self. The one true spiritual teaching is the state of *being*. It is the ever-present eternal life, beyond the myriad of lives. It is the true nature of all life in the universe. It is ancient, yet ever new, knowledge that is within each of us.

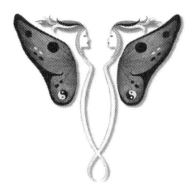

## Chapter Nine:
## Man-Made Religion

One day, I asked Cathy, "If there is universal truth within all religions, then how has religion gone so far off track?" A distinct thought came to me: "Religion has become man-made."

I wondered how I would introduce such a subject. Before I began typing, I decided to check my e-mail. My husband and I received a monthly newsletter from "Father John," who used to be a parish priest in Jack's hometown. He has asked me not to reveal his real name because he fears retribution from the Catholic Church.

Father John works with the desperately poor indigenous people of Mexico. His newsletters normally recount the accomplishments of the month, such as the building of houses, schools, and churches. But this month, Father John's newsletter was different.

He compared his quest to help the poor and his frustrations with the Church to the journey taken by two young men in the movie *Motorcycle Diaries*. The movie chronicles the true story of a medical student from Argentina, Ernesto, and his friend Alberto. They rode across South America on an old dilapidated motorcycle they nicknamed "the mighty one." The trek across Latin

America was a life-changing event for the young men and fostered their deep concern for the poor of Latin America.

The motorcycle represented hope for the men as they began their journey. However, as time passed, it got in the way and became an obstacle. It kept breaking down and eventually the mechanics could no longer repair "the mighty one," so it was put to rest.

At that point, the two men went their own ways and assumed their own identities. They realized that they were no longer on a thrill ride but had each found their life's purpose in helping the poor and downtrodden.

Father John wrote: "Last night, at about 3:00 a.m. I realized just who or what 'the mighty one' is for me: the Church. Years ago I started out full of wonder and excitement. What a ride I was on, the thrill of a lifetime. But then reality hit. 'The mighty one' was falling apart. Things weren't working like they were supposed to. There were more and more crashes. The mechanics couldn't do the necessary repairs, and I had to go out on my own. My eyes are more opened to the reality of life. Neither the Church, nor the government nor any other structure is 'the mighty one'...The people are hurting, and we cannot abandon them...We have to build new structures, new systems, new societies, which do not depend on 'the mighty ones' but rather enable the 'the mighty ones' to change their focus, abandon their fears, and build a new and hopeful world."

I was intrigued by the synchronicity between what Father John had written and what I was about to write. This was not the first time I had the feeling that information had appeared at just the right time.

In their book *On the Wings of Heaven*, G.W. Hardin and Joseph Crane described an amazing encounter Joseph had with an angel who revealed startling information about the current state of religion. The angel told Joe that great teachers have been sent to people of all faiths, yet all faiths have strayed from the truth.

140

## Religious Dogma Vs Direct Experience

One Sunday during the Mass, the priest decided that instead of giving his homily (sermon), he would have a question-and-answer session. A woman in the back raised her hand and asked whether she could speak to God directly about her sins. My mouth fell open when I heard the priest say that there are certain sins that God will only forgive if a priest is used as an intermediary. I knew that this was part of the Catholic Church's teachings, but I just couldn't believe that anyone could possibly believe that something like that was true.

Yogananda lamented in *The Second Coming of Christ* that religion has been hijacked by scripture-quoting dogmatists who focus solely on literal translations rather than the spirit of the religious scriptures. He warned that religious dogma has gotten in the way of common sense.

Yogananda explained that God's divine teachers never come to bring new or exclusive religions, which separate man from God and each other. Their purpose is to restore the unity among the religions and bring people to a direct experience with God.

He explained that the messages of the world's great religions outwardly appear different and that this is a necessary part of human diversity. It is only rigid narrow-mindedness that causes religious bigotry and divisiveness.

In creating competitive religions, the world has constricted the truth. Instead of the one true universal religion of unity and brotherhood we have misunderstandings and anger, which only serves to keep us separate and in conflict with each other.

In the case of Christianity, Yogananda was distraught by the lack of understanding of Jesus' purpose on earth. He said that Christ did not come to provide sermon material for Sunday church services. Jesus' life and death was meant as an inspiration to others to live rich and spiritual lives and to encourage humanity to experience the oneness with God that he did. Yogananda wrote that Jesus Christ was crucified once but his teachings are crucified on a daily basis by religious dogma, misinformation, and misinterpretation.

Through his direct contact with Christ, Yogananda could feel Jesus' disappointment. Although the churches erected in his name are often vast ornate buildings, filled with large congregations, few souls are really in touch with Christ through deep prayer and meditation.

According to Yogananda, people of all faiths, especially those in the West, have been taught to rely on external information about God instead of trusting their inner insights. Neale Donald Walsch wrote in *Conversations with God* that all religions ultimately fail because they are based on someone else's ideas and words. Spirituality, on the other hand remains constant because it urges people to seek God through their own experiences.

According to Yogananda, the more spiritually advanced a soul becomes, the less he or she relies on religion. In his book *In God's Truth*, Nick Bunick described a vision he had of God waiting at the top of a mountain. He saw people traveling up the mountain. The vehicle in which each person traveled comprised his or her religious and spiritual beliefs. As an individual came close to the top of the mountain, he or she abandoned the vehicle to avoid being bound by religious dogma and doctrine. At that height, a soul would find a true, one-on-one relationship with God.

Eleanor told me during my astrology reading that part of my life purpose was to study religion, philosophy, science, and spirituality. She said that my true learning would happen on the deepest levels through direct experience versus what I read or someone told me. I believe that a direct connection with the Divine is the only way to really see the oneness behind the world's religions.

142

## Fear and Separateness

My husband was acting particularly fearful about the decision I had made to quit my job and work part time so that I could spend more time writing. I knew that the decision was perfect and that everything would work out, but my husband didn't see it that way. I finally got angry and yelled at him, "Your religion has failed you! You sit, stand, and kneel every Sunday and you have been doing that for forty years, and yet you know nothing about what Jesus taught about faith." I was fuming mad for a while until my sister reminded me how fearful I had been for many years. It was true that I had been as fearful as my husband until I began my own spiritual journey. And even though I understand now that fear is a myth, I still struggle with it.

I remembered a similar comment Cathy had made about me. She wrote to Tom: "My sister goes around calling herself a Christian and yet she doesn't seem to know what Jesus' teachings about faith were really about. I have noticed that with a lot of people."

"That was harsh," I told her, but I knew it was no more harsh than what I had said to my husband. However, it is evident, particularly in Western culture, that fear is deeply ingrained in our religions and therefore our lives.

One day a relative of my husband's who was a lifelong Catholic, unexpectedly began telling me stories about his experiences with religion growing up. I was surprised by the deep bitterness he expressed regarding the fear that was instilled in him as a small child.

When he was seven years old he attended Catholic school. He described how the nuns marched him and his classmates to confession on a weekly basis. I wondered what sins a seven-year-old could possibly have committed.

The children were lined up around three confessionals. "Jim" and his friends would tremble and pray that they would not get the Monsignor. Once the unlucky child would confess his or her sins to the Monsignor, he would sternly berate and lecture the child for several minutes. Each week the children became more and more fearful of confession and of God.

Another fundamental problem is that religion instigates separateness. For in order for one religion to be right and the others wrong, God would have to take sides. This is a small, humanized vision of the One Universal Source of love and light.

Walsch wrote in *Conversations with God* that religion has created a false hierarchy. The religions have taught that God is above man, that man is above woman, and that human beings are above animals and nature. But this hierarchy is a myth. The reality is we are all one with God and with one another. No separation exists.

Separateness has not always been a part of the world's major religions. For Christians, the idea appeared almost four hundred years after Jesus died. Church leaders got together and created a new set of teachings, which included the theology that the human spirit is not part of God. This decision was based on a desire for the Church to hold onto its power. If Christians saw themselves as being created separately from God, then they would have no other alternative than to flock to the Church for salvation and entry into heaven.

One Sunday during Mass, our well-meaning deacon gave a passionate and creative sermon regarding the light of God and His son, Jesus. He held up a flashlight and compared the light of the flashlight to God and the batteries to Jesus. He told the congregation, "We are not the light, but we can be reflectors of God's light." Many people were nodding their heads and most seemed pleased with the analogy, but I felt very frustrated with it.

This simple story is a perfect example of how religion has taught separation. It is so ingrained that it is not even questioned. I believe that since we are one with God, and

God is light, and God is within us, then we are the light, not just a reflection of the light.

## Original Sin & Adam and Eve

According to Stevan Davies in *The Gospel of Thomas*, there are actually two creation stories in Genesis. Genesis 1:1 begins with, "In the beginning God created the heaven and earth." Genesis goes on to describe how God created light and darkness and the earth and all its inhabitants including nature, animals, and human beings.

This creation is perfect and God declares it "good" seven different times. Davies wrote that this story of creation is about primordial humanity, which was made in the image of and likeness of God. It speaks of goodness and perfection of all of God's creations and the origin of light.

The second version of creation, which begins at Genesis 2:4, says that man—called Adam—was created from dirt, and woman—called Eve—was created from the rib of man. Apparently both creation stories were meant to exist simultaneously. Davies wrote that it is only when humans choose the first version that they can truly be in the original image and likeness of God.

The early Church leaders were able to persuade the uneducated masses that unless they became members of the Church and were baptized they would not be absolved from sin and would be destined for hell. It was reasoned that the public would believe this fallacy because the Church could tie original sin to the story of Adam and Eve. As the story went, Adam committed the first sin when he ate the apple in the Garden of Eden, so it would follow that everyone born from the original man would be born in original sin. The idea was not immediately accepted, but two decades later, it became an official Church doctrine and has not been questioned since.

When attending Catholic Mass on Sundays, I would cringe to my core when I heard a room full of people dutifully repeating the phrase: "Lord, I am not worthy to receive you; but only say the word and I shall be healed." Much to the chagrin of my husband, I would repeat the phrase my own way: "Lord, I am worthy to receive you, you have said the word, and I am healed."

My sister helped me to see that God is within each one of us and therefore to say and believe that we are not worthy of God is a sad and misguided fallacy.

Matthew Fox wrote in *Original Blessing* that the Western view of a "fall/redemption" spiritual model is dualistic and patriarchal. Fox explained that this model begins with original sin and ends with some form of redemption that human beings must seek and then be found worthy to receive. Redemption is granted by some outside source (usually the Church).

This view of spirituality does not allow for creativity, play, social transformation, pleasure, or delight. It excludes the idea that we should love and care for the earth and the cosmos. It denies science as a means of discovery and enlightenment and is steeped in fear and pessimism. Fox says that it is unfriendly to Native Americans and woman. The fall/redemption ideology that has dominated theology, Biblical scholarship, religious studies, and psychology for centuries completely eliminates the joy of passion, spirituality, and mystical experiences.

Fox advocates that our religions take another look at a spiritual model that is far more ancient than the concept of original sin. Creation-centered spirituality is open to all people and all religions because we each share the concept of creation. Creation-centered spirituality focuses on the divinity within all things. It celebrates unity and oneness and allows for the inherent goodness of mankind.

Mahatma Gandhi believed that humanity's true nature is one of honesty, faith, love, and caring. Cathy reminded me that this was demonstrated in an astounding way during the 9/11 attacks on the United States in 2001. Hundreds of ordinary people, who happened to be public

146

safety and rescue workers, ran into burning buildings to save others, knowing that they would probably not survive. This was a vivid testimonial of the inherent goodness of man.

In his book *The Prophet's Way*, Thom Hartmann stated that the root cause of the world's problems is a basic flaw known as *original sin*. It is evident in the atrocities that have taken place throughout history that people who believe that they are inherently bad will and have acted accordingly.

## The Myths of Hell and the Devil

Walsch wrote in *Conversations with God* that Hell does not exist. Because the religions wanted to justify a punitive and angry God, they invented a torturous place called Hell.

In his book *In God's Truth*, Bunick described a garbage dump that existed two thousand years ago, outside the city of Jerusalem, called Gehenna. The garbage burned twenty-four hours a day. When someone got mad at another person he would say, "Go spend the rest of your life burning in Gehenna." The English translation became "Hell." This became the model for the fourth-century church's creation of a place of fiery torment and punishment.

Yogananda wrote in *The Second Coming of Christ* that a kind and merciful God would never damn a sinner to a place of eternal torment. Even those who commit the most heinous of crimes have an immortal soul that cannot be burned by any physical fire.

According to Yogananda, most souls have great peace and freedom when their spirit leaves their bodies at death. However, those who have become so attached to the physical world will feel frustration and lack of fulfillment. These ego-bound souls will struggle to stop the life force from leaving their bodies. But when they realize that they cannot stop themselves from leaving the earth's plane,

147

they feel great agony from their own self-induced hell. But ultimately God's angels and beings of light coax the souls to remember their true nature of love and light.

Bunick compared the many levels in the spirit world to the many grades of academic education. The souls who are at the lowest spiritual dimensions spend all of their time "in kindergarten" preparing for their next incarnation on earth.

They evaluate their misdeeds and are helped to understand the pain and suffering they caused others. When a soul is ready, with the help of his guides, he will decide what lessons he must learn on earth and what challenges he will face in order to heal the scars on his soul.

I learned that God has given us the power to create the things we desire in life but we have a difficult time believing this so we have created an imaginary man with red horns, a pitchfork, and tail running around thwarting God's will.

Jesus used a metaphor to personify the devil when he said, "From the very beginning he was a murderer and has never been on the side of truth, because there is no truth in him. When he tells a lie, he is only doing what is natural to him, because he is a liar and the father of all lies" (John 8:44).

*Maya* is a word Hindus use to describe the ignorance and unenlightened thinking of mankind. Prophets of the Old Testament called this same principle "Satan." The literal Hebrew translation is "the adversary."

Modern science has discovered that there is a certain unreality that pervades all matter, and man is subject to the same unreality. To conquer the unreality (maya) and to realize our oneness with the Creator is the task of all humanity.

## The Ego

"The meek shall inherit the earth because their egos are humble," wrote the authors of *A Course In Miracles*. The "*Course*," as it is often called, is a remarkable spiritual system, which teaches the way to universal love and peace.

Dr. Helen Schucman, a professor of medical Psychology at Columbia University, was anything but spiritual. However, one day William Thetford, the head of her department, announced that he was tired of the anger and aggressiveness that pervaded their environment. He felt there had to be a better way. Schucman agreed to help him find it.

Dr. Schucman began having inexplicable visions and dreams. She was compelled to write down these unusual events. One day she surprised herself when she sat down and wrote, "This is a course in miracles." Thus, she became Jesus' scribe as she took down rapid, inner dictation of a universal theology for a world in desperate need of healing and understanding. Although the *Course* is written in Christian language and style, it clearly embodies the ancient wisdom found at the core of the world's great religions.

The *Course* spends much time on the concept of the ego. Some call this the "lower self." Many believe that the ego is "the devil," which Jesus spoke about.

The lower self is the part of a person that manifests itself as a feeling of isolation and separateness. According to the *Course*, God and the ego are diametrically opposed. The idea of God and anything eternal dispels the myth of the ego so the ego seeks to deny that we are part of God.

The ego fears the joy of the spirit because once we have experienced it we will withdraw from the ego. The ego keeps us off balance so that we do not remember our true nature.

The most important thing the *Course* says about the ego is that it is an illusion. It appears to be a demonic force because it can deceive and trick us. While we cannot take the ego lightly, it is nothing more than a belief about ourselves.

Whenever we stay at a dead-end job or in a negative relationship, that is the ego telling us that we can't have more and we should stay out of fear that things will only get worse if we leave. But fear is the opposite of the higher self and of God.

## Our Biggest Downfall

It is the man-made elements of our religions that hold the world in a state of constant fear and keep us from fully experiencing the divine. Walsch learned in *Tomorrow's God* that other people are not terrorizing us. We are being terrorized by our own beliefs. Religion in its present form has been humanity's biggest downfall. Our fallacies about God have created a world full of anger, violence, and terror.

According to Matthew Fox in *Original Blessing,* the religions are now being called upon to bring back the importance of the earth and cosmos. If we want to remove hatred from the world, our religions must promote a less arrogant and chauvinist way of viewing the world. The world's religions must stop making one another wrong. If we truly want peace and harmony on our planet, the religions must stop promoting dogma, fear, and separateness and begin to focus on the spirit of universal love that has been passed down throughout the ages by the world's great prophets. The *Course In Miracles* says that there are really only two basic human emotions: love and fear and that only love is real. Cathy and I say it is time to move away from fear and all its related emotions such as blame, guilt, shame, anger, and separateness to love and all that comes with love such as joy, hopefulness, cooperation, and unity.

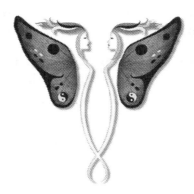

## Chapter Ten:
## Revelation Re-visited — A Warning
## for the Church?

"Revelation is a remarkable disclosure of the soul's intuitional perception of the deepest truths garbed in metaphor," wrote Paramahansa Yogananda in *The Second Coming of Christ*. He believed that the apostle John was Jesus' most spiritually advanced disciple. During deep meditation, John experienced a powerful vision, which he recorded in the Book of Revelation. Yogananda also believed that John had a deep understanding of the Eastern yoga sciences, which was evidenced by his symbolic description.

Revelation 1:19-20 says, "Write the things which thou hast seen, and the things which are, and the things which shall be hereafter; the mystery of the seven stars which thou sawest in my right hand, and the seven golden candle sticks." Revelation 5:1-2 states, "And I saw in the right hand of him that sat on the throne a book written within and on the backside, sealed with seven seals."

The number seven, referred to repeatedly throughout Revelation, symbolizes the seven energy centers in the body known as the chakras. Yogananda called them the centers of divine consciousness through which the Holy Spirit enters and exits the body during meditation.

## An Angelic Messenger Reveals the Truth

After reading G.W. Hardin and Joseph Crane's *On the Wings of Heaven: A True Story from a Messenger of Love*, I put it among my growing stack of books and forgot about it. But I felt as though Cathy were nagging me to dig it out and read it again. I knew the book had something to do with the Book of Revelation, but I wasn't clear exactly what the message was. I went through the pages again, writing down the important ideas, and then started to move on to another book. But I heard her say, "You are not done with this book yet. Look deeper." I re-read it a third time and felt as though I finally had the approval of my pushy twin sister as I did a side-by-side comparison with the Book of Revelation and carefully studied the true meanings that Joe had been given by the angel. I was in awe of the message and thrilled when I saw how closely it coincided with all the other information I had gathered.

Joseph Crane first felt a spiritual presence and heard a voice guiding him in July 1967, while he served in the Vietnam War. He survived the bombing of his ship by following the calm voice, which led him and several of his fellow shipmates to safety.

Many years later, he heard the same voice calling his name. Not knowing what to do, he sought out the advice of a spiritual friend and mentor. His friend told him about the biblical story of Samuel.

After Samuel had gone to bed one night, he heard someone calling his name. He got out of bed and asked his spiritual teacher, Eli, if he had called him. But he hadn't, so Samuel went back to bed. This sequence of events occurred twice more until finally Eli told Samuel that the Lord must be calling him, and if he heard his name called again he should say, "Speak, Lord, for your servant hears." Samuel did this, and the Lord spoke to him.

152

Joe felt a little odd saying those words, but the voice was persistent, and so he repeated Samuel's words. Suddenly a circle of light started forming in his darkened bedroom. The whole room became filled with a blue-white color. A being with brilliant blue eyes appeared.

Joe felt the same sense of calm that had washed over him that day in 1967, when he was rescued from his burning ship. He knew that this was a messenger of peace when his four bullmastiffs looked inquisitively at the angel but continued to lie calmly on the floor.

Joe was unable to pronounce the celestial name of the angel, so he nicknamed him "Michael," although it was not the famed Archangel Michael.

Michael told Joe, "*I Am* has given me the words to tell you what is truly said in the Book of Revelation." Joe was stunned that he had been chosen to reveal the truth behind St. John's words.

Joe was told that he should not think of himself as a Christ or a prophet but a servant of God. God would give Joe the words that he was to write through Michael. Joe learned that Revelation was a message given to the apostle John to relay to the seven early Christian churches.

During that time, there were seven influential cities: Smyrna, Pergamum, Thyatira, Sardis, Philadelphia, Laodicea and Ephesus (the same city Cathy visited while in Turkey). Each city had its own church. The apostle John saw a vision that was intended to be a warning for each church that they were misusing the gifts that God had given them. They had become self-serving and were more concerned with maintaining their power than their message to the people.

The churches failed to hear Heaven's message and thus the idea was formed that people could not have a one-on-one relationship with God, and all further writing in the Bible was halted.

Two thousand years later, an angel appeared to Joseph Crane to set the record straight. The angel instructed Joe to write exactly what he said and not any other version. The angel said that many had been called up to receive God's words but had lost all meaning of God's truths when they wrote them down.

Joe learned that the Whore of Babylon referred to in Revelation 17:6 is a creation of man that has taken on a life of its own. It is the institution of religion. ("On her forehead was written a name that has a secret meaning: 'Great Babylon, the mother of all prostitutes and perverts in the world.'") Like a whore, it gives the illusion of love, and yet the love is not real.

Michael gave Joe a very pointed message to send to the Whore of Babylon (the institution of religion). He was to tell the "whore" that if God really were a God of punishment and vengeance as she had told people, then the wrath of God would be on her doorstep because she had led people away from God.

The angel explained that the ransom God's son was said to have paid was not to Satan but to the churches. The ransom was Jesus' treasured teachings, not his life. God sent Jesus as the ransom for the freedom of God's people from the churches. The whore twisted his message of enlightenment and used his words to instill fear in the people.

Michael instructed Joe to tell the whore to go and confess to the people that she had lied to them and demanded their presence in her churches and insisted that people obey her interpretation of the scriptures. She told people that if they did not obey they would be banished to Hell and eternal damnation. She had added the Book of Revelation to her scriptures to make her more powerful.

The angel revealed to Joe what the apostle John was told and what he had seen in his famous vision. Joe knew that the truth was being revealed. He was shocked by the simplicity of the original intent of Revelation. He saw that Revelation has been misunderstood and misused for millennia and that as the world enters a new age, the

154

"whore's" actions are now being exposed for the whole world to see.

Joe laughed at the thought of the world's religious leaders standing before God, trying to explain why they had chosen to teach such silliness as the apocalypse with its mythical, demonic armies locked in a final battle.

## The Meaning of Revelation

The following are excerpts from the Book of Revelation and their corresponding meanings according to Joe's angel:

"I saw a scroll in the right hand of the one who sits on the throne; it was covered with writing on both sides and was sealed with seven seals. And I saw a mighty angel, who announced in a loud voice, 'Who is worthy to break the seals and open the scroll?' But there was no one in heaven or on earth or in the world below who could open the scroll and look inside it" (Revelation 5:1-4).

The angel lamented to Joe that none of the churches were worthy to open the scroll. But the scroll could be opened with the Christ Consciousness that had been given to all people. Jesus had come to let the people know that they, like him, were one with the Christ Consciousness.

"After I saw four angels standing at the four corners of the earth, holding back the four winds so that no wind should blow on the earth or the sea or against any tree. And I saw another angel coming from the east with the seal of the living God. He called out in a loud voice to the four angels to whom God had given the power to damage the earth and the sea. The angel said, 'Do not harm the earth, the sea or the trees until we mark the servants of our God with a seal on their foreheads'" (Revelation 7:1-4).

Michael explained the symbolic nature of this passage. When John spoke about the four winds, he was describing the mental north, emotional south, physical west, and spiritual east. These are the four natures of mankind. Jesus came to balance these attributes.

155

Joe learned that the mark on the forehead has been misused by the religions for centuries for the ritual of baptism. The angel declared that baptism is a lie and that all of God's children are treated equally and none shall be denied entry into Heaven. The marked forehead in Revelation served a similar purpose to the dot on the forehead of Indian women, which indicates the third eye chakra or spiritual eye.

"When the Lamb broke open the seventh seal, there was silence in heaven for about half an hour. Then I saw the seven angels who stand before God, and they were given seven trumpets...There were rumblings and peals of thunder, flashes of lightning and an earthquake. Then the seven angels with the seven trumpets prepared to blow them.

"The first angel blew his trumpet. Hail and fire, mixed with blood, came pouring down on the earth. A third of the earth was burned up, a third of the trees and every blade of green grass...How horrible it will be for all who live on earth when the sound comes from the trumpets that the other three angels must blow!" (Revelation 8:1-4, 6-8, 15).

Michael explained that there was silence after the seventh seal was broken because all who had heard the words of Christ were one with God and did not need to hear more. The seven angels stood before God and were again given a message to give to the churches. But again the message was distorted, and the teachings of Jesus were not understood.

Ignorance and superstition were born. With the loss of spiritual enlightenment, it was foretold that the churches would battle one another. The earth and all of God's people would suffer at the hands of one another. The destruction described in Revelation was a prediction of religious wars, famines, plagues, and poisoning of the earth due not to the punishment of God but because of the actions of mankind.

156

"I was then given a stick that looked like a measuring-rod, and was told, 'Go and measure the temple of God and the altar, and count those who are who are worshipping in the temple. But do not measure the outer courts, because they have been given to the heathen, who will trample on the Holy City for forty-two months. I will send my two witnesses dressed in sackcloth, and they will proclaim God's message during those 1,260 days'" (Revelation 11:1-4).

The rod was given to John to measure what the churches said. He was told not to measure the enlightened ones outside of the temple because they would overcome the false teachings of the churches. Joe learned that Jesus in body and spirit were the two witnesses. He wore sackcloth as a sign of mourning for the consciousness of mankind.

Joe saw a vivid image of exploding light, and then a magnificent, jewel-encrusted walking stick appeared. On its side was a rule for measuring. Joe watched as it measured each religious object: a statue, an altar, or a place of worship. Each time, the rod made a terrible hissing sound. The measuring stick moved faster and faster as it measured the temples and scriptures. Finally Joe saw the Vatican, the Dome of the Rock, the temple in Jerusalem, and the Wailing Wall. The hissing sound was so loud it was unbearable.

Suddenly he saw a burst of intense white light. Peacefulness enveloped him. He had never felt such love before. Joe looked again into the light and saw Jesus, both in body and in spirit. As the rod measured Jesus, a sound of gentle music and the scent of flowers filled the air. Michael told him that this was only the beginning of the love and light of God.

"Then a great and mysterious sight appeared in the sky. There was a woman, whose dress was the sun and who had the moon under her feet and a crown of twelve stars on her head. She was soon to give birth and the pains and suffering of childbirth made her cry out.

"Another mysterious sight appeared in the sky. There was a huge red dragon with seven heads and ten horns and a crown on each of his heads. With its tail he dragged a third of the stars out of the sky and threw them down to the earth. He stood in front of the woman, in order to eat her child as soon as it was born" (Revelation 12:15).

Joe understood that the woman was not a person but represented the feminine aspect of God. She was clothed with the moon and the sun. Both are symbols of light to the world. She was pregnant and crying, not because of the pain of childbirth but because of the pain humanity was experiencing due to the lack of spiritual understanding. She would bring enlightenment and end suffering in the world. Joe also knew that she represented the women who were honored as teachers of light in earlier times.

The dragon represented the old teachings of ignorance. The seven heads are the seven churches with headdresses, which symbolize unenlightened thinking. The ten horns are the Ten Commandments on which the churches impale humanity. The dragon waited to devour the child that was to be born so it could keep its hold on mankind.

"Then I looked, and there was the Lamb standing on Mount Zion; with him were 144,000 people who have his name and his Father's name written on their foreheads... The 144,000 people stood before the throne, the four living creatures, and the elders; they were singing a new song, which only they could learn...They are the men who have kept themselves pure by not having sexual relations with women; they are virgins" (Revelation 14:1, 4&5).

To Joe's astonishment, the angel told him that this passage refers to homosexuals, not celibates, as the religions would have us believe.

158

Joe was shown a scene of some gay friends who had died of AIDS. They were with Jesus and looked whole and happy. He cried tears of joy for his friends as the angel explained to him, "They are in touch with the male and female natures in all things." The angel said that they were chosen to take on this role before they came to earth to teach tolerance to others. The religions have cast them out and denied them God's love. But Michael said that they are blessed because the love of God was all they had. They were set free so that they could feel the connection with God without the religions.

Joe was saddened by the centuries of religious bigotry and intolerance against gays and women. He saw that the prejudice came from fear and ignorance.

He was shown the importance of the yin and yang, the unity of opposites, and he saw that there are elements of dark and light, night and day, and masculine and feminine within all things.

Joe saw how humans have created an imbalance in the world. Foolishly, walls have been erected between East and West and male and female. The angel conveyed to Joe that ultimately it is an imbalance within the self, as we are all interconnected.

"After this I saw another angel coming down out of heaven. He had great authority, and his splendor brightened the whole earth.

"He cried out in a loud voice: 'She has fallen! Great Babylon has fallen! She is now haunted by demons and unclean spirits; all kinds of filthy and hateful birds live in her. For all the nations have drunk her wine—the strong wine of her immoral lust. The kings of the earth practiced sexual immorality with her, and the businessmen of the world grew rich from her unrestrained lust.

"Then I heard another voice from heaven, saying, 'Come out, my people! Come out from her! You must not take part in her sins; you must not share in her punishment.

For her sins are piled up as high as Heaven, and God remembers her wicked ways'" (Revelation 18: 1-6).

Joe was shown what looked like a city with the temples and places of worship he had seen being measured by the rod earlier. The streets were filed with idols, altars, and crosses. Joe understood that all the holy artifacts were just things that people chose to worship.

He saw fire falling upon the city. The altars and idols were burned to the ground. Books, scrolls, teachings, and commandments melted into black liquid. He saw people running out of the city.

Joe learned that this was the fate of the religions that have lied to the people. The angel said that those who spoke of end times spoke of their own end times. When they spoke of final judgment and punishment, they were speaking from ignorance. Michael told Joe that God does not judge and that all judgment will wither in the light of God's love.

Michael explained that time and again Heaven gave the message "fear not" to people of all faiths. But "fear God" was the repeated message given by the religions.

Then Joe saw everything disappear except a circle of sound in a pool of silver water. The wave of sound was traveling across the world, touching each person, and everyone became connected to one another. Joe knew this was the oneness he had heard about.

"Then I saw a new heaven and a new earth. The first heaven and the first earth disappeared, and the sea vanished. And I saw the Holy City, the new Jerusalem, coming down out of heaven from God, prepared and ready like a bride dressed to meet her husband. I heard a loud voice speaking from the throne: 'Now God's home is with mankind'" (Revelation 21:1-4).

The angel instructed Joe to look again. Joe looked and saw a new clean world. He peered into a valley with the most beautiful trees and flowers he had ever seen. He saw fields of grain, which were watered by rivers and streams

160

flowing down from the mountains. The air was clean, the water so pure he could see the bottom. Green fertile lands replaced the deserts. He saw that the earth itself was alive. He realized that animals and all creatures with red blood have souls. The angel explained that God's love would care for each individual according to his or her needs.

Joe saw a city coming down from the heavens. Michael explained that it was not a city of buildings but it represented a state of being that mankind had risen to.

Michael said that the city's brilliance was the enlightenment coming from within. The walls represented the masculine, and the foundation was the feminine aspect of God. Joe did not see a temple, and he understood that mankind had become one with God and did not need a temple.

"I, John, have heard and seen all these things. And when I finished hearing and seeing them, I fell down at the feet of the angel who had shown me these things and I was about to worship him. But he said to me, 'Don't do it! I am a fellow servant of yours and of your brothers the prophets and all those who obey the words in this book. Worship God!' And he said to me, 'Do not keep the prophetic words of this book a secret, because the time is near when all this will happen'" (Revelation 22:9-12).

Michael said that this last chapter of Revelation is a warning to those who would change the meaning of what is written. Joseph Crane and his co-author, G.W. Hardin, came to the conclusion that the earth is being given a second chance to receive the gifts that were originally given to the seven churches.

## Age of Aquarius

Joe's angel indicated that Revelation is a prediction for the new Age of Aquarius. There is much debate regarding what year the Age of Aquarius actually began, but most people agree that the year 2000 was the beginning of what has been called "the Golden Age."

Astrologers have foretold that all of humanity will step out of the superstitious Age of Pisces and will move into the enlightened Age of Aquarius. It has been predicted that mankind will move away from dogmatic religions and there will be a coming together of all true religions and spiritual systems.

The revolutionary symbol for the Age of Aquarius shows a man pouring water onto the earth. This symbolizes the pouring forth of wisdom and knowledge onto a world thirsting for enlightenment.

The new age will bring a balancing of male and female energies. Every person, regardless of gender, has aspects of both male and female as part of his or her makeup. As people become enlightened, they will embody a perfect combination of both. The Age of Aquarius will move humanity away from competition, aggression, and symbols of outward power, to an era where feminine characteristics such as intuition, cooperation, and compassion will be emphasized. At the same time, there will be great growth of the higher male attributes such as knowledge, intellect, and expansion of the mind. The Gnostics call this coming together "the doctrine of synthesis." This change is predicted in Revelation and within many other prophecies throughout history

"In the days of the voice of the seventh angel, when he is about to sound the trumpet, the mystery of God shall be completed" (Revelation 10:7). The passage is referring to the opening of the seventh and last crown chakra, the energy center at the top of the head. This represents the human connection to the Universal Mind and the crowning of the human evolutionary process.

According to Yogananda, The Second Coming of Christ will not be in physical form but will be an amazing evolution in which humanity will finally come to realize the Christ Consciousness within.

I asked my sister, "What is to become of churches and religion?" I suddenly remembered something I read in

*Conversations with God*: The well-meaning people of the world do not need to tear down their churches. They simply need to examine each belief or doctrine, one at a time, and decide if each element is beneficial to the whole structure. If it is not, then it should be thrown out. The idea is to expand our views about God and about life and to see the spiritual connection that exists among all things.

Walsch learned that while there are no wrong paths to God, some are more efficient than others. The more direct contact a person has with the Eternal Source through meditation and prayer, the more enjoyable and swift the journey will be up the mountain.

I stopped attending Catholic Mass because I could not bear to hear words spoken that I knew were not true. I felt a sense of loss, and I pondered what it was I was missing. I realized it was not the teachings of the Church that uplifted me but the sense of belonging and community I felt by being part of a church. I believe that churches can be centers for positive energy and resources for charity work in the world.

Michael told Joe that religion is man-made, and its intent is to create dependence and to grow more powerful. But a church is a gift from God and a place where like spirits can come together to serve humanity.

Religion often focuses on rules and obligations. According to Dr. Wayne Dyer in *The Power of Intention*, we should simplify our lives and take out all the things that we believe we should do or that we have to do. Dyer said that by removing unnecessary obligations we are able to become still and quiet and allow our minds to be open channels for divine guidance. I believe that every hour, every minute, and every second is holy. We should cherish and honor every day we are alive.

Joseph Crane's angel said that a true church of God would give light and love abundantly to every person without fear or obligation. Cathy and I hope that in the future religions will acknowledge life as a wondrous gift, free for all people to enjoy equally.

## Chapter Eleven:
## Man-Made Armageddon

Cathy spent many of her last days rushing around San Diego, leaving books for people to find and, she hoped, read. She begged me to read the books, many of which describe the impending problems looming on the horizon for our planet. I brushed her off, saying, "Why would I want to read something like that?" I scoffed at what I called the "alarmists."

But now, four years later, I see with complete clarity what Cathy was talking about. I understand that Armageddon is not being thrust upon us by God as punishment for our sins but is something that we, as a collective on this planet, have created.

### The Warning

One of the books my sister most wanted me to read was *The Last Hours of Ancient Sunlight* by Thom Hartmann. After Cathy died, I resisted reading it for almost three years. However, it was clear that even though my feisty twin sister was no longer around physically, she was with me full-force in spirit and would not let up on me until I read it.

Tears streamed down my face as I sat reading in the park. I put my head in my hands as the disgust and horror of what I was learning sunk in. The book describes in great detail the ravages of poverty, starvation, famine, war, disease, and natural disasters on our planet. Sadly, all of these things have been brought on by the limited vision and ignorance of human beings, exactly as predicted in the Book of Revelation.

"Oh my God, Cathy," I sobbed, "This is all true, isn't it?" She silently acknowledged to me that it is true, and that she, like many others have been trying to warn the world before it is too late.

## The Elder Brothers and Red Brothers Speak

In his book *The Prophet's Way,* Thom Hartmann described a story he had heard during a trip to Colombia, about an Indian tribe called the Kogi, which changed his view of the world. Hartmann met a British journalist who had come to Colombia in 1988 to hear the message of the Kogi tribe.

Hartmann had always assumed that Western civilization was more valuable than "primitive cultures." He was not interested in hearing what such simple people had to teach the "civilized world." After all, he reasoned, we have conquered disease, outer space, and even the atom. Yet when he was told the story about the Kogi Indians, he realized that they have lived in complete harmony with the earth and all other creatures for thousands of years. This is not something the "civilized world" can boast.

High in the Sierra Madre Mountains of Colombia, a secret priesthood exists among the Kogi tribe. They are known as the "elder brothers of the world." They have been given the awesome task of keeping the earth alive. Their story was told in a PBS film called *From the Heart of the World* and in a book called *The Elder Brothers* by Alan Ereira.

166

The Kogi tell a symbolic story to illustrate the warning. It began long ago with two brothers who lived on earth. The younger brother caused so many problems that he was sent far away over the ocean. But he found his way back and has been wreaking havoc ever since.

The elder brother sent a messenger out to try to make contact with his wayward younger brother to warn him that he must listen to the elder brother and stop destroying the planet or there would be dire consequences. The younger brother did not listen.

Hartmann learned that the Kogi know many secrets about the earth that would change the way scientists view the universe.

The Kogi tribe had been given a revelation by the Creator several thousand years ago that the earth is a living organism, with a life and consciousness of its own.

According to Hartmann, many other tribes around the world also have been given this knowledge and are tasked with the safekeeping of the earth. All the tribes were given a sacred technique for living in harmony with Mother Earth, which they were supposed to teach the rest of the world, but to no avail.

Although these groups do not have a way to communicate with one another, all of them spend their time in constant prayer and meditation in tune with the heartbeat and spirit of the earth. They are attempting to keep alive the delicate thread that connects humanity with the consciousness of the planet.

The Kogi say that a great wound has opened on the earth's surface, and its skin is literally being torn off. They claim that the earth can feel the pain of the wound.

Meanwhile man is ripping out the earth's core in search of minerals, and the filth of pollution is choking the planet's lungs. Possibly the worst attack of all is the draining and discarding of the blood of the earth—oil and water.

Eleanor once told me that at times I might not feel well or have a feeling of uneasiness because of my strong connection to the consciousness of the earth. She said that I can feel the wounds of the earth.

The planet has always been resilient, but now the tribes who watch over the earth say there is a true threat, which could even mean the extinction of mankind.

In his book *The Voice of the Great Spirit: Prophecies of the Hopi Indians*, Rudolph Kaiser wrote about a similar prophecy of the Hopi Indians of North America: Mother Earth and the Great Spirit created two sons, a red brother and a white brother. The red brother was to stay home and watch over the land and keep it in a sacred trust. The white brother was sent abroad to see the world and to make many discoveries. He was supposed to come home and share the new inventions and technologies with the red brother, and the two were to balance each other. But the white brother's ego became so large that he did not listen to the wisdom of the red brother. The Hopi say that if the white brother refuses to listen to the red brother, the end of the world will be right around the corner.

While in Africa, Hartmann received a similar warning from a group of twelve shriveled and starving old men at a refugee camp. They pointed at the dead trees, barren ground, and starving children and said that what Hartmann was seeing was the future of mankind.

In his book, *World War III*, Michael Tobias wrote that we are already engaged in a third World War. It has been going on for some time. It is the clash between human beings and the environment. He likened it to a cancer that has no outward signs until the very end. Yet the cancer is being felt and seen now; this is a very critical time for our planet. Again I felt as if my sister wanted me to know that the decisions we make right now, today, will determine the fate of the earth and all its inhabitants.

## Older Cultures Versus Younger Cultures

According to Thom Hartmann in *The Prophet's Way*, the difficulties facing the planet are due to the way most people view the world. After 100,000 years of cooperation on earth, people began enslaving and dominating one another. Hartmann calls these two ways of understanding life the *older culture* and the *younger culture*.

### Older Cultures

Older cultures feel an intrinsic connection to the earth. Like the Kogi, they know it is a living organism with a destiny of its own. An older-culture view of the world is broad and long-term. It is understood that things that damage the earth will not work in the long run. Those with this view also understand that there are no true possessions in the world, and that the earth and everything else has been entrusted to us for safekeeping.

Older cultures view all things with reverence and pray for the souls of all living things, including the animals they kill for food.

People of older cultures do not isolate themselves from one another. They work together to create enjoyable, meaningful, and productive lives for all the people in their communities.

It would be unheard of for anyone to starve to death in an older-culture environment. It is considered to be the greatest affront to God to eat without sharing with others in need.

According to Hartmann, one of the most famous spokespersons for the older culture was Jesus. Even in his time, his message was not well received. He told people to stop worrying, that God would provide all things, and that we should forgive and bless people regardless of how many times they harm us.

He directly challenged the younger-culture idea of killing one's enemies. He disputed the younger-culture notions that man is separate from God and Heaven is a faraway place up in the sky. He promoted ancient laws, which protected the earth. He was murdered for these older-culture views.

Religions have kept the words of Jesus but have lost the wisdom behind the words. They speak of these principles as symbolic lessons and parables, not real-life instructions for behavior.

## Younger Cultures

Younger cultures view themselves as separate from the earth and from one another. Their viewpoint is narrow, and is only interested in short spans of time. The damage being done to the earth is too slow for the younger culture to notice.

Younger-culture people are focused on themselves and believe that they have dominion over the earth and all other living things. Resources are to be used and discarded. Younger cultures are egocentric and believe that the creation of humans was the beginning of all creation.

Younger-culture religions invented the idea of original sin, and this have created the belief by many that they are not worthy of doing good work in the world. This keeps people separated from their true purpose.

The impact of younger-culture ideas on older cultures is evident around the world. For example, many believe that India is a spiritual place full of holy men and yogis. This was the way Yogananda described his India in the 1920s. But today most of India is overrun with poverty, overcrowding, and disease.

## "Right" and "Wrong" Don't Work

Neale Donald Walsch learned in *Conversations with* God that it would be beneficial for people to stop focusing on what is right and wrong and start focusing on what works and what does not work. The concepts of right and wrong have changed drastically over time and are seen differently by each person, so they are not a good indicator of what should or should not be done.

We cannot use religion as a measuring stick because, as stated in the last chapter, God does not have preferences for one religion over another. The question is whose idea of right and wrong are we going to follow? Some believe dancing is wrong. Some believe it is wrong to celebrate birthdays and holidays. Some people believe using birth control is wrong. Some people believed it was wrong to eat meat on Friday but then they changed their minds and now it okay to eat meet on Friday. People used to believe that slavery was right, and there are places in the world where slavery is still seen as right. Some believe it is right to kill people because they have land and resources that are desirable. Some believe it is right to fly airplanes into buildings because they believe their way is the only right way. Whose right will be right and whose wrong will be wrong?

Certainly things that are considered to be "right" by the majority of people are things that work, and those that do not work would most likely be seen as "wrong." For example, the Golden Rule is a good guideline for what works in order to have peace and harmony on our planet.

As I thought about the many heated arguments my sister and I had over this subject, I heard her say, "Common sense is a God-given gift."

## Overpopulation

The overpopulation of the world is a perfect example of humans defying logic and common sense. People have taken literally the biblical order: "be fruitful and multiply." This edict came down at a time when the population was very low. The groups with the greatest numbers had the highest chance of survival. Because many refuse to see that this no longer applies to our current world, the earth is in great peril. Many religions around the world still believe that it is wrong to limit procreation. The results of these religious beliefs speak for themselves.

According to Hartmann in *The Last Hours of Ancient Sunlight*, at our current growth rate the earth's population will reach 10 billion people by the year 2030, 20 billion by 2070, and 80 billion by 2150. At 10 billion people, there will not be enough food, and there will only be enough fuel for 3 billion people.

According to James Howard Kunstler in his book *The Long Emergency*, we are now stuck with a problem that has very few solutions. I doubt that our all-knowing, all-loving Creator ever had these ungodly and inhumane conditions in mind.

## Poverty and Famine

The scenes of poverty, desperation, and starvation described in Thom Hartmann's books are horrendous.

While in the Philippines, Hartmann was shown a rotting garbage dump. At first glance, he thought he saw a swarm of insects on the pile of garbage, but then he realized it was not insects he saw but children. Thousands of them were scavenging for food for their families.

The human misery in Bombay, India, was overwhelming. Families were sleeping on urine-and-feces-soaked sidewalks. Small toddlers ran through the streets begging.

In Uganda, skeletons of dead human beings lay in the gutters, their bones being picked clean by buzzards. A United Nations truck fed hundreds of naked children who were shrieking and crying for food.

In Haiti, 99 percent of the trees have been cut down to use for cooking and boiling water. The land is covered in sewage due to rainwater runoff. International corporations use cheap labor from the overcrowded cities, while businessmen exploit inexpensive child prostitutes.

In Bogotá, Colombia, the overcrowding and poverty is so bad that children live in sewers and are hunted at night by middle-and upper-class men and off-duty police officers, purely for sport and amusement.

Wealth and poverty were other subjects that Cathy and I argued over. I was incensed at her criticism of the distribution of wealth in the world. After all, I reasoned, the people who work hard and are innovative should receive the most money. It is the natural order of things. But now I see it is not that simple, and that there is a serious flaw in a world that allows such great disparities between the rich and the poor.

According to United Nations statistics, in 2003 the richest 20 percent of the population controlled 87 percent of the world's wealth. The poorest of the world's people have access to only 1.4 percent of the wealth.

I read in *Conversations with God* and *A Course in Miracles* that there are currently enough resources, including food, in the world, but we have chosen not to make it a priority to help the needy or feed the hungry, or most important, to change the circumstances that cause these conditions.

## Destruction of the Environment, Trees and Rainforests

Without trees, our atmosphere would become toxic to us. Rainforest trees have a much larger leaf area and therefore provide much of the world's oxygen. Rainforests are essential to maintain life on our planet. According to Hartmann, at the current rate of destruction, the world's rainforests will be wiped out in our children's lifetime. The main reason for cutting down these trees may at first seem to be for the wood, but Hartmann said that the purpose is to clear the forests to make way for the raising of cattle for the fast-food industry.

A rainforest tree draws millions of gallons of water through its roots and releases it into the atmosphere as water vapor. This complex cycle prevents desertification, a destructive domino effect in which the rain stops falling, crops fail, and topsoil blows away. A once-fertile land becomes a desert. The destruction of the rainforests has already caused desertification in northern and eastern Africa, leading to massive starvation.

According to Thom Hartmann, approximately 1,500 acres of land are becoming desert worldwide every hour, due to the destruction of forests.

## Lack of Diversity

Timber companies advertise the planting of new seedlings, but this is misleading. Not only does the stripping of trees create a ten-year-long gap in the water cycle, but the logging companies are also setting up an ecological disaster by re-planting forests with the exact same species of trees in an area that used to be full of diverse species.

Hartmann explains that when systems are small and widely scattered, they are usually immune to failure. Yet in America and worldwide there is a push for the centralization of products and services, which promotes a lack of diversity. Diversity supports our survival, and we're losing it in every aspect of society. We are facing an implosion of our ecological and economic systems due to this shortsighted process.

## Erosion of Topsoil

There are many signs of environmental destruction, some less obvious than others. For example, our planet is developing a shortage of soil due to erosion. The topsoil that still exists has been stripped of many important nutrients essential for a healthy diet.

For centuries, farmers understood that it was necessary to alter their fields each season to give the earth time to regenerate before planting again. But large corporations that mass-produce food do not have the time. In order to counteract the less fertile topsoil, farmers dump chemicals into the earth.

Thus, humans are eating food with more chemicals and fewer nutrients. The long-term effects on the body are irreversible.

## Natural Disasters

The world has seen an increase in natural disasters, from earthquakes and tsunamis to hurricanes. Many people call these things "acts of God." But in reality they should be called "acts of mankind."

*Conversations with God* says that these events are due in part to naturally occurring phenomena and to the negative collective consciousness of the world, which will be discussed in later chapters. But mainly these disasters are caused by the mistreatment and poisoning of the earth.

## Climate Changes

According to Kunstler in *The Long Emergency*, global warming is no longer disputed by the scientific community. The causes for this change in temperature are extremely complex, but it is believed that the ultimate cause is human activity and greenhouse emissions.

There are many consequences of global warming. For example, the thin protective layer above us is dropping. According to Hartmann in *The Last Hours of Ancient Sunlight*, a 1998 *Science News* article showed that scientists have discovered that the average ionosphere height dropped by eight kilometers. Increased carbon dioxide levels trap heat close to the earth, preventing the upper atmosphere from being heated. As predicted by computer models, the cooling of the upper atmosphere causes the heat to be trapped in the lower atmosphere.

According to Hartmann, the climate change, driven by increased carbon dioxide levels, is producing swings in weather all over the planet. Heat is energy, and increased energy in the atmosphere means more unstable and violent weather. The average temperature of the planet is going up. The change, though seemingly very small, has had a huge impact on the environment.

One of the most drastic predictions is the shutdown of the Gulf Stream, a warm, freshwater undersea river that loops around North America and ends off the coast of Europe.

The effects of the shutdown could vary, but among them are a new ice age for Europe and North America and the desertification of major crop-growing areas. Another consequence could be the invasion of tropical diseases in places that once enjoyed more temperate climates.

According to the Intergovernmental Panel on Climate Change (IPCC), there is a heightened risk of severe flooding due to increased storms and the rise of sea levels.

The devastating effects of global warming on the environment are far-reaching and unpredictable. What is clear is that we must do something to change our patterns of destructive behavior before it is too late.

## The End of Fossil Fuels—What Is Oil?

Hartmann writes that everything is made of sunlight, which pours energy on the earth and is converted from one form to another. For thousands of years, our source of energy came from sunlight that was immediately available and local. But humans discovered ancient sunlight (oil) stored in the ground and began using it for heat and raw materials.

Oil comes from an organic substance made of algae, which lay on the ocean floor approximately 300 million years ago.

### Why Is Oil Important?

Kunstler says that oil and natural gas have temporarily allowed humans to extend the carrying capacity of the earth. The discovery of oil was like an enormous savings account. Because of oil, humans have been able to build billions of machines. Oil is essential to maintain every modern benefit that we now enjoy, including central air conditioning, heating, cars, airplanes, lighting, affordable clothing, supermarkets, surgery, and national defense. There is nothing more versatile than oil.

### So What's the Problem?

The problem is, we're running out of oil. Some may say that we are not expected to run out of oil in our lifetime, so why worry about it? Some experts predict that the world will run out of oil around mid-century, although others say that time frame is hugely inflated.

### Cheap Oil Will Become Inaccessible

According to Hartmann in *The Last Hours of Ancient Sunlight*, long before we run out of oil, we will no longer have access to inexpensive oil, and that will cause market disruptions and a multitude of other calamites.

The oil crisis of the 1970s produced frantic drilling, which gave us a two-decade long glut in oil. This has led many people to the dangerous notion that oil is in abundant and ever-flowing supply.

Scientists have learned that oil is found mainly in the "oil window" between 7,500 and 15,000 feet beneath the earth's surface and is not likely to be found outside of those depths.

Sometimes oil seeps up to the surface as it has in the Middle East, but this is rare. Most of the oil found recently has been in the "oil window."

In order to reach these depths, extensive drilling is necessary. When an oil field has been drilled to its halfway point, it becomes increasingly difficult to extract the remaining oil. The costs become prohibitive, and the well is sealed and closed down.

Another fallacy is that we will discover a huge supply of oil somewhere on the planet. Hartmann says that most of the earth's surface has been digitally "X-rayed" using satellites. All of the wells that have shown promise are already included in the estimates that the oil industry uses for oil reserves.

## Ignoring the Facts

While working the graveyard shift as a 911 dispatcher, I often listened to a late-night radio talk show called "Coast-To-Coast A.M." The program is advertised as a "freak show," but when I listened I discovered interesting, intelligent conversations with cutting-edge scientists, physicists, medical doctors, paranormal experts, mystics, and mediums. It seemed that every time I turned on the radio I was receiving a message from my sister to pay attention. I heard numerous people talking about this upcoming emergency. I wondered how so many could know about these converging disasters, while nothing was being done about it.

According to Kunstler, every administration, Republican and Democrat, has been well aware of the looming oil crisis. Neither political party wants to spoil the American dream by telling the truth. If they did, the economy would implode. The oil companies know bad news is not good for investors, and they have no reason to believe that the future of the planet is their responsibility.

Many say that alternative sources will come to the rescue. But Kunstler disagrees. Based on everything we know right now, no combination of alternative fuels will allow us to maintain daily life as we have known it. There is no alternative that will allow us to operate our systems at even a fraction of their current level.

## Consequences

Declining oil supplies could ignite battles among nations who have oil and those that do not. This would only exacerbate an already tenuous situation.

The suburban sprawl, which makes up most of the United States, only works when there are abundant

178

supplies of cheap oil. Kuntsler calls suburbia a "prodigious, unparalleled misallocation of resources."

Kuntsler says that big cities won't fare well either without affordable oil. If an energy shortage and an economic collapse were to occur, a big city would become a desolate place; everything would grind to a halt. There would be no food in the grocery stores, gas would be scarce, there would be no work, and people would become desperate.

On my trip to a conference at Bard College in New York, I made a stop in New York City to visit my cousin Mela. She was unable to get time off work, so I walked alone through the streets and rode the subways, feeling the discontent and separateness all around me. I used to love the hustle, bustle, and anonymity of big cities, but now it just seemed like a sad, dirty, and lonely place. I had a sudden vision of a futuristic city I'd seen in a movie. As I rode the subway downtown to meet my cousin for lunch, I randomly opened *The Last Hours of Ancient Sunlight* and read that Thom Hartmann had also envisioned America's largest cities transformed into scenes of chaos and destruction from a futuristic movie.

## Wake Up, America

While working with my first editor, Jill, she said to me, "Your topic is very interesting, but you keep mentioning this strange thing about 'the world is in big trouble.' You'll need to be more specific or delete it because no one is going to know what you are referring to."

She had no idea that the planet and all of its inhabitants are in grave danger. But I didn't fault her. I hadn't known the severity of the problem until after my sister died and she forced me to become informed. I became even more aware of how deeply troubled our world is while answering 911 calls. Every day at roll call, a list of serious crimes was read from the current day and the day before. It seemed to me that the list got longer and more horrible every day.

I was thoroughly disgusted at the calls I took daily on the non-emergency line from people complaining about the homeless. While I understood that they did not want a homeless person impeding their business or residence, they seemed to forget that the person was a human being. It was my job to ask for a description of the person. A common indignant reply: "I don't know what he looks like; he's just dirty, and I want him out of here."

These calls reminded me of Betty Eadie's *Embraced by the Light*. While on her near-death journey, she was shown an old drunken bum on the side of the road. She was asked what she saw when looking at the man. She replied that he was just an old bum who didn't want to work for a living. But then she was shown who he really was, a highly evolved spiritual master who had chosen to come to earth to teach others about compassion, tolerance, and kindness.

So if you don't believe our world is in trouble, my recommendation is to set up an appointment at any big-city police department, sit with a 911 dispatcher, and hear the desperate state of humanity.

My first response upon realizing the severity of our problems was to feel guilty. But then I quickly realized that guilt is a wholly inappropriate response. Guilt is an offshoot of fear, which is the very emotion that causes problems in our world. As a collective, our mass feelings of anger, fear, blame, and hatred have caused all of these events to occur. So the first thing that we must *not* do is to point fingers or feel guilty. As Dr. Wayne Dyer said in his audio series *The Secret of the Power of Intention,* feeling bad does not make other people feel good.

I love my country and do not buy into the notion, as many people seem to, that America is to blame for all the world's problems. But as Americans, we are startlingly uninformed about the state of the world. We call this the information age, yet most Americans can't answer simple questions about history. We have evolved into a country that elects political candidates based on which one has the best thirty-second advertisement on TV or who has the nicest looking hair.

I was deeply pained when I read in *Conversations with God* that as Americans we have lost the vision of our founding fathers. We have lost our sense of unity and even worse, we have lost the idea that "I am my brother's keeper."

Kunstler agrees. He wrote that it is difficult for Americans who are so caught up in the mundane of our daily lives to make sense of the gathering forces that could change the way everything is done in our highly technological society. Kunstler said that even after the terrorist attacks of September 11, 2001, America is still sleepwalking into the future. We have walked out of our burning house and are now headed off the edge of a cliff.

The world is in trouble. The American way of life is in jeopardy. There are solutions, but changes must occur immediately. I believe that Americans are innovative, resilient, and compassionate people, but we must become educated and we must take action.

All human beings must see the planet as being on loan to us. It is not ours to dominate, use, and discard. It is a living organism to be preserved and cared for. We must view others as part of our world community and seek to find ways to help those in need. Our job on this planet is to serve others. Masters and prophets have come to earth throughout history to remind us of this.

Until each person as an individual feels responsible for the world's problems, nothing will change. Every great spiritual teacher has understood this higher truth.

It is time to listen to the ancient wisdom of our elder brothers: We must change our way of life or face our own man-made Armageddon.

## Chapter Twelve:
## The Bible — Old Misunderstandings,
## New Insights

After writing Chapter Eleven, Man-Made
Armageddon, I realized that many of the problems we face
are due to humanity's misunderstanding of religious
scriptures. The books that I read dealt mainly with long-
standing misinterpretations of the Bible, but I believe
people of all faiths should take another look at their own
scriptures. All religions should allow the sacred truths
behind the words to shine through. After thousands of
years of violence and destruction, it is clear that taking
these texts literally doesn't work.

### The Bible
What is the Bible? According to Nick Bunick's book
*In God's Truth*, the Bible is the history of the human race.
The authors were men who wrote down the stories that
had been passed down to them from friends, family, and
teachers.

Theologians reference the New Testament gospels
when speaking about the life and teachings of Jesus. But
what are the gospels? They were written by four
individuals; two were disciples of Jesus, one was ten years

old when Jesus died, and the other never even met Jesus. After Jesus died on the cross, not a single word of the gospels was written down for almost forty years. While the gospels are of huge historical value, scholars say that they were never meant to be a biography about Jesus.

The original documents were written in Aramaic. Then they were translated into ancient Greek. Then the words were transferred into ancient Latin. In the fourth century they were translated into contemporary Latin. Fifteen hundred years after the original writing, the gospels were translated from Greek and Latin into English. It is easy to see how much misunderstanding, mistranslation, and misinformation has been spread regarding the original words spoken by Jesus.

Many people have been taught that the Bible was not written by men but by God. Every word, they say, was inspired by God and therefore is never to be challenged on any level. Some have even gone so far as to suggest that those who do question the writings are dangerous because they are being influenced by the devil. I believe nothing is more dangerous than the idea that man's interpretations of religious scriptures can't be questioned. To regard the Bible as infallible is a form of idolatry, the very thing Jesus preached against.

Yogananda wrote in *The Second Coming of Christ* that to be an unquestioning believer in any doctrine without scrutiny is to be immersed in dogmatism. He warned people not to waste their beliefs on false teachings and to maintain their common sense. God may have inspired the Bible and all other religious scriptures, but when man wrote these inspirations down, he did so through the filter of the human mind and experience.

### Misinformation
According to Mark and Elizabeth Prophet in their book *The Lost Teachings of Jesus*, much of the New Testament writings were deliberately altered due to

184

changes in theological beliefs. One of the world's oldest Bibles, written in 340 A.D., was found in 1859 in a Greek orthodox monastery. It appears to historians to be one of the most authentic versions of the New Testament. It shows that the New Testament we read today is significantly different than the original version.

Some of the discrepancies can be explained by the errors and misinterpretations by the scribes, but many appear to be intentional edits and deletions. For example, in two of the world's oldest versions of the New Testament there are no references to the ascension of Jesus' physical body into Heaven. It is clear that most of the changes were made to make Jesus seem less human and more divine.

### The Problem with Parables

Another reason for misunderstandings was that Jesus' teachings were often shrouded in symbolism and allegory. He taught in parables so that the masses might understand his messages. But people have taken these parables literally and have not understood the deeper meanings behind the parables.

"Then the disciples came to Jesus and asked him, 'Why do you use parables when you talk to the people?'... 'The reason I use parables in talking to them is that they look, but do not see, and they listen, but do not hear or understand...Because their minds are dull, and they have stopped up their ears and have closed their eyes'" (Matthew 13: 10, 13, 15).

Unfortunately, people are still looking but not seeing, listening but not hearing. I am sure that Jesus never would have guessed that 2,000 years later, people would be quoting his parables as fact and demanding that others do the same or be punished by God.

According to Paramahansa Yogananda in *The Second Coming of Christ*, Jesus spoke of the universal Christ Consciousness to his disciples, apostles, and others who had attained the ability to withdraw their minds from their bodies into the depths of meditation. But for the unenlightened souls who were not prepared to receive deeper truths, he taught by telling stories.

## Jesus Is God

Yogananda wrote that God does not take on corporal form to walk amongst the people but rather shows Himself to the world through worthy instruments.

The idea that Jesus is God began with a simple mistranslation of St. John's Gospel: "In the beginning was the Word, and the Word was with God, and the Word was God. The same was in the beginning with God.

"All things were made by him; and without him was not any thing made that was made. In him was life; and the life was the light of men" (John 1:1-4).

For ages, Christian churches have interpreted the Word to be referring to Jesus himself. But according to Dr. Elaine Pagels, professor of religion at Princeton University, in her book *Beyond Belief*, scholars have found that John's original meaning of the Word was vibratory sound waves of divine energy flowing down from God. Other philosophers of John's time used Word in the same manner. In Greek, nouns are masculine, feminine, or neuter. The Greek noun *logos (word)* is a masculine word, which apparently caused the early English translators to substitute the word *him* instead of the correct translation, *it*, meaning the Divine Intelligence.

In her book *A History of God*, Karen Armstrong wrote that the Aramaic translations of Hebrew scriptures called *targums*, which were written at the same time as John's Gospel, showed that the word *memra* (word) was used to describe God's activity in the world.

This slight misinterpretation in the intended meaning of John's gospel has had far-reaching implications. The same fourth-century church leaders who did away with reincarnation and brought us the doctrines of original sin,

Hell, the devil, and separateness also decided that Jesus was God. They used the simple equation: God = Word = Jesus and therefore God = Jesus. Any other interpretation was considered a blasphemy.

## The Holy Trinity and the Nicene Creed

Early church leaders came up with the idea of the Christian Holy Trinity, and Jesus became three persons in one substance. He was not only God the father but also the Son of God and the Holy Spirit. At the infamous fourth-century council at Nicea, the bishops wrote the Nicene Creed, which is the most widely held and accepted statement of the Christian faith. It is repeated every Sunday in all Catholic, Lutheran, Anglican, Eastern Orthodox, and many Protestant churches.

The Nicene Creed basically reiterates the Holy Trinity: "...We believe in one Lord, Jesus Christ, the only Son of God...begotten, not made, of one being with the father. Through him all things were made..."

This section of the creed clearly states that Jesus, the only Son of God, was not created like everyone else but rather is an agent through whom all created things exist.

Yogananda wrote that Hindu scriptures have a more universal version of the Holy Trinity as Sat, Tat, Aum. Sat means God as the Creator. Tat is the Son, meaning God's omnipresent intelligence existing in creation or the universal Christ Consciousness. Aum, also known as the Holy Spirit, is the vibratory power of God that became creation. Aum is also called the Word, meaning vibratory sound.

According to K.C. Cole, in his book *Mind Over Matter: Conversations with the Cosmos*, a team of astronomers at the California Institute of Technology recently collected data that shows that during the first 100,000 years after the universe was formed, nothing but a deep vibratory sound existed, identical to the sound Aum.

According to Yogananda, the sacred sound of Aum became the word Hum of the Tibetans, Amin to Muslims, and Amen to the Jews and Christians.

Christians say that the Holy Trinity is a mystery and cannot fully be explained. Yogananda agreed, saying that the Holy Trinity is completely inexplicable without differentiating between Jesus the body and Jesus the vehicle in which the only begotten son or the Christ Consciousness was manifested.

## The Only Son of God

"For God so loved the world that He gave his only begotten Son, that whosoever believeth in him should not perish, but have everlasting light. For God sent not his Son into the world to condemn the world; but that the world through him might be saved. He that believeth on him is not condemned: but he that believeth not is condemned already, because he hath not believed in the name of the only begotten Son of God" (John 3:16-18).

Many believe that the greatest misinterpretation of all is that Jesus was the only Son of God. Yogananda wrote in *The Second Coming of Christ* that the confusion between the "Son of Man" and the "only begotten Son of God" has created much bigotry because the human element in Jesus is not understood. Yogananda said that he was a man, born in a mortal body, who evolved his consciousness to become one with God.

Jesus made this distinction when speaking about his body as the "son of man" and his soul as the "Son of God."

Yogananda said it is a metaphysical mistake to confuse the man Jesus with his honorific title "Christ." In the little human body called Jesus was born the vast Christ Consciousness of Self-Realization, also known as "the only begotten Son."

I found a book in my sister's collection called *The Masters and the Spiritual Path*. The authors, Elizabeth and

188

Mark Prophet, channeled the great Indian master, El Moyra, who conveyed to them that one of the most egregious errors of the Christian orthodoxy is that Jesus is the *only* Son of God. The belief that Jesus came into his body in full mastery of Christhood and that he did not have to realize his own inner God-potential before beginning his mission, is a grievous misunderstanding.

Yogananda wrote in *Autobiography of a Yogi* that it is a form of spiritual cowardice that leads people to believe that Jesus was the only Son of God. It is comfortable to believe that Jesus was uniquely created so that we as mere mortals could not possibly emulate him. But Yogananda said that all men have been divinely created and are sons of God. I believe that this was one of the most important messages that Jesus brought to the world. This is clearly evident in his words: "Behold, what manner of love the Father hath bestowed upon us, that we should be called the sons of God" (I John 3:1).

Jesus repeated the same thing again in a later section of St. John's Gospel: "As many as received him, to them gave he power to become the sons of God" (John 1:12).

Yogananda said that in urging people to believe in the only begotten Son, Jesus was not referring to his own body but to his state of universal Christ Consciousness, which was fully manifest in him and all God-realized masters throughout the ages.

The church's dogmatic interpretation of John's Gospel is that if people do not accept Jesus as their savior, they will be condemned. But as Jesus conveyed to Yogananda, the real meaning was that whoever does not realize himself as one with the universal Christ Consciousness is condemned to live as a struggling mortal who has disengaged himself from the Creator.

Nick Bunick, whose remarkable life story as the Apostle Paul was told in *The Messengers*, remembered Jesus as being deeply humble. He would never have had the ego to demand that people accept him or be condemned to live without God's love.

## Resurrection on the Last Day

After Cathy died, a well-meaning chaplain told me, "Your sister Cathy will rise again." What the heck did that mean? The Christian concept of the "resurrection on the last day," comes from several different biblical scriptures. In John 11:23-24, Martha was grieving over the death or her brother Lazarus. Jesus told her "...Thy brother shall rise again. Martha saith unto him, I know that he shall rise again in the resurrection at the last day."

Multiple passages in both the old and New Testament talk about the resurrection on the last day and the raising of the dead from their graves. For example, "Verily verily I say unto you, the hour is coming, and now is, when the dead shall hear the voice of he son of God...all that are in the graves shall hear his voice" (John 5: 25-28).

Somehow the rising of the dead from their graves became entangled with a story from the book of Revelation in which seven angels stood before God, each blowing their trumpets. The seventh and last angel, who was unidentified in Revelation, but is believed to be Gabriel, heralded the reign of Christ. "In the days of the voice of the seventh angel, when he is about to sound his trumpet, the mystery of God shall be completed" (Revelation 10:7).

Quite frankly, the idea that Cathy would "rise again" wasn't all that comforting. It sounded to me like the return of the zombies. Thankfully, I learned in Yogananda's *The Second Coming of Christ* that "resurrection on the last day" is not a fixed day in time when all souls will reappear in their dead bodies at the sound of Gabriel's trumpet. Yogananda said that after death, there is often a period of rest for the weary soul who has just come from a difficult life on earth. Resurrection signifies the rising of souls from the after-death state of rest to the state of full wakefulness and

190

higher consciousness. Resurrection also indicates the elevation of consciousness from the lower state of consciousness we have during life to the higher form we take after death.

This reminded me of Kim's description of Cathy's state of confusion immediately after death. She needed to spend time processing her death before she could make her full transition.

A similar concept to "the resurrection on the last day" is the idea of the last judgment or judgment day. The Nicene Creed says that Jesus will "come again in glory to judge the living and the dead..." But *A Course in Miracles* says that the last judgment is not an action taken by Jesus or God and has nothing to do with punishment. It will be a day when the world will reach a state of such enlightenment that there will be no more judgment of one another. It is simply a process by which everyone will finally come to understand what is worthy and what is not. The last judgment is a doorway into a new life.

## Jews Versus Christians

The misunderstanding of a single verse has led to a disagreement between Christians and Jews: "For the law was given to Moses, but grace and truth came by Jesus Christ."

Through Yogananda's connection with Jesus in *The Second Coming of Christ*, he learned that this verse was not intended to define any difference in the degree of spirituality between Jesus and Moses. The point was that every prophet has a special purpose and mission to fulfill. Moses' gift from God was the Ten Commandments, universal laws that make man's journey on earth more harmonious and spiritually fulfilling. The phrase "an eye for an eye, and a tooth for a tooth" is attributed to Moses and is often used to justify killing as a means of justice. But Yogananda said that Moses was not speaking about punishment but merely stating the law of karma—we reap what we sow. Moses himself was disturbed by the misuse of his words. He said that the people had corrupted themselves: "They are a perverse and crooked generation...neither is there any understanding in them" (Deuteronomy 32:5, 28-29.)

The phrase "Grace and truth came by Jesus Christ" means that all truth, goodness, and power behind universal laws flow through the divine Christ Consciousness, which was present in Jesus and every master. Because people had taken "an eye for an eye" literally and were brutally killing and maiming one another, Jesus came to show a gentler, more forgiving way to live.

### The Ten Commandments

"There are no such things as the Ten Commandments," God told Neale Donald Walsch in *Conversations with God.*

"Oh my God, there aren't?" Walsch responded.

Walsch learned that it is a human fallacy to believe God needs something from us. A deity has no needs and therefore would command nothing. The idea of commandments directly contradicts the idea of free will. It is difficult to conceive of a God who would give us the freedom to make our own choices but at the same time command us to act in a certain way.

God told Walsch that the Ten Commandments should actually be called, "The Ten Commitments." In this context they would not be taken as orders for obedience, but as instructions for how to know if we are in resonance with our own Godself. For example, when one is in resonance with God, the commandment, "Thou shalt not steal" is no longer necessary because a person would no longer feel the need to take something from another because of the knowledge that there is enough for everyone.

Yogananda said that the word *commandment* gives an incorrect connotation of the spiritual laws given to Moses.

God is not a dictator, and human beings are not God's servants. According to Yogananda, the Ten Commandments should be seen as a code of natural righteousness. If man does not follow these spiritual laws, he will create great suffering for himself and others.

### The Way to the Kingdom of Heaven

"I am the way, the truth and the life, no man cometh unto the father but me" (John 14:6).

"Except a man born of water and of the Spirit, he cannot enter the Kingdom of God" (John 3:5).

"Do your best to go through the narrow door; because many shall not be able" (Luke 13:24).

"I am the door: by me if any man enter in, he shall be saved, and shall go out and find pasture" (John 10:9).

At first reading, these biblical passages seem to say that the only way into Heaven is through Jesus. They have also led to the misinterpretation that Heaven is a physical place and that only a few shall be allowed in.

Yogananda disputed this idea. What these verses actually indicate is that Heaven is not a place up in the sky but a state of being. Jesus was saying that through the attainment of Christ Consciousness, one would attain the Kingdom of God. Jesus repeatedly said that the Kingdom of Heaven couldn't be found through the five senses, or through the mind, but by reaching the eternal soul within and by seeing the perfection that was already on the earth:

"His disciples asked him, 'When will the new world come?' He answered, 'What you are looking forward to has come, but you don't know it'" (the Gospel of Thomas, verse 51).

"Jesus' disciples asked him: 'When will the kingdom come?' He said to them, 'It will not come by waiting for it. People will say, 'Look! Here it is! Or 'There it is!' But the kingdom of the Father is spread out upon the earth and people do not see it'" (the Gospel of Thomas, verse 113).

"If those who lead you say, 'Look! The kingdom of heaven,' then the birds of Heaven will precede you. If they say to you, 'It is in the sea,' then the fish will precede you. But the kingdom is within you and it is outside you. If you will know yourselves, then you will be known, and you will realize that you are children of the living Father. But if you do not know yourselves, then you dwell in poverty and you are the poverty" (the Gospel of Thomas, verse 3).

In his book *The Gospel of Thomas*, Stevan Davies described Jesus' message as emphasizing the value of the present. His sayings show that the Kingdom of Heaven is not beyond death but is here and now and has been here since the beginning of time.

*A Course in Miracles* says to be in the Kingdom is merely to focus full attention on it. In his book *The Power of Now*, Eckart Tolle agrees, saying that remaining in the state of the "ever-present now" is eternal life in the Kingdom of Heaven and is accessible to all people immediately.

According to Davies, there are two streams of thought in the Christian tradition. One view, put forth by orthodox Christians, discourages self-discovery and self-reliance. This view encourages people simply to have faith and wait for the unearned grace of the Kingdom of Heaven to arrive. Davies believes that this was not Jesus' true perspective but that a group of first-century followers made the decision that these ideas would be the official views of the Christian Church. Since that time, people who call themselves "keepers of the faith" have strived to keep this viewpoint at any cost.

The second stream of thought is found in the Gospel of Thomas. This view urges people to find the Kingdom in the here and now and promotes the idea of "seek and find." This viewpoint indicates that the Kingdom of God resides upon the earth and within each soul.

It is clear, from Yogananda's communion with Jesus in *The Second Coming of Christ* and the communication received

194

from Jesus in *A Course in Miracles*, that the latter version not only represents his original intent but the intent of all the world's great teachers.

## The Gnostic Gospels and the Gospel of Thomas

According to Davies in *The Gospel of Thomas*, the censorship of Jesus' teachings began in the first century and continued throughout history. The early church leaders decided which scriptures would represent Jesus. Any writings that they did not agree with were discredited, suppressed, or destroyed.

For centuries, this effort was remarkably successful until an interesting coincidence occurred in 1945. While the first bombs were being dropped on Hiroshima and Nagasaki, a collection of extraordinary ancient texts, rolled up inside a piece of pottery, was found in a cave near Nag Hammadi in Upper Egypt. These texts are now known as the Nag Hammadi Library. It was as if the most horrific destruction of mankind came together with one of the most enlightening discoveries of our time.

The fifty-two ancient texts are known as the Gnostic Gospels and the Gospel of Thomas. A fragment of the Gospel of Thomas was found earlier in Egypt in the 1890s.

Conservative religious scholars discredit the Gnostic Gospels because much of the information contained in the writings is mythological and mystical in nature. Some of the writings give some rather outlandish stories. But Marvin Meyer wrote in his book *The Gnostic Gospels of Jesus* that the Gnostic Gospels offer the world a rich variety of viewpoints of the Christian message.

The Greek word *gnosis* means insight or knowledge, which involves the intuitive process of knowing oneself. The Gnostics said that knowing oneself on the deepest level was to know God. It is easy to see why many believe that the Gnostics were influenced by Eastern philosophies. Trade routes with the East had begun to open up during the time Gnosticism flourished (80-200 A.D.). The influence of Eastern thought led the Gnostics to emphasize the idea of seeking God through inner reflection.

Meyer wrote that the more mythological texts such as The Gospel of Mary and The Holy Book of the Great Invisible Spirit are merely interpretations of the story of creation given in Genesis. These ancient writings reflect ideas similar to contemporary beliefs regarding quantum physics, metaphysics, astronomy, astrology, and the limitless universe.

Many church leaders have vehemently opposed the Gnostic Gospels throughout religious history. To say a text is Gnostic is their way of saying it is irrelevant. The Gnostic Gospels were declared a heresy in the second century but remained in circulation until the fourth century, when the books were again forbidden or destroyed. It is believed that a monk hid the banned books in Egypt, where they remained buried for 1,600 years.

But many regard the Gnostic Gospels, and the Gospel of Thomas in particular, to be the most important discovery ever made regarding Jesus of Nazareth. Davies said that the Gospel of Thomas is the clearest guide to the vision Jesus held for the world.

Conservative Christian scholars, who have been severely threatened by the Gospel of Thomas, have included it with the Gnostic Gospels so that it would be ignored. It is often seen as a Gnostic Gospel because it was found with the others and has a Gnostic perspective.

But according to Davies, the Gospel of Thomas should not be included as a Gnostic Gospel. None of the complicated metaphysical theorizing of the Gnostic Gospels appears in the Gospel of Thomas.

Another theory put forth by skeptics is that Thomas's Gospel was dependent on the New Testament gospels of Matthew, Mark, and Luke. Although Thomas's Gospel refers to information within the Old and New Testament, it does not contain any references to the usual Christian themes such as Jesus as the Messiah and Christ or the crucifixion and resurrection. Davies believes the reason for this is that Thomas's Gospel was written before these themes were fully developed.

The Gospel of Thomas is written in such a primitive form, it is thought to have possibly pre-dated the New Testament gospels. The author of the gospel calls the list of 114 sayings "the secret sayings which the living Jesus spoke."

In the Gnostic Gospels and the Gospel of Thomas, Jesus led people to enlightenment through inner wisdom. His intent was to show people that they had fallen asleep and forgotten who they were. They had been seduced by the pains and pleasures of the world.

In the Gospel of Thomas, Jesus' focus was not on sin but on ignorance and showed that knowledge was the key to God. I was reminded of the spiritual masters who spoke to Brian Weiss through his patient Catherine in *Many Lives, Many Masters*. They said that it is through knowledge that we approach God.

## God as a Warrior

Many Christian theologians have criticized the Gnostic Gospels for making what they believe are outrageous claims. But I believe there is nothing more outrageous than the idea put forth in most of the world's religious scriptures that God is a warrior.

Throughout the Bible and other religious texts are stories of God waging war and leading people into battle. For ages, people have acted in the same manner because they have believed that God condones it. But Walsch learned in *The New Revelations* that nothing is more ungodly than killing another human being. And no act is farther from God than killing others in God's name.

In his book *In God's Truth*, Bunick said that people should exercise their God-given intelligence and inner wisdom when reading the Bible and other religious scriptures. It is imperative that readers distinguish between the words inspired by God and those that reflect the words of individuals who are sharing their own fantasies and views of the world.

## Creation Versus Evolution

"You don't really want me to take on creation versus evolution, do you?" I asked my sister. I didn't get an answer right away. A few days later, as my husband and I flew to Ohio to visit my in-laws, I picked up a copy of *People* magazine. For once I was looking forward to reading something that did not involve deeper thinking. But I wasn't getting off the hook that easily. I randomly opened the magazine to an article about the town of Dover, Pennsylvania, which had become so embroiled in the argument over intelligent design (I.D.) versus evolution that people on opposite sides of the debate were no longer speaking to one another.

The evolution people were upset because the intelligent design people were insisting that a statement be read to students in class that claims there are other theories of the origins of life besides evolution and that students should keep an open mind. A group of parents sued to stop the statement from being read. The evolutionists argued that students of other religions, such as Hindus, should not have to hear a Christian account of creation.

Cathy reminded me of Yogananda's comparisons of the story of creation in the Old Testament, the New Testament, and the Hindu scriptures.

Yogananda wrote in *The Second Coming of Christ* that St. John's Gospel in the New Testament could also be called "Genesis according to St. John." Yogananda found that the opening of St. Johns Gospel shows the same view of scientific evolution and cosmic creation that is given in the ancient scriptures of India.

Both Genesis and St. John's Gospel open with, "In the beginning..." Yogananda discovered that "the beginning" was a reference to the birth of everything finite, the beginning of the realm of the relative. In the realm of the Absolute, there is no beginning or end.

In *Conversations with God*, Walsch learned that life evolved through a series of steps. Yet these steps occurred in one instant in the realm of the Absolute. Walsch discovered that scientists' Big Bang theory is fairly consistent with what actually occurred. However, human beings would see this blink of an eye as billions and billions of years. So both views are correct. It all depends on how you look at it.

Gary Zukav wrote in *The Seat of The Soul* that the view of evolution taught in schools is incomplete. According to this definition of evolution, known as "survival of the fittest," an organism that is most able to ensure its survival is the most evolved.

However, these ideas come from a purely physical point of view and focus solely on dominance and power when characterizing evolution. This perspective has negatively influenced the way people view and treat each other and completely ignores the spiritual aspect of humanity.

Zukav says it is time to expand our view of human evolution. If a person sacrifices his or her life for another, he or she is said to be a highly evolved being.

Jesus knew what was going to happen to him and could have stopped it, but he didn't. He valued love more than his own body and placed his divine mission over any human desires to remain living. Most would agree that Jesus was one of the most highly evolved beings ever to walk the earth, yet he did not fight to survive.

It is only within a larger understanding of evolution that we can explain people like Gandhi, Mother Theresa, and Martin Luther King, Jr., who spent their entire lives in the service of others.

According to Zukav, our purpose for taking on physical form is to evolve from being what he called five-sensory humans to multi-sensory humans. Evolution occurs when we raise our consciousness beyond our own body and realize our unity with all other living things.

## Allow the Truth to Shine Through

Yogananda said that the saviors of the world did not come to foster divisions and their teachings should not be used for that purpose. He believed that it was a misnomer even to use the term "Christian Bible" because it was never intended to belong exclusively to one sect but was for the enlightenment of all. The Christ Consciousness is universal, and therefore Jesus Christ and his teachings belong to all people.

According to Yogananda, the Christian churches of today have strayed from the true path of Christ, and any revival of the true teachings of Christ would only take place when the Christian churches change their focus from Sunday sermons to quite meditation and inner stillness.

The prophet El Moyra revealed in *The Masters and the Spiritual Path* that the layers of misinterpretation have removed the keys to the true and original intent of Jesus and have given Christians today a watered-down religion that will not meet the challenges facing our civilization.

I asked Cathy, "Why does it really matter what someone believes? Why is it a problem if someone wants to believe that Jesus is God or that he is the only Son of God? People have believed these things for centuries. Why is this information about Jesus so important now?"

She reminded me of an incident that occurred on my fourth wedding anniversary. Somehow my husband and I began discussing the subject of religion and Jesus. My husband, a lifelong Catholic, became very upset.

"If you don't believe that Jesus is God and that He is the only Son of God, then maybe we aren't really married in the eyes of the God."

I was tremendously hurt and angry with my husband for saying something so cruel, especially on our anniversary. After I stewed for several hours, I finally realized that he only knew what he had been told all his life, and he was reacting out of fear. I remembered something Brian Weiss said at his seminar: "Just because you have been told something all your life doesn't mean it's true." He had learned this in his own life.

I understood what Cathy was alluding to. If people choose to believe something that causes divisions among people, religions, and nations, then that belief is not working.

If we believe that Jesus is God and not a great master who came to teach the world, then we are not only betraying Jesus' message that we are all divinely created, but we are essentially saying that God created millions of mistakes in people of other faiths.

I would argue that anything that divides and excludes people is not truly of God and anything that promotes unity and universal truth is of God.

The teachings of the world's greatest sages have been repeated over and over again like the game of telephone and have become distorted. These misconstrued ideas became the basis for the world's most influential religions and have filled humanity with fear and hatred.

"If the world is going to move into the new age of enlightenment, these misunderstandings must be put to rest," Cathy said. "It is time to allow the light of truth to shine through."

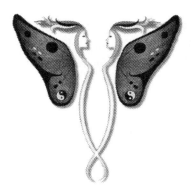

## Chapter Thirteen:
## The Master of Galilee

While writing *Twin Souls* I realized how much misinformation and confusion has been spread about Jesus. I understood that his original message to the world was extremely important, especially at this time in history, so I spent time researching little known facts about his life and mission.

It is common knowledge that Jesus was born in Israel, in the small town of Bethlehem in Nazareth. Much has been written about his birth and his ministry, beginning at age thirty. He spent many of his days at Capernaum on the Sea of Galilee.

His first disciples were Galilean fisherman: Simon Peter, Andrew, James, and John. Jesus preached to large audiences about the Kingdom of Heaven, performed miracles, and healed the sick to the amazement of the crowds. The people were not only astonished at his abilities and the things he was saying but also at the authority with which he spoke.

Not much information can be found about Jesus' childhood years. Luke's Gospel moves quickly from Jesus' birth to the age of twelve, where he was seen in the temple in Jerusalem sitting among the scribes and learned men asking questions. At that point, Luke's story jumps to Jesus' baptism by John at age thirty. Matthew's Gospel provides details of Jesus' family, their flight to Egypt after his birth, and the visitation of the three Magi.

## The Lost Years of Jesus

Scholars and Eastern philosophers point to an abundance of evidence that supports the idea that the "lost" seventeen years of Jesus' life were spent studying in India and the orient.

Scholars and historians have found nothing that supports the idea that during those years Jesus worked as a carpenter around Palestine and Nazareth. In fact, early church leader Origen disputed that Jesus was a carpenter. Nowhere in the gospels or other writings is Jesus depicted as a carpenter, except by the churches. The orthodox view that Jesus did nothing noteworthy between the ages of thirteen and thirty has not been substantiated either.

Many believe that Jesus was an Essene. The Pharisees, Sadducees, and Essenes were Judaic sects living in Palestine. They practiced their faiths in the same temples and churches even though they had differences of opinion on how the Jewish religion should be observed.

One of the Essene colonies existed near Mount Carmel in Samaria, where Jesus studied as a child. The Essenes were greatly influenced by Eastern philosophies and astrology. Some believe that this may have influenced Jesus to travel to the East to learn more about these ideas.

According to Elizabeth Prophet in her book *The Lost Years of Jesus*, a Russian journalist, Nicholas Notovich, wrote a book in 1894 called *The Unknown Life of Jesus Christ*. The journalist claimed that while traveling in Ladakh, often called Little Tibet, a city set deep in the Himalaya Mountains, he found a copy of an ancient Buddhist manuscript that plainly stated that Jesus studied and taught in India, Nepal, Tibet, Ladakh, and Persia during the "lost years."

204

Notovich visited a Buddhist convent hidden away at an altitude of 11,000 feet in the Himalayas. The journalist asked the Chief Lama about the "prophet Issa," the Eastern name for Jesus. The Lama replied that the Buddhists greatly respected Issa and said that there were many scrolls locked away in the monastery regarding the Buddha Issa, who "preached the doctrine in India and among the children of Israel."

Notovitch persuaded the Lama to allow him to read the manuscripts. From these volumes he compiled a text he called *The Life of Saint Issa: Best of the Sons of Men.*

The story began in Jesus' thirteenth year, the beginning of the "lost years." Apparently at that age an Israelite man would normally "take a wife." But Jesus wanted to travel east to the "Divine World" to perfect himself.

Jesus spent six years studying with Brahmin priests who taught him the holy Vedas (Indian scriptures). He learned that by tuning into the divine Christ Consciousness within, he could heal the sick and perform other miracles.

Jesus later created conflict among the Brahmins and Kshatriyas (the priestly and warrior classes or castes) by teaching the Vedas to the lower castes. The upper castes said that the lower castes could only hear the Vedas during certain ceremonial times and that the lowest caste, the Sudras, were not allowed to hear the teachings at all.

Some in the upper castes even plotted to kill Jesus, but he was warned by the Sudras and took cover in the Himalaya Mountains in Southern Nepal.

From there he traveled west, spreading the great truths he had learned until he returned to Palestine at age twenty-nine.

Elizabeth Prophet wrote in *The Lost Years of Jesus* that in 1925, Swami Abhedananda, a member of India's ancient monastic order, went to the same convent to inquire about Notovitch's discoveries. The Swami interviewed the Chief Lama, who not only verified the journalist's story but also helped Abhedananda translate the writings, which he later published in Bengali.

According to Prophet, several others have also traveled to the monastery and found both written and oral accounts of Jesus' journey to the East.

Yogananda learned during the writing of *The Second Coming of Christ* that Jesus went to India to return the visit of the three "Wise Men from the East" who came to pay homage to him at his birth.

Yogananda believed that the three Magi were guided to the Christ child not by a physical star in the sky but by the light of the omniscient spiritual eye within. Yogananda explained that the adoration of the Wise Men was far more significant than just another scene from the holy birth. It was a defining moment that would characterize Jesus' future mission and message. It was meant as a reminder that Christ was born in the Orient and that his teachings would be influenced by Eastern philosophies.

### The Missing Links

In their book *The Lost Teachings of Jesus*, Mark and Elizabeth Prophet gave several examples of what they called the missing links to Christianity. Several passages within the New Testament show Jesus teaching and speaking for several hours. But very few words he spoke were included in the gospels.

Mark 6:35 describes a scene in which Jesus talks to a large crowd that was said to have been so spellbound that it did not leave even when night fell. Jesus took pity on the people and multiplied five loaves of bread and two fishes so that the group could eat. All four gospels mention this incident, but none of them reveal what Jesus said.

Luke tells a story about an in-depth discussion Jesus had with his disciples on the road to Emmaus: "And Jesus explained to them what was said about himself in all the scriptures, beginning with the book of Moses and the writings of all the prophets" (Luke 24:27). Apparently none of the disciples wrote down what Jesus said.

John's Gospel tells the story of Jesus' trip to Jerusalem for the Feast of Tabernacles. The feast supposedly lasted for seven days. John depicts Jesus as teaching at the feast, yet the only words recorded in the gospels were Jesus' answers to the queries of the Jews, who were amazed at what he was saying. Surely there must have been many things said that were noteworthy because when the officers of the temple were questioned as to why they did not arrest Jesus for his blasphemy, they responded, "Never a man spake like this man" (John 7:46). What did Jesus say that was so astonishing? We may never know.

When Jesus sent his disciples out to teach, he said, "What I tell you in the dark, utter in the light; and what you hear whispered, proclaim upon housetops" (Matthew 10:27). But no one knows what Jesus whispered in the dark and what they were to shout from the rooftops.

According to Mark and Elizabeth Prophet, Jesus' post-resurrection teachings were also sparsely recorded. In Acts 1:3, we hear about Jesus' contact with his disciples after his death: "He had shown himself alive to them after his Passion by many demonstrations: for forty days he had continued to appear to them and tell them about the Kingdom of God." It is difficult to believe that no one would have taken the time to write down such important communication.

A year after his ascension, Jesus reappeared to teach the Apostle Paul and stayed in constant contact with him for a number of years.

Paul wrote in his first letter to the Galatians, "I want you to realize this, the Good News I preached is not a human message that I was given by men, it is something I learned only through a revelation of Jesus Christ" (Galatians 1:11).

It is clear that what Jesus taught Paul had not been heard before, and Paul believed the information would be met with shock and even scorn. "I have to boast, even though it doesn't do any good. But I will now talk about visions and revelations given me by the Lord. I know a certain Christian man who fourteen years ago was snatched up to the highest heaven (I do not know whether this actually happened or whether he had a vision—only God knows)...and there he heard things which cannot be put into words, things that human lips may not speak" (II Corinthians 12:4-5).

There is no known record of this one-on-one tutoring of Paul. It is common knowledge that many of Paul's letters were lost.

Another issue is the literacy of Jesus. Many have assumed that Jesus wrote nothing. But according to some biblical scholars, it was highly unlikely that Jesus was illiterate. During Jesus' time most people could read and write. The gospels depicted Jesus as a literary genius. He easily engaged in complicated debates regarding the Old Testament scriptures, so it is clear that he could read. It seems unlikely that Jesus would have neglected to write his teachings down.

Scholars believe that the writers of the New Testament relied on several other sources of information when writing their gospels. Researchers have found that there was another document known as *Q* for Quelle, a German word for Source. There is significant evidence that the gospel writers relied heavily on Q and other documents because the chronology of events and Jesus' sayings in all four gospels are almost identical. The gospels were written almost forty years after Jesus died, so there had to have been another written source of information.

There is little doubt among scholars that other texts existed. The obvious questions are: Who wrote these other gospels, and why were some kept and others conveniently lost? Some say that the early Christians were expecting Jesus' imminent return and that the end of the world would soon follow. They were too caught up in spiritual pursuits to write anything down.

Mark and Elizabeth Prophet believe that most of the information that did not make it into the New Testament gospels was discounted, suppressed, and destroyed. I believe that this is the reason Jesus gave the apostle John a stern warning at the end of Revelation to discourage whomever would try to add or delete words from the prophetic book.

## The Secret Teachings

There is evidence that Jesus and his apostles deliberately withheld certain teachings. Biblical scholars recognize that Jesus had esoteric inner teachings that he gave his disciples in confidence. The gospels do not reveal these confidences.

"But without parable spake he not unto them. And when they were alone he expounded on all things" (Mark 4:34).

In Paul's first letter to the Corinthians, he wrote, "We speak wisdom among them that are perfected: yet not the wisdom of this world, nor of the princes of this world, that come to nought: But we speak the wisdom of God in a mystery, even the hidden wisdom, which God ordained before the world unto our glory..."(I Corinthians 2:6-7).

Jesus also had secret spiritual practices. It is said that when he healed a man, he always took the sick man aside. Very few knew what he said and did, and he often told the people close to him not to reveal his methods.

I learned that authors Mark and Elizabeth Prophet, who are well known for channeling the ascended masters, wrote about their contact with Jesus in their book *The Lost Teachings of Jesus*. I immediately ordered it and eagerly waited for it to arrive. But I was dismayed when the book arrived because it was almost 500 pages, and that was just Volume One. I wondered how I would possibly have time to read the entire book. I asked Cathy what I should do.

"You already know what the teachings are," she said and advised me to thumb through the book. As I did, I realized the information was almost identical to the revelations Jesus gave to Yogananda in *The Second Coming of Christ* and the authors of *A Course in Miracles*.

Jesus said that all of humanity should remove the masks of their egos and allow their true selves to shine through. He encouraged people to keep their thoughts focused on the present.

He suggested that we remove all ideas of self-importance and realize that no one person is more or less important than another.

Those who do not realize that God is within them will suffer from negative thinking and doubt. Jesus said that finding God's inner presence would provide humanity with all the qualities needed to find the Kingdom of Heaven.

Jesus warned against judging others. He said that those who condemn the spirituality and religion of others would suffer a heavy burden of karmic debt because of the negativity they have spread in the world.

He explained that regardless of what we believe through our myriad lifetimes, we will all eventually reach the perfected state that many call the Kingdom of God. This will happen more quickly for some, but even those who choose to take great detours will find the straight path of inner wisdom sooner or later.

Jesus spoke about intuition and the ability of human beings to develop their sixth sense. He said that it is perfectly natural for people to communicate with those in spirit and that all human beings have this ability. He encouraged people to seek out their spiritual guides, angels, and master teachers so that they are able to move more quickly toward their divine life purposes.

He talked about the importance of the seven energy centers in the body known as the chakras. Each chakra is a hub of life-giving energy that radiates throughout the body.

Mark and Elizabeth Prophet said that the chakras are the missing dimension in physical fitness and heath, especially in the West. Universal life-force energy called *prana* flows through the chakras. Without this process, life cannot exist. This light energy, also called *chi*, flows through the meridians, which are manipulated in the ancient art of acupuncture. The chakras nourish the organs and nervous system and are part of the main energy current for the body, which runs vertically up and the spine.

Many believe that diseases are caused by a shortage of prana. An imbalance of prana will affect emotional and spiritual well-being.

I experienced this firsthand when I began having great difficulty breathing due to tightness in my diaphragm. I learned that the cause was emotional and spiritual.

The solar plexus chakra is related to control and power. My sister told me that to cure the problem I had many things to work through. She told me, "Stop trying to muscle the universe! You're not going to win that battle."

I have a tendency to take on all the world's problems and feel that I have to make everyone's difficulties go away. In 2005 my dad began having anxiety attacks when he turned seventy-two. He had just retired and said he felt lost. He didn't know what his purpose was. I, of course, could not stand by and watch him suffer, so I immediately ran to his aid, telling him what I thought his purpose was and giving him stacks of books to read. But Kim told me that part of his purpose was to go through the struggles and that I couldn't give him the answers. He had to find them on his own.

Eleanor said that because my energy is so open and fluid like water, I am like a sponge. She said I had to be careful because I could take on the grief of the world if I wasn't careful.

I also heard Cathy say, "Stop giving away your power." I realized that because I was taking on everyone's problems I felt a lack of control. This lack of control was causing a blockage of energy in my solar plexus chakra. I also discovered that worrying about the external approval of people around me instead of following my intuition was also a way of giving away my power. As soon as I told myself that it wasn't my job to fix things for other people, and that I didn't have to rely on other people's approval, I immediately breathed easier.

One of the most important chakras is the "third eye" between the eyebrows. It is the center of spiritual vision Jesus spoke about when he said, "If therefore thine eye be single, thy whole body shall be full of light." The spiritual eye is the focus of Eastern mediation and is often marked with a dot on the forehead of Indian women.

Jesus wanted humanity to understand that we have been given free will, and because of God's laws we can create anything we want in our lives. Each person is solely responsible for his or her own circumstances. There are no victims.

Before we are born, we make decisions about our upcoming lives based on what spiritual lessons we want to learn. Our only purpose is to advance our souls closer to God-realization while in our physical bodies.

We are all created in the image and likeness of God and therefore we are all co-creators with God. We are masters of our own destiny with God's help. This idea is met with vehement criticism by the Christian orthodoxy. But Jesus said that those who do not realize this do not understand God.

Through special meditative techniques, masters in the East are able to do all the miraculous things that Jesus did. They can do this because they understand their connection with God. Most remarkable of all, Jesus said that every person would do these things and more.

212

Yogananda believed that through the meditative practice of aligning the body and mind with the universal Christ Consciousness and Divine Intelligence, a human being is able to experience his or her oneness with God. This was the secret that Jesus taught his inner circle. Yogananda said that these ancient teachings were also kept secret in the East for thousands of years.

But according to Yogananda in *Autobiography of a Yogi*, the entire world will soon be introduced to these Eastern meditative practices. When this occurs, the heightened level of human consciousness will have the power to transform the world.

## Who Was Jesus?

Jesus has appeared throughout the centuries to numerous people, including St. Francis, St. Teresa, and many others in the East and West. Yogananda said that his appearances mean that he has an ongoing role to play in the destiny of the world and that he is very much alive in spirit and is active in the world today, guiding those who seek his help regardless of religious affiliation.

Yogananda wrote in *The Second Coming of Christ* that he had reverently read the Bible to gain an understanding of the historical person of Jesus. Through extensive study, meditation, and his contact with Jesus, Yogananda came to believe, as many biblical scholars do, that John the Baptist was in a past life the guru and teacher of Christ. The term *guru* has a negative connotation in the West as a charlatan who preys on weaker people looking for guidance. But the true meaning is teacher or mentor. A guru is not an ordinary spiritual teacher. Eastern religions believe that a guru is an agent appointed by God in response to a student's readiness to move toward enlightenment. The guru/disciple or teacher/student relationship is very common throughout history in Eastern traditions.

According to Yogananda, many passages in the Bible imply that John and Jesus were, in their past incarnations,

Elijah (John) and his disciple Elisha (Jesus). Greek translators used the names Elias and Eliseus in the New Testament. Elijah and Elisha are Old Testament spellings for the same names.

In his book *Autobiography of a Yogi*, Yogananda discussed a prediction given by the prophet Malachi at the end of the Old Testament, which many believe was a prophecy of the return of Elijah and Elisha: "Behold I will send you Elijah the prophet before the coming of the great and dreadful day the Lord" (Malachi 4:5). John the Baptist (Elijah) was sent before Jesus (Elisha) as a herald for the coming of Christ.

An angel appeared to John's father, Zacharias, to let him know of the coming of his son John who was the great prophet Elijah (Elias in the New Testament).

"But the angel said unto him, fear not, Zacharias: for thy prayer is heard; and thy wife Elizabeth shall bear thee a son, and thou shalt call his name John...And many of the children of Israel shall he turn to the Lord their God. And he shall go before him in the spirit and power of Elias, to turn the hearts of the fathers to the children, and the disobedient to the wisdom of the just; to make ready a people prepared for the Lord" (Luke 1:13-17).

Yogananda pointed out that Jesus twice unequivocally identified John as Elijah (Elias): "Elias is come already and they knew him not...Then the disciples understood that he spake unto them of John the Baptist" (Matthew 17:3).

Jesus also said, "Until the time of John all the prophets and the Law of Moses spoke about the Kingdom; and if you are willing to believe their message, John is Elijah, whose coming was predicted" (Matthew 11: 13, 14).

Some Christian scholars dispute this by pointing to the fact that John the Baptist denied he was Elijah (Elias). But Yogananda learned through his contact with Jesus that by denying he was the great guru Elijah, John was saying that in his current humble garb of John, he was no longer the revered Elijah.

214

In his former life, Elisha (Jesus) had asked the great guru to give him his "mantle" of spiritual wealth so that in the next incarnation, Elijah (John) the guru and Elisha (Jesus) the disciple could exchange roles. Jesus would no longer need his teacher because he had become divinely perfected.

"And Elisha [Jesus] said, I pray thee, let a double portion of thy spirit be upon me. And he [Elijah] said, Thou hast asked a hard thing: nevertheless, if thou see me when I am taken from thee, it shall be so unto thee...And he took the mantle of Elijah that fell from him" (II Kings 2:9-14).

Although Elijah (John) was a great master, he agreed to incarnate in a lesser role just so that he could witness and prepare the way for his disciple, Jesus, to carry out his divine purpose of revolutionizing the spiritual destiny of mankind.

While John agreed to play a less significant role than Jesus, his imprisonment and beheading was arguably as horrendous an ordeal as Jesus' crucifixion.

When Jesus lay dying on the cross, he is said to have called out to his mentor, Elijah (Elias): "Eli, Eli, lama sabachthani?" This translates to "My God, My God, why has thou forsaken me?"

"Some of them that stood there, when they heard that, said, 'this man calleth for Elias...Let us see whether Elias will come to save him'" (Matthew 27:46).

Jesus had a very clear understanding of the Old Testament and often referred to himself and his mission as the fulfillment of the Old Testament prophecies.

"Think not that I am come to destroy the law of the prophets: I am not come to destroy, but to fulfill" (Matthew 5:17).

The Indian master El Moyra spoke extensively about Jesus through his scribes, Mark and Elizabeth Prophet, in *The Masters and the Spiritual Path*. He said that in order to have a true relationship with God, it is important to realize who Jesus was and who he was not. Jesus did not come from God as a new soul, born for the first time in his incarnation in Nazareth.

El Moyra and many others have said that, in a former life, Jesus was Joshua, a military hero to the Hebrews. Then he was Joseph, one of the twelve sons of Jacob. In Genesis, we hear a story about Joseph and his coat of many colors, which many believe signified he was passing through certain tests prior to his wearing the garment of the Christ, which represents the unity of God and man.

In the Gospel of Thomas, we learn that Jesus was a mystic and a teacher. *A Course in Miracles* tells us that Jesus was a man who remembered his divinity.

In the *Course*, Jesus distinguished himself from God by saying that he would substitute for our ego if we asked him to but never for our spirit. He explained that, like a father who leaves a child with an older brother, the older brother can protect the child but he does not confuse himself with the father because he helps watch over child.

What set Jesus apart from other people was that he had reached perfection. He had attained a state in which his spiritual mind and his conscious mind had become one.

In the Gospel of Thomas, we see a very different view of Jesus than the version given today in most Christian churches. According to Stevan Davies in his book *The Gospel of Thomas*, Jesus was not dogmatic or prosperity-conscious, and he rejected all religious rules. In many instances the New Testament gospels and the Gospel of Thomas show Jesus as defiant when it came to conventional religious customs of his day.

His disciples questioned him: "Should we fast? In what way should we pray? Should we give to charity? From which foods should we abstain?"

Jesus responded, "Do not lie. If there is something that you hate, do not do it, for everything is revealed beneath the heaven. Nothing hidden will fail to be displayed. Nothing covered will remain undisclosed" (the Gospel of Thomas, verse 6). This verse reveals that Jesus believed finding truth should take precedent over religious concerns and rituals.

As I was finishing this section, my husband and I received Father John's December 2005 newsletter. Again I was amazed at the synchronicity. He wrote, "God loves us all, without reservation. Jesus showed us that love in simple and real ways. He came as a little child—helpless and poor. He grew up, lived, and died as a Jew. He never identified with the power-hungry leaders of his religion or his state. Nor did he accept their restrictive moral and legalistic attitudes. He didn't talk about sex. He talked about love. He didn't condemn people to Hell. He offered salvation to all. He embraced prostitutes, he sat down with the men and women, and everyone rejoiced."

I sent Father John an e-mail telling him how timely his newsletter was. He wrote back: "I keep realizing that the images a lot of us have of Jesus are taken from myths, which we grew up with, rather than what was probably reality..." He echoed my feelings when he wrote: "I keep discovering a new and better Jesus."

## What was Jesus' Purpose?

"Is it not written in your law...ye are gods?" Jesus said to the Jews, as they were about to stone him because they believed he had made himself God. Jesus was quoting from the Old Testament: "I have said, ye are gods; and all of you are children of the most High" (Psalms 8:26).

In response to his followers' shock over his abilities, he said, "Why are you so amazed? These things and more shall you do."

Jesus came to show that all people are divinely created and that all people can attain the level of Christhood that he did. Ironically the so-called "guardians of the faith" have continually demanded the world believe the exact opposite of Jesus' mission.

Another misunderstanding is that Jesus died for the sins of man. But I believe that Jesus lived for humanity. He chose to die on the cross to show his love of God and his commitment to the message that he came to deliver.

The viewpoint given in the Gospel of Thomas is startlingly different than the traditional Christian ideas about Heaven. Thomas wrote that the Kingdom already exists on earth and within all humanity and has been there since the beginning. These ideas mirror the teachings of many Eastern traditions.

Jesus' own disciples showed their confusion in the Gospel of Thomas when they asked him, "Tell us about our end. What will it be?" Jesus replied, "Have you found the Beginning so that you now seek the end? The place of the Beginning will be the place of the end" (the Gospel of Thomas, verse 18a).

Jesus rejected the idea of the future Kingdom in this passage and refers to time in the eternal present, a theme that is central to the teachings of Zen Buddhism.

Jesus lamented the world's lack of desire for what he came to give. "I stood in the midst of the world. I came in the flesh. I found all of them drunk. I found not one of them to be thirsty. My soul was saddened by the sons of men for they have come into the world empty and they will go out of the world empty. But now they are drunk. When they sober up they will repent" (the Gospel of Thomas, verse 28).

But Jesus was forgiving of mankind's spiritual ignorance and lack of knowledge. "Father, forgive them; for they know not what they do," was Jesus' mantra as he opened his arms to all people and rejected no one. He promoted universal love of every person, enemy or friend.

In *Tomorrow's God*, Walsch wrote that Jesus taught his followers about the unity of God and man. Jesus was a savior to all of mankind, and his message was that everyone could be a savior. But this message did not serve the human agenda. So his message was changed.

218

Jesus understood that people would have great difficulty believing in their own divinity, so he asked people to believe in him.

He had such an incredible understanding of who he was that he was able to make the promise that anything asked in his name would be. He knew there was no limit to what he could do, and he came to teach that there is no limit to what any of us can do. But his ultimate message was that people did not need him in order to be who they really were—one with God.

## The Coming of a New Age

Again I asked my sister if this information about Jesus was important for the book. I wanted to make sure that I was not somehow fulfilling my own agenda. She assured me that the information is vitally important and reminded me that Jesus is a pivotal figure in history. All time is divided by his life and death (B.C. and A.D.). In order to promote true change in the world, all people must know who Jesus is.

I thought about a lecture our priest gave at Mass about a woman who had left the church in search of "all kinds of New Age ideas." She went to hear a "New Age guru" speak. But the woman was unable to find what she was looking for and came back to the Church.

My grandmother, who was a very religious person, used to warn my sister and me to "stay away from that 'New Age' stuff. It comes from the devil." Cathy always tried to argue with her, but she refused to even discuss it.

People often label Eastern ideologies as "New Age," so I asked Cathy, "What about people who will write off and belittle this information as 'New Age' thinking?"

Cathy said that when people talk about "New Age" ideas they are really saying that people in this new age are returning to ancient wisdom. The Eastern philosophies that influenced Jesus are not new. Most were in existence several thousand years before the time of Christ.

"Like so many great truths, these teachings have been suppressed and obscured to cater to the powers that be," Cathy told me.

The pieces of the puzzle were beginning to fall into place. I understood that the teachings in the Gospel of Thomas and the Gnostic Gospels regarding self-discovery, wisdom, and knowledge matched the predictions for the Golden Age.

The prophecies at the end of the Book of Revelation foretold of a new heaven and a new earth. The first heaven and the first earth would pass away. The old ideas that are preventing the world from uniting will pass away. In this new age, the timeless and treasured teachings of Jesus will finally be restored and understood.

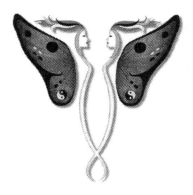

## Chapter Fourteen:
## The World's Teachers

"We have a habit of making Gods out of our teachers instead of listening to the messages that they bring us," Cathy wrote to Tom.

I learned that all of the world's teachers have come to deliver the same message, each in a different way. Most souls come to earth to experience their true selves and realize their own divinity. But a few select souls come back to the earth to help others. There are always advanced souls among us who have made the choice to come back even though they have finished their own work on earth.

### The Masters

When I first began reading Cathy's books, I encountered the word *master* repeatedly. Initially it was difficult to understand what the term actually meant.

According to Mark and Elizabeth Prophet in *The Masters and the Spiritual Path*, the state of mastery is having expert skill or proficiency in a given field or area of knowledge. There are those who are masters in philosophy, science, and music.

I learned that a spiritual master is one who has gained mastery over the cycles of life and death. The Bhagavad-

Gita describes an enlightened master in the following words: "the self shines forth like a sun in those who have banished ignorance by wisdom" (V:16).

Yogananda said in *The Second Coming of Christ* that a master does not identify with his limited body but with the great universal force of the Creator and is an extension of deity for mankind.

A master will always choose the highest option and is unflappable in the face of what most would consider a disaster or terrible tragedy.

Masters have lived through enough fear, rage, and grief that they no longer react to these things. They understand these emotions are illusions. They see the bigger picture and know that in the end, a perfect outcome is assured. Masters have always chosen love and do so even when their love is not returned. This is often the most difficult lesson on the road to mastery.

Neale Donald Walsch wondered in *Tomorrow's God* how we could send messages of love to those whose only desire is to kill us. He learned that all masters see themselves and others for who they truly are and by doing this, they have changed the world.

Someone who has reached this heightened level of spiritual growth has discovered the secrets of the physical world and refuses to acknowledge the ups and downs of the drama we call "life."

Yogananda explained in *The Second Coming of Christ* that every master has come for a specific mission. Moses came to emphasize the downfalls of reckless and selfish behavior. Jesus came to demonstrate God's love and compassion. Before Jesus was Gautama Buddha, "the enlightened one," whose purpose was to remind a forgetful generation of the forces of karma, the law of cause and effect, and mankind's responsibility for his present condition.

Bhagavan Krishna came during a time of great wisdom and understanding. He taught God-realization and union with God through the spiritual science of yoga and meditation.

The prophet Mohammad taught, "Not one of you is a believer until he desires for his brother what he desires for himself." Many of the things Mohammad said have been misunderstood. In *On the Wings of Heaven*, Joseph Crane's angel said that when Mohammad spoke of the infidel, he was speaking of those who say they believe in God but do not.

An infidel was not one who was outside Mohammad's own religion. There are infidels in every religion. The angel told Joe that anyone seeking an infidel should look no further than his or her own reflection in the mirror. Mohammad would advise us to enlighten ourselves instead of seeking to enlighten others.

There are numerous masters who are not as well known. Most people include Paramahansa Yogananda among the ranks of the great masters. All masters have taught mankind of their inherent divinity. Every master's message has been the same: *What I am, you are. These things and more shall you do.*

## What Is Ascension?

Another frequently used word in spiritual literature is *ascended master*. Many have heard the word ascension used in reference to Jesus. And Jesus is indeed an ascended master. But what is ascension?

According to Mark and Elizabeth Prophet in *The Masters and the Spiritual Path*, ascension means to go back to the heart of God after having overcome all karmic debt through many lifetimes.

Walsch learned in *Conversations with God* that while in spirit, a soul cannot know itself experientially. So we take on physical form so that we might know who we truly are. As souls we intended to go out and create on earth the love and eternal peace that is in Heaven. But while in physical form we forget why we came and we identify ourselves as human bodies first instead of souls first.

In order to go back to the realm of God, the soul must merge its lower self (ego) with its higher self (soul) and become one again while in physical form. Nick Bunick described this in *In God's Truth* when he said that Jesus was a man who had merged his conscious mind with his spiritual mind and that this is the goal of humanity.

I learned in *The Masters and the Spiritual Path* that during ascension, an enlightened master consciously increases the vibratory rate of the electrons that make up his physical existence. Like an exploding star, the master merges his consciousness with the Christ Consciousness of the Creator.

When the ascension takes place, the soul becomes so full of light that it can no longer be attached to the earth. The spirit no longer needs a physical body in order to know itself.

Some people are afraid that this final blending of consciousness means the end of individuality. But Jesus told Mark and Elizabeth Prophet, in *The Lost Teachings of Jesus*, that oneness does not mean sameness. He said that there is no greater freedom than to leave the physical body behind permanently. After the ascension, the soul can fly with the birds or swim with the fish in the rivers and oceans. An ascended soul can walk the earth or be anywhere else in the universe and eternally experience the divine state of being one with all creation.

## The Ascended Masters

People who have had near-death experiences have seen a group of white-robed advisors who look like the Supreme Court. Some have also seen these wise souls while under hypnosis, in dreams, or during meditation. According to Mark and Elizabeth Prophet, these are the ascended masters. They are beings of light, teachers, angels, and masters who guide mankind. Their task is to help us prepare for our next embodiment, and they greet us upon our return between lifetimes.

The Western saints and Eastern masters make up the ascended masters. They are both male and female and come from every race, culture, and religious background. Regardless of what part of the world in which they made their ascension, they have chosen to be the teachers of the world. There is no competition among them.

Unfortunately, many of the world's religious organizations attempt to discredit the service of all other masters and are loyal to only one ascended master. But in doing this the religions have cut themselves off from those who represent the consciousness of God. Every ascended master has something important to contribute to the world.

### El Morya Kahn

I discovered that my sister had been influenced by the teachings of the ascended master El Morya Khan. I learned that the great teacher had an illustrious past. He was Abraham of the twelve tribes of Israel. He then returned as Melchior, one of the three Wise Men of the East. Later he became King Arthur, king of the Britons who summoned the Knights of the Round Table and the ladies of the court of Camelot to find the Holy Grail. He came back to Britain twice more as Thomas Becket and Thomas More. He was born as King Henry II and VIII. In the sixteenth century, he chose the East again and became the mogul Emperor Akbar. Finally, he appeared as one of the most renowned Tibetan mahatmas, El Morya Kahn.

I believe that Cathy and I have been guided to his teachings because, like Paramahansa Yogananda, he is known for his efforts to merge the spiritual truths and traditions of the East and West. El Moyra's mantra was that everyone could become like Christ and that God has no favorite sons. In 1898 El Moyra became an ascended master. His message is universal and it is helping to usher in the coming of the new age.

## Mother Mary

Most of the ascended masters I have been learning about are male. I knew that there were many female ascended masters but I was not acquainted with many of them. According to Doreen Virtue in *Archangels and Ascended* Masters, Mary, the mother of Jesus, is an ascended master just like her son.

Mary has appeared over the ages to many people. A friend who is a life-long Catholic had an astounding encounter with the Blessed Virgin. He had tears in his eyes when he told me the story. He had always felt a loving affinity with Mary. His wife affirmed this, saying that "George" had spoken often about the Blessed Virgin.

One night he woke up out of a deep sleep. His eyes were drawn to a picture of Jesus with a crown of thorns that hung on the wall. He fell back asleep but later woke up again and saw the picture of Jesus on the wall. The next morning he opened his eyes and lay in bed for several minutes reflecting about his nighttime vision of the picture of Jesus. He heard his wife in the kitchen preparing breakfast when suddenly it seemed as though the ceiling were opening up to a blue sky with white fluffy clouds. He shook his head to see if he were dreaming but he was wide-awake. To his awe and amazement the Blessed Virgin Mary appeared to him, smiling and then she was gone.

George asked me tearfully, "Why me?"

"Why not you," I responded. Sadly, after a lifetime as a devout Catholic, he truly believed that he was not worthy of the encounter. I assured him that he was worthy. According to Virtue, like all the other ascended masters, Mary comes to anyone who calls upon her, regardless of religious background.

226

Virtue said that Mary's personality is very similar to the sweet, compassionate image that is portrayed in Christian teachings. She is the most loving, kind, and patient of the ascended masters, although Virtue says that behind her gentleness is a firm "mother bear" attitude. She is lovingly warning the world to shape up.

In her book *Archangels and Ascended Masters*, Virtue described her travels around the world to places where she could feel the strongest connection with each ascended master. Virtue spoke to Mary at a shrine dedicated to her at the Cologne Cathedral in Germany.

Mary told Virtue that what humanity needs most at this time is compassion. She said that compassion is love combined with an understanding of the other person's perspective. Mary lamented that there is entirely too much energy being wasted on aggression. She explained to Virtue that we will all soon realize that those we resent and fear the most are merely children who are also afraid.

Mary wants all of humanity to lay down our arms. She believes that we are weary from constantly defending ourselves against dangers and problems of our own making.

## Unascended Masters

Unascended masters are those who have reached mastery over their physical bodies and their emotions but have not yet taken their ascension.

*The Masters and the Spiritual Path* describes an unascended master as one who has come so close to the I Am presence that he or she can be one with God without leaving his or her body in death. Some agree not to ascend and to stay on earth to help move other souls closer to their own ascensions.

There are many masters on earth, especially in the East, who have not yet perfected themselves, but they frequently reach very high states of consciousness through meditation. A few unascended masters can, like the ascended masters, perform miracles.

Once a master goes through the ascension process, he or she usually does not go back into a physical body again. A master is able to appear in spirit to those on earth and has done so many times throughout history.

The prophet Elijah (John the Baptist) was a rare exception. He was allowed to take on physical form after his ascension so that he could prepare the way for his disciple Elisha (Jesus Christ).

## Avatars

The word *Avatara* is a Sanskrit word meaning *descent of God*. In Hindu scriptures, it means Divine Incarnation, or one who attains oneness with Spirit and agrees to stay on earth to help mankind. Avatars are like earth angels, and their goal is always to raise the consciousness of the earth and its inhabitants.

I learned in *The Masters and the Spiritual Path* that many avatars were born in the 1960s and 1970s. The vibrations of these souls could be felt for hundreds of miles. These masters did not have to reincarnate again, but they volunteered to help raise the planet from one of its lowest points in history, and they came to move the world to its highest point in history known as the Golden Age.

Yogananda said that in order to understand the divine incarnation of an avatar, it is necessary to understand the source and nature of the consciousness of these souls. The level of consciousness can best be described by Jesus' words, "I and my Father are one" (John 10:30) and "I am in the Father and the Father in me" (John 14:11).

I recently met one of these rare masters named Siva Baba. I attended a seminar that he was teaching and was immediately taken by the immense energy I felt in his presence. We were told that Siva Baba would enter the room and would look each one of us in the eyes and he would know what our soul needed and would send us energy that would help us on our soul's path. As he looked at me I suddenly felt faint. The outer edges of my vision became blurry. It was as if reality were fading in and out.

Later I heard his staff telling stories about the amazing things they had witnessed while traveling with Siva Baba. They had seen him shape shift and take on the physical characteristics of Jesus and other masters. At times he would meditate until his physical body simply disappeared as it turned to light. I was filled with gratitude for the opportunity to have met an avatar face to face.

### Mahavatar Babaji

According to Yogananda in *The Second Coming of Christ*, there are those in India and other places who have attained such mastery that they possess phenomenal powers and can remain in their bodies for thousands of years. They are not subject to the laws of nature and are free from the bondage of the material world.

When I first heard this, it sounded rather farfetched. But Yogananda said that the rare souls who stay in their bodies for prolonged periods of time do not readily make themselves available to the public. In fact, many of them remain in constant meditation, sending out powerful vibrations to help balance the ills and evils of the world.

One such avatar is Mahavatar Babaji. He is known as the deathless saint because he has been in his body for hundreds of years. Mahavatar means great avatar. Babaji means revered Father. The word *Baba* is a generic word meaning father, and the suffix *ji* is a title of respect.

Yogananda explained in *Autobiography of a Yogi* that masters like Christ, Buddha, and Krishna come to earth for specific purposes and leave when their missions are complete. But avatars like Babaji are concerned with more slow, evolutionary issues of humanity. Babaji's mission is to help other prophets carry out their special dispensations.

In *Autobiography of a Yogi*, Yogananda wrote about the sparse details of Babaji's life. He has lived for centuries in the most spiritual place on earth, the Himalayan Mountains. He is constantly on the move with a close-knit circle of disciples.

Yogananda said that a few spiritually advanced Americans are among his small group and that Babaji can hear people in the West calling out to him. One of Babaji's disciples, Lahiri Mahasaya, was the mentor and guru to Yogananda's mentor, Sri Yukteswar. According to Mahasaya, whenever someone utters Babaji's name, they receive an instant blessing.

Babaji commissioned Sri Yukteswar to write an analysis of the unity between the Hindu and Christian scriptures. The work was called *The Holy Science* and was later published by Yogananda's Self-Realization Fellowship.

Babaji instructed Sri Yukteswar to send Yogananda to the West to reveal the harmony between the original yoga science given by Bhagavan Krishna and original teachings of Christ.

According to Yogananda, Babaji is constantly in communion with Christ. They work together to send high-frequency vibrations to the world. Yogananda wrote that the two great masters—one in body the other in spirit—have been working tirelessly to inspire the nations of the world to discontinue anger, hatred, and war. They spend the majority of their time encouraging humanity to let go of intolerance and resolve our religious differences.

As a Westerner, I was skeptical when I first heard about these Eastern mystics. I wasn't sure if Babaji, Lahiri Mahasaya, and Sri Yukteswar even existed.

But when Helle and I met our friend Lena, she told us a story that changed my mind. Lena lives near the Self-Realization Center in Encinitas, California. She told us that she didn't know anything about Yogananda but was drawn to the colorful gardens overlooking the ocean. She often went there to meditate and to sketch pictures that came to her while she sat in the beautiful setting.

She matter-of-factly stated that one day while she sat meditating, Sri Yukteswar appeared to her. She thought, "Who is this Sri Yukteswar?" She decided she should go to the Self-Realization Fellowship bookstore to pick up a book about Yogananda and Sri Yukteswar.

She stood in the bookstore trying to decide if she wanted to spend the money to buy a book and which book she should buy. Finally she decided to purchase Yogananda's *Autobiography of a Yogi*. As she left the bookstore and headed up the street, something in the gutter caught her eye. There was a twenty-dollar bill lying on the ground. She looked around to see who might have dropped them. No one was around, and no cars were in sight. She picked up the money, delighted that she had been reimbursed for her purchase. She found out that Sri Yukteswar was Yogananda's revered teacher.

### Affinity with Four

Every person is drawn to certain masters depending on his or her life purpose. Our attraction to teachers may change depending on what is happening in our lives. While writing *Twin Souls* I felt a strong affinity with Jesus, Babaji, Yogananda, and El Moyra. I spoke to them often and asked them for guidance, and feel their presence around me.

One day I was feeling distraught over my father and brother's problems. My father was having anxiety attacks because of his retirement. He wanted to find a part-time job so that he would feel that he still had a schedule to follow. My brother, who did independent contract work for several large telecommunications companies, was upset because a large contract had just fallen through and he was out of work. Every penny he had was tied up in running his business, and he was broke.

Beside myself, I told the four great masters that I was at my wits' end. I thanked them for helping me with a special intention for both my father and my brother so that I could stop worrying about them and focus on my book.

Two days later, I received an excited message from my brother. Not only had he found a well-paying job in his field, but he also found an advertisement in the paper for a performing arts school looking for a part-time music professor.

My father sent his resume and was hired less than a week later. My brother was stunned by the turn of events and even more so when I told him about my special intention. While our teachers can help us with special intentions they will not intervene with the karma or free will of an individual. I remember Kim telling me that my father and brother came to this life to overcome obstacles like all people do. And she reminded me that it was not my job to "save" them from suffering.

A while later the company my brother was working for was removed from the project and he was out of a job again. My father decided not to take the teaching job because there were not enough students.

I believe our lives would be much richer if we allow the ascended masters, both male and female, to help us instead of limiting ourselves to only one teacher. I had chosen to receive specific guidance from these four great teachers while writing *Twin Souls* because their purpose is to bring love back to the world. I believe that *Twin Souls* is one of the many ways they are encouraging humanity to do this. By demonstrating the unity of opposites, they are showing that when we come into communion with our opposite, we become one.

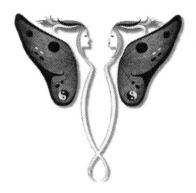

## Chapter Fifteen:
## The World's Messengers

### Earthly Messengers

According to Sanaya Roman in *Spiritual Growth*, one of
the greatest challenges a soul can undertake is to come
into the dimension of the earth. The denseness of the
being in physical form creates a veil of forgetfulness. Even
highly evolved beings sometimes forget who they are. It is
as if we are operating "blind" with a very dim awareness of
our true purpose. Because of the immense challenge of
taking on a physical body, God sends us many messengers
who always encourage us to make the highest choices
possible.

Many of our religions have taught us that no one living
today other than clergy are inspired directly from God and
that no person is worthy of communicating with God.
They have said that books written today could not
possibly contain sacred truths. I believe that the religions
do not want their followers to expand their ideas because
that might cause them to believe that they don't need the
religion any more.

The idea that great truths have come from God
through human beings is accepted, but the religions say
that this only occurred in ancient times. According to this

view, everything important has already been said, and there is nothing further to add. I believe that progress on this planet will be very difficult while we still subscribe to this point of view.

Neale Donald Walsch learned in *Conversations with God* that nothing is further from the truth than the idea that God has stopped communicating with us. He is continually sending us messages through a variety of channels, and it is an enormous mistake to discount the messengers who have come to earth at this time.

I believe it is important to understand that messages come in many different forms and from many different people. Some examples of today's messengers are: Neale Donald Walsch, Dr. Wayne Dyer, Deepak Chopra, Dr. Brian Weiss, Nick Bunick, medium James Van Praagh, and angel therapist Doreen Virtue.

Messengers come in both genders and from all faiths and cultures. Yogananda wrote in *Autobiography of a Yogi* about his journey to meet a Catholic mystic named Therese Neumann of Konnersreuth, Bavaria. Her life purpose was to send a message to Christians and people of all faiths that Jesus really did exist and that the account of his crucifixion given in the gospels and other documents is real and historically accurate.

Therese was born on Good Friday in 1898. At the age of twenty she was injured in an accident and became blind. She regained her sight and the use of her limbs by praying to the Catholic saint Therese of Lisieux, known as "The Little Flower," who is known for her healing abilities.

Beginning in 1923, she abstained completely from all food and drink except for one consecrated wafer a day. Every Friday, she experienced within her own body the Passion of Christ. People came from all over the world to witness the stigmata (sacred wounds of Christ), which appeared on her head, breasts, hands, and feet. A simple peasant, she spoke only the native German of her village, but during her Friday trances she uttered words in

Aramaic while she experienced the horrendous suffering that Jesus endured.

Yogananda witnessed her transformation and saw the blood running down her face, her forehead, and her hands. He realized that although she suffered greatly, she looked forward with great expectation to her divine connection with Christ.

Yogananda also met a female Indian yogi named Giri Bala who, like Therese, never ate. She used a special yoga technique in which she connected her consciousness with God and this enabled her to live without eating or drinking for many years.

A local investigation was done to see if the woman was a fraud. She agreed to live for several months locked in one part of her home while others monitored her. Her story was deemed authentic. Yogananda interviewed the woman's brother and learned that for fifty years she had not eaten one bite of food. She told Yogananda that she received her sustenance from a much higher source. Her message was to show that man is made purely of spirit and that through meditation, prayer, and faith, a human being can live by the light of God alone.

Walsch learned in *Tomorrow's God* that the days of the one-man savior are over. In order to face the great challenges and expectations of the new age, a large number of messengers are necessary. What is most needed is for many people to begin their journeys to mastery. As more people start to move down the path toward ascension, a monumental shift will occur in the energy of the planet, and this will change the direction of the human race.

My friend Helle took an extensive, seven-day angel therapy class with Dr. Doreen Virtue. Helle is extremely intuitive and resonates with optimism and light. Everyone who has met her can see a rare sparkle in her. When she told me that she took the class, I was thrilled because my friend Lena had told me that Helle was herself an earth angel and that she already had a gift for communicating with heavenly angels.

I readily agreed to a reading with Helle and felt an angelic presence almost immediately. Helle said that the night before the reading she heard an angel say, "Tell her she can't save the world by herself." Helle had laughed, knowing that the message must have been for me. Helle sensed that I was overwhelmed because I felt as if I had to single-handedly save the world. I admitted to feeling this immense pressure, and I knew that Cathy had felt the same way.

One person can't save the world but one person can change the world with the help of kindred spirits on earth and in Heaven. *Twin Souls* is one of the many messages given to humanity to help usher in the transformation to higher consciousness.

## Our Higher Selves

Author Sanaya Roman has been channeling Orin, a teacher and spiritual guide, for more than ten years. Orin has been speaking through Sanaya Roman at this time to help the world go through a major spiritual awakening and period of great change. Roman explained in *Spiritual Growth* that Orin is a being of light who exists in the realm of our higher selves, and his purpose is to assist us in receiving guidance from our higher selves while on earth.

"What is the higher self?" I wondered. According to Roman, the higher self is that part of a human being that is connected to the spiritual dimensions. Our goal is to become immune to the negative emotions of others and to open our higher intuitive centers so that we can receive guidance, inspiration, and information from our higher selves. The lower self, also called the ego, is something we have created and usually works in opposition to the higher self.

In his book *Journey of Souls*, Dr. Michael Newton described his discovery of the higher self and the levels of human consciousness. A traditional hypnotherapist, Newton was extremely skeptical of anything metaphysical in nature. But he inadvertently stumbled across the gateway to higher consciousness and the spiritual dimensions while hypnotizing a client.

Walsch learned in *Tomorrow's God* that there are four levels of human consciousness. The *subconscious* handles all the automatic tasks of the body. The *conscious* mind is assigned to data collection in each moment. It also handles decision-making and data analysis. It creates our present-moment experience.

The *superconscious* mind is in charge of the body-mind-spirit connection and the purpose of the soul. The *supraconscious* handles all of these tasks simultaneously. At the supraconscious level, we are connected to God and all others without losing our individual identity.

The higher self is part of the superconscious and supraconscious states of being. In this way, our higher selves are part of a different dimension than our conscious minds.

According to Virtue in *Divine Guidance*, it is important to distinguish between the messages we receive from our true higher wisdom versus the fearful thinking of our lower selves.

Virtue said that divine guidance comes from God and all of His creations, including ascended masters, angels, spirits, deceased loved ones, and our higher selves.

All false guidance comes from our ego, or lower selves. Virtue lamented that our current worldview at this time is immersed in scarcity, fear, and separation, all created by our lower selves.

According to Virtue, there are some very clear-cut ways to determine whether guidance is coming from our lower or higher selves.

## Messages from Our Lower Selves

Messages that we receive from our egos are always negative, insecure, competitive, and focused on fears about the future. The lower self warns us that there is a lack of everything and that we live in a dog-eat-dog world. For example, our egos tell us that there is not enough money, jobs, or other resources to go around so we must get ahead at any cost, with little concern for the welfare of others. Our lower selves try to delay us from our divine life purpose and are filled with worries of all kinds.

## Messages from Our Higher Selves

According to Virtue, the wisdom that comes from the higher self is always loving, mature, confident, positive, repetitive, powerful, familiar, and focused on the present. Our true selves remind us that we are equal with others, push us to fulfill our life purpose, and bring us great joy. When we receive divine guidance in any form, it is usually in the second person—"You should pay more attention to your health." Virtue said that these messages often come suddenly, and are often in response to our prayers.

Virtue wrote that people often struggle to hear their spiritual voices. But struggle of any kind blocks the still, small voice within. Other inhibitors to spiritual guidance are poor diet, lack of exercise, drugs, and alcohol.

As small children, we are open to all possibilities because we have not yet developed any preconceived notions about the world. Children are very aware of spirits, angels, their higher selves, and God. But as they get older, they become filled with fear and anxiety, and they often lose their spiritual insight. Sadly, when they tell their parents about seeing spirits, angels, or visions from past lives, they are often told that this is just their imagination or, worse, that they have done something wrong. This will cause a child to shut down his or her spiritual vision, sometimes permanently.

Medium James Van Praagh wrote in *Heaven and Earth* that many people's lives are more tedious and difficult than necessary because they go through life without the precious, God-given gift of spiritual intuition. If people would develop the ability to receive divine guidance from their higher selves, they would go from living a life of uncertainty to one of great peace and calm, as it was intended to be.

## Mediums and Psychics

According to Nick Bunick in his book *In God's Truth*, this time of great spiritual growth and change has produced more mediums, psychics, and mystics on earth than any other period in history. These gifted souls are messengers who bring great hope, joy, and guidance to the world. Bunick believes that many of these mystics are the prophets of the Old Testament who have returned to earth to aid in the great spiritual transition.

But many people do not believe that it is possible to communicate with those in spirit, nor do they believe that is it possible to use inner intuition and insight to predict future events. I used to be one of them.

A friend of my husband's family had a very difficult time with the death of his wife. I had never met him, but my husband told me about his sadness and confusion. I decided to send him some books that might help him with his grieving process. I collected all the books I had read immediately after Cathy died. Most of them were written by famous mediums such as Sylvia Browne, James Van Praagh, Rosemary Altea, and John Edwards.

After Cathy died, my ideas and beliefs began to change when I read story after story of gifted mediums making contact with deceased loved ones. I even went to see Sylvia Browne and James Van Praagh in person. And it was clear to me that I too was having communication with my sister and others on the other side.

I didn't know what "Tim's" beliefs were until my husband told me that he had considered becoming a priest although he had not grown up in one particular religion. After hearing about his religious views, I regretted sending him the books for fear he would be turned off by the stories of mediums and psychics.

Several weeks later, I got an e-mail from him saying that he was grateful that I had given him the books but that he was still struggling with his beliefs. "I would like to believe that there is something more after this life, but I have a hard time believing in these types of things because of my faith," he wrote.

That statement floored me. "Wouldn't someone's faith allow him or her to believe in life after death?" I wondered. But I remembered my own initial response to my sister's death. My religious "faith" was what caused me the most terror and confusion.

In my opinion, Western culture and religious teachings do not give an adequate explanation of death or of life after death. I think this is tragic, given the fact that there is so much information available about death.

Our religions have taught us that there is life after death. But for Christians, it is a very dicey situation because we don't know if our loved ones have gone to Heaven or, God forbid, Hell. We can hope our loved ones are in Heaven, but it is not appropriate to believe that we or someone else can communicate with him or her.

I pondered where these ideas came from. After all, I knew that I had been in constant communication with my sister, and I had witnessed other people communicating with her. I knew I wasn't crazy, and I was quite sure she had died.

All we have to do is recognize what science and spirituality have already proven—that the spirit, which is made of pure energy, never dies but leaves the body whole and intact, and it is very possible to communicate with someone in this state.

240

## Mediums

Cathy was a big fan of medium John Edwards. She often talked about wanting to go see him. She told Tom that she believed more and more people on earth are realizing that they too are able to communicate with those in spirit. She wrote, "I believe that now is a time of great awakening in all respects. The organizations that don't want us to know about these things are going to have an increasingly difficult time stopping people from seeing the truth. What you feel and experience is real. Don't doubt yourself," she instructed Tom.

Orthodox Christianity and other religions forbid communication with spirits and the use of mediums. According to Van Praagh in *Heaven and Earth*, this idea began when Moses declared it was against religious law at that time for a person to communicate with spirits for any reason other than for the purpose of helping Israel. These ideas led people to believe that it was wrong to communicate with someone in spirit for any reason. Moses' edict became permanent religious law and later became part of the Judao-Christian ideology.

Van Praagh explained that there is nothing strange or superhuman about communicating with those in spirit. In fact, it is quite natural. It is simply a matter of tapping into the God-force energy that exists in the fourth dimension, or spiritual realm. The mind, body, spirit and the entire universe is made up of this energy. Our minds are connected to this life energy and the Universal Mind, which has no boundaries or limits.

All people have spiritual intuition. I came to realize this truth after my sister died. We communicated quite easily through our thoughts. A medium is someone who is either naturally gifted or has fine-tuned his or her psychic abilities and extrasensory perception to such a heightened degree that he or she can interact with many spirits in other dimensions by manipulating and raising his or her energy to a higher vibration.

While attending Van Praagh's seminar, I witnessed just how much energy it took to communicate with those in spirit. He wore a wireless microphone with a large battery pack. Before the show was over, the entire battery pack went dead and had to be replaced before he could continue. Van Praagh explained that the enormous amount of energy he used to communicate with the large number of spirits, plus the higher energy vibrations of the spirits themselves, depleted the battery pack, which ordinarily would have lasted for several days or weeks.

According to Roman in *Spiritual Growth*, once people learn to access the Universal Mind and become more aware of their higher selves, they will also become more conscious of the dimension in which the higher self resides. And they will find that the spiritual beings who are part of this realm can be quite helpful in their daily lives.

According to Virtue in *Divine Guidance*, in Western cultures we are not taught to use our inner eyes and inner hearing. We have almost completely turned off our spiritual senses. They lie dormant and misunderstood.

Virtue says that our spiritual abilities will increase through meditation. We will realize that everything we do has more levels than what we see, and if we pay attention, we will become aware of subtle energies at work all around us.

### Psychics

For centuries, there have been religious stories about prophets foretelling the future. Bunick pointed out in *In God's Truth* that the Old Testament was full of tales about the greatest prophets in history: Daniel, Isaiah, Elijah, Ezekiel, and Malachi, who were revered and respected teachers.

Yogananda wrote in *The Second Coming of Christ* that the scribes of the New Testament may not have used the word *intuition*, but the New Testament is replete with references to intuitive knowledge.

According to Yogananda, there have been certain periods of ignorance throughout history in which God has sent his saints and prophets to guide weary souls out of the darkness. Yogananda spoke about the Universal Mind when he said that future events could be predicted by tapping into God's all-knowing consciousness.

Walsch learned in *Conversations with God* that there are certain rules that govern psychic phenomena. First, all thoughts are made of energy. This is a very important concept and will be discussed in later chapters. Second, all things are in motion; and third, all time is now.

The way we see time on earth is different than the way time is perceived once a person has crossed over into the spiritual realm. I heard about this during my first reading with Kim. My mother told me through Kim, "Soon you will understand that time is not what you think it is."

Time is actually vertical, not linear. Everything exists simultaneously. There really is no beginning or end. People who have had near-death experiences have expressed this sensation of everything being now instead of past, present, and future.

This is a very advanced concept and is difficult for the human mind to grasp, but it is this element of time that allows people to "see" what we perceive as the past or future.

Yogananda explained that prophecy does not mean that all events on earth are predestined. It is the karmic law of cause and effect that projects vibrations into the ether. Sensitive people can pick up on these vibrations and can see or feel a probable outcome. However, these outcomes can change drastically due to man's power of free will.

Bunick said that we choose our paths before we come to physical form. For many years we may walk down a narrow road where many things are predetermined. We use our free will to make smaller, everyday decisions. But every so often, we come to a major crossroads in our life where our God-given gift of free will becomes very important.

I experienced this firsthand when Kim and Sonia, my psychic friends, both told me that they saw me having two children. They both saw a daughter first.

One of the initial things Kim said in our first reading was, "Who has two kids? Your sister is talking about two kids." I told her that no one I knew had two kids. Kim concluded that they were going to be my kids. Kim said she was not sure of the year, but she that saw my first child would be a daughter and that she would be born in December, which would mean she would be conceived in March.

Two years later, in February of 2005, I felt déjà vu during a reading with Sonia when she said, "Who has two kids?" She felt sure I was going to have two kids, and she definitely saw me getting pregnant before April.

"Well," I thought, "this must be the March that I am going to get pregnant."

That same night at work, my husband responded to a radio call. As he was taking a statement from one of the witnesses, she asked him, "Do you want me to tell you what I see for you?"

"Ah, sure," he responded, not knowing what she was talking about. My husband is not a big believer in psychics.

"You are going to have a baby soon," she told him.

The next morning, I was describing Sonia's prediction when he said, "My psychic told me the same thing."

At first I thought he was joking around, but then he told me what the woman had said. He didn't think much about the coincidence, but I knew that coincidences don't exist and that my daughter was around us waiting to see if the timing was right for her to come.

March arrived and I wondered if I was going to get pregnant. But a problem arose when I developed a severe cold. I was so miserable that I broke down and took some very strong cold medicine even though I knew it would not be beneficial for conceiving a child. My cold was so bad that I took the medication for more than a week. I hoped that it would not harm the baby if she were conceived.

March came and went with no pregnancy. I had a very strong feeling that my daughter had used her free will and decided not to come because of the danger of birth defects related to the medication.

Six months later, in September of 2005, I went to see Kim for the second time. I asked her what she saw for me in regard to pregnancy. I didn't remind her of her prediction of my pregnancy from two years earlier.

She sat silently for several minutes then asked me, "Were you taking some kind of medication? I think it was about six months ago. Your daughter is saying that she was going to come, but it was not part of her life purpose to have special needs, so she didn't come."

"I knew it," I told Kim and explained to her about the cold medication.

"Yes, she's showing me that she has been waiting. It's like she's showing me this long chute and she is waiting to go down. I feel that somehow she has missed the window of opportunity."

"So am I still on track to have children, and if so, when will this all occur?" I asked Kim.

"Well, things have shifted; let me see if I can find out. I will ask your mother." After several seconds, she looked perplexed.

"I can't figure out what your mother is saying. She keeps mentioning '1989'...okay, I see what the problem is; your mother has not been in touch with the earth's plane for many years. Let's ask your sister."

Kim started laughing. "Your sister says, 'It's just like her to worry about this!'"

"I'm forty years old!" I protested.

"Well, Cathy, maybe she does have reason to worry; she's forty years old." Kim laughed. "Your sister wants you to focus on the book and not worry about how many children you will have. I am being told that things are changing in your life and you will just have to wait and see on that one."

I had to admit to myself that I was somewhat relieved. I had never been a person who desperately wanted children and there was a part of me that realized I wanted kids because I felt that I should want them.

I knew that if I did get pregnant I would be thrilled, but I was glad my daughter had used her free will and decided not to risk a situation that did not suit her life purpose.

Walsch learned that psychic power is merely the ability to step away from our limited experiences and our view of ourselves as limited individuals and tap into the larger truth that exists around us. Psychic power is something we must use or we will lose. To develop this power, we must pay attention to every hunch and intuitive feeling. We should act on those feelings before there is time to talk ourselves out of them.

Psychics are able to tune into very subtle, fleeting energy patterns. It is the slightest flicker of an idea or image, and then it is gone. Walsch wrote that psychic intuition does not reside in the mind but in the soul. The soul is the only instrument sensitive enough to pick up on these slight waves of energy.

Kim explained this to me on my first visit. I asked her if she wanted to see a picture of my sister or of my other family members. She told me that it wasn't necessary. She was tuning into my soul, and she got a picture of these people directly from me. The way she described my brother, mother, and father were startling accurate.

The soul is more powerful than we can imagine, and we have only begun to understand the vast reaches of the human mind. We are on the edge of a time when humanity will remember its God-given spiritual gifts of intuition and sixth sense. People will rediscover their higher selves and the enormous wealth of information and guidance that is always available. Many messengers have been sent to earth at this time to promote a greater understanding of these truths and to move humanity toward a spectacular spiritual renaissance.

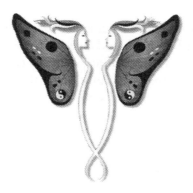

## Chapter Sixteen:
## Heavenly Helpers

According to Jerry and Esther Hicks in their book *Ask and It Is Given*, all physical beings have non-physical counterparts. But most people have forgotten about their connection to the spiritual realm. Many mediums are able to communicate more successfully with spirits by working with or channeling their spiritual counterparts. For example, psychic Sylvia Browne uses her spirit guide, Francine, when writing books about the afterlife. Medium Rosemary Altea's guide, Grey Eagle, assists her in doing clairvoyant readings for clients.

Other clairvoyants, such as Doreen Virtue and my friend Helle, who are now called angel therapists, have perfected their ability to interact with angels to bring love, light, and guidance to others.

### Spirit Guides
According to medium James Van Praagh in his book *Heaven and Earth*, spirit guides are highly evolved beings who have chosen to help others on their spiritual paths. Spirit guides are souls who have incarnated on earth and in other realms. Every person has at least one spirit guide. Some people have several spirit guides, depending on their

life purpose. Specialized guides come and go throughout our lives to assist us on specific projects. We may not recognize their help and guidance, but they are always there and are always part of any creative task.

Some believe that spirit guides are the same as guardian angels, but I believe they are different. An angel is a being that has never incarnated on earth. According to Doreen Virtue in *Divine Guidance*, a spirit guide can often be a great-grandparent or someone who passed away before we were born. It is important that a spirit guide be experienced in issues regarding our physical lives on earth as well as our spiritual paths.

Our guides know how to help us without interfering with our free will or karmic lessons. They will not make decisions for us, but they will help us see different options and urge us to make all decisions out of love and compassion.

In *Journey of Souls*, Michael Newton presented several case studies that showed how souls planned their upcoming lives with their spirit guides. We have one spirit guide who stays in mental contact with us throughout our lives. He or she also greets us when we die, along with our deceased loved ones, soulmates, and friends to help us make our transition.

I visited Kim a short time after Cathy died. She told me that Cathy had several guides and that they were with her. She explained that because of Cathy's sudden death, Cathy was still processing her death and making her transition. Kim described a blue, fluffy, cloud-like substance that surrounded her. I had read about this "cocoon" that is sometimes used after a sudden death to help a person calmly accept and understand his or her death. Sometimes people are literally thrown out of their bodies and may be very disoriented.

"I see your sister. Her guides say she is still processing her death. Her guides are waiting for her," Kim said.

According to Michael Newton in *Journey of Souls*, our spirit guides also help prepare us for our meeting with the council of ascended masters who gently and lovingly help us through reviews of our lives.

According to Sanaya Roman in *Spiritual Growth*, guides are at different spiritual levels, like we are. They begin by working with one person. As they become more adept at guiding people, they work with larger groups. The most advanced beings, such as the ascended masters, are involved in guiding people on earth and in other realms simultaneously.

In *The Messengers*, by Julia Ingram and G.W. Hardin, Jesus explained that he could be seen as a spirit guide for everyone. Yogananda realized this when he interacted with Jesus. He described his encounter in *The Second Coming of Christ*: "The whole universe I saw glistening in those eyes. They were infinitely changing, and with each transition of expression I intuitively understood the wisdom conveyed. In his glorious eyes I felt the power that upholds and commands the myriad of worlds."

According to Virtue in *Divine Guidance*, the role of a spirit guide is a highly esteemed role and requires much training from both the earth and afterlife's planes. I was thrilled when Helle told me during an angel reading that Cathy had moved up significantly in her spiritual level so that she could become a spirit guide for the writing of *Twin Souls*.

## Angels

According to *The Shorter Oxford Dictionary*, an angel is "a ministering spirit or divine messenger superior to human beings in power and intelligence, who are the attendants and messengers of the Deity..."

Theologian and intellectual St. Thomas Aquinas was given the name Doctor Angelicus, or Angelic Doctor, because he wrote volumes about the angels. He said that angels are experts in intuition. They see things more clearly than we do and therefore they represent knowledge and truth.

Virtue wrote in *Divine Guidance* that angels are composed of God's love, light, and intelligence. In essence, they are the loving thoughts of God.

Virtue said that angels appear to us as beautiful beings with elegant wings, their bodies surrounded by gold or white light. She wrote that angels actually come in all shapes, sizes, and colors, and they do not really need wings, but they take on this form so that we will recognize them. In reality, they are formless beings of pure love and light.

Angels have been part of religious stories for centuries. They played a large role in both the Old and New Testament, from Genesis to Revelation. In Genesis, we hear a story of Jacob, the son of Isaac: "He lay down to sleep, resting his head on a stone. He dreamed that he saw a stairway reaching to Heaven, with angels going up and coming down on it. And there was the Lord standing beside him" (Genesis 28:12-13).

In Revelation, John wrote, "Then the angel said to me, 'these words are true and can be trusted. And the Lord God, who gives his Spirit to the prophets, has sent his angel to show his servants what must happen very soon" (Revelation 22:6.)

According to Mathew Fox and Rupert Sheldrake in their book *The Physics of Angels*, the function of an angel is to teach humankind about spirituality and to move souls toward their ascension. Unfortunately, our religions, which first brought us these heavenly beings, have become secularized and no longer allow angels to be part of our lives. Fox and Sheldrake say that to secularize something means to suck the joy and awe out it.

According to Fox and Sheldrake, the machine-like cosmology of the last few centuries, seen in both science and religion, has left little room for spirits, angels, or even souls. A huge void occurred when our religions withdrew from the realm of the spiritual.

Angels in particular were banished and marginalized. It became embarrassing for theologians even to mention angels. Fox and Sheldrake explained that in the Baroque era of the seventeenth and eighteenth centuries, churches portrayed angels as fat, cute little babies instead of the elegant, powerful beings they are. Fox and Sheldrake point to the fact that whenever an angel appeared in the Bible, the first words that were usually spoken were, "Be not afraid." People who can see angels say that many of them are as large as ten feet tall.

According to Bunick in *In God's Truth*, every person has at least one angel, if not many more. Angels provide us with comfort, guidance, hope, and courage. They inspire us to choose the highest versions of ourselves in every situation.

According to Virtue in *Healing with the Angels*, every angel has a particular purpose. There are angels who help with healing the sick, angels whose job it is to insure our safety while driving, angels who protect our homes, angels who help us heal past-life traumas, and even nature angels who protect the trees, plants, and animals.

Virtue says there is a hierarchy of angels. Archangels oversee other angels and also have specialized functions of their own.

Archangel Michael is a leader among archangels and angels. According to Virtue in *Archangels and Ascended Masters*, his chief job is to rid the earth of the toxins brought on by fear. He enlists humans called lightworkers to inspire others to release worry and anxiety from their lives. He also assists people in finding their life purpose. According to Rudolf Steiner in his book *A Reader's Journal: The Archangel Michael, His Mission and Ours,* we are currently in the age of Archangel Michael, which began in 1879 and will span 350 years. Steiner believes that we are now at the height of the Archangel Michael years.

Archangel Michael was canonized in 1950 as Saint Michael, the patron saint of police officers because he is a great protector. His job is to inspire courage and heroic deeds. I have a strong connection to Archangel Michael, which will be described in later chapters.

Archangel Raphael is a powerful healer of pain and physical challenges. He encourages people to become healers like him.

Archangel Gabriel, or Gabrielle, is known as the angel who came to Elizabeth and Mary to tell them about the impending births of their sons John and Jesus. Her secondary purpose is to help those who are involved in communication, writing, and the arts. According to Virtue, she was responsible for dictating the Koran to Mohammad.

Archangel Uriel's name means "God's light" because he is the wisest of the archangels. He gives prophetic information and warnings. Virtue wrote in *Archangels and Ascended Masters* that Uriel warned Noah of the impending flood and helped the prophet Ezra to interpret mystical predictions about the coming of Christ. Virtue wrote that Uriel also brought the Jewish mystical teachings of the Kabbalah to mankind.

My friend Helle gave me a stack of Doreen Virtue's *Messages from Your Angels Oracle Cards*. I found out that oracle cards are an ancient tool, which help people receive clear messages from God, spirit guides, deceased loved ones, and angels. According to Virtue, every card is drawn out of the deck for a specific reason. With the help of the angels and the law of attraction, a person automatically picks cards that mirror his or her thoughts and emotions. Virtue explained that because our thoughts and emotions influence the future, the cards can accurately guide us and predict the future.

I wasn't really sure if I would receive messages from the angels by using the cards but I decided to try it. I began by thoroughly shuffling the cards. I turned the picture side away from me and chose any card that stuck up out of the deck. I did this multiple times over several weeks. Out of 44 cards, I continually pulled the same seven cards whose messages are summarized below:

*Omega* let me know that I had chosen to follow my divine guidance and indicated that powerful universal forces were flowing behind my decisions. The card encouraged me to keep up the good work and victory would be mine.

*Archangel Michael*'s card told me that he was guiding and protecting me and helping me to ensure that my divine life purpose would come to fruition.

*Mystique* let me know that I was on the right path and that I should stay firm and not stray from my divine purpose. He instructed that I should resist the pressure to bend to please others because in the end people would be pleased with the outcome. The card also reminded me that I was following a divine plan, which others were not privy to. I should not explain or defend my actions and remember that Heaven was backing me up one hundred percent.

*Aurora*'s card told me that I was flying high, which might threaten others, but I should not descend because many would soon follow.

*Arielle*'s assured me that the psychic and spiritual experiences that I was having were not my imagination. The card indicated that I really had connected with the spirit world and that these experiences were occurring because of my increased willingness to communicate with angels and those in spirit. I had been asking for the angels to guide me with my life's purpose and I should continue to study, pray, and meditate.

*Sonya* brought messages of love from my deceased loved one. She reminded me there was still a great bond of love between our souls.

*Archangel Gabrielle*'s card said that my divine life purpose involves communication, writing, and creativity.

She instructed that I should not allow doubt to interfere with my life purpose. She was helping me to improve upon my natural talents so that I could help others.

Every day for months I used the cards. I often got other messages that pertained to my life, but the same basic cards kept appearing.

When I asked about my brother, father, or husband I picked very different cards than the ones I pulled for myself. I could see that the angels really were guiding and encouraging me.

Another way that angels communicate with us is through numbers. Doreen Virtue and Lynnette Brown channeled angels and the ascended masters to write their book *Angel Numbers*, which explains the meanings behind the numbers that are used to send messages of guidance and love to earth.

According to Virtue and Brown, numerology is an ancient science that can be traced back to Plato, Hermes, and Pythagoras. These wise philosophers taught that everything in the universe is mathematically exact. Doreen Virtue, a student of Pythagoras in a past life, said that every number possesses its own specific vibration.

The angels guide us by subtly sending messages to look at the clock at a certain time or cause us to look at a particular license plate. I bought *Angel Numbers* because I noticed that I always looked at the clock at 4:44, 1:11 or 11:11, and every waking hour of the day I am drawn to look at the clock at 44 after the hour. After I bought the book I continued to see these numbers and also began to see other numbers on signs and license plates. I decided to keep track of how many times I saw each number sequence. Finally I gave up because it happened so frequently.

The following is a list of numbers and their meanings, according to Virtue and Brown:

- $0$ = God is talking to you, and you are encouraged to meditate or pray.
- $1$ = We are all one, and we are all associated by our thoughts so be sure to focus on intentions and desires and not fears.
- $2$ = Have faith and courage. Your prayers are being answered even if we can't see the results yet.
- $3$ = A sign from the ascended masters such as Jesus, Moses, Yogananda, and Buddha. This lets us know that they are with us, helping us to manifest our desires.
- $4$ = Many angels are with you.
- $5$ = Big changes are occurring in your life. Hold on because a transformation is imminent.
- $6$ = Balance your thoughts of earthly materials and worries with spiritual thoughts and faith.
- $7$ = Congratulations; the angels applaud you for listening to your divine guidance.
- $8$ = Financial abundance is coming to you.
- $9$ = You are a lightworker, so get to work.

I told the angels one day that the numbers that came in groups of three were especially inspirational for me. A few minutes later a car drove by with 333 on the license plate. After that, I constantly saw sequences of three numbers.

One day, while driving to a doctor's appointment, I saw four license plates across all four lanes in front of me. The last three numbers of their plates read: 111, 333, 444, and 777. A few minutes later I saw plates that read 999 and 888.

When I arrived for my appointment, I was early so I decided that I would take my dog for a walk around the block. I started to walk one direction but suddenly changed my mind and walked the other way. I soon realized why. I saw license plates with 555, 222, and 000.

These numbers always seemed to pertain to something I was thinking about. For example, I tend to worry about things more than I need to. Almost every day, I see 1:11 or 11:11, which advices me to be careful of my negative thoughts. Every clock in my house is set to a different time, so I get many reminders from the angels that I have opened an energetic gateway and that I need to focus only on positive intentions and not fears or worries so that they won't become a reality.

The angels found very sneaky ways to get me to look at the clock. One day I was driving in my car when I heard the radio make a strange static sound. I looked at the radio to see if it had changed stations and realized the clock read 3:33. I had been writing about Jesus and knew that the number 3 had to do with the ascended masters. For several weeks, I saw 333 continuously. If I was looking up a verse in the Bible or looking for a quote in one of my other books, the page always fell open to 333 or 111.

One day I was sitting in my office writing. I was very tired and wanted to stop but I felt that I needed to continue to push myself so that I could finish the chapter I was working on. I thought I heard my cell phone ringing and got up to answer it. When I got to it I saw that it was not ringing. I looked at the front panel to see if maybe I had missed a call. The time read 4:44 p.m.

Another night I went to bed very early because I had to get up at 4:00 a.m. to go to work. Something woke me out of a dead sleep. I turned on the light and looked at the clock; it was 11:11 p.m.

A new trainee at work named Jennifer asked me about my *Angel Numbers* book. I told her about it and also about *Twin Souls*. She was very intrigued and told me she had always been very afraid of death, so she was interested to hear about my communication with my twin sister.

A few months later, Jennifer told me that she was having difficulty in her later phases of training and wasn't sure if she was going to make it. She told me that she kept seeing 11:11 everywhere. I explained to her what 11:11 meant, and I instructed her to think positively no matter what and to tell God and the angels that she intended to pass and to thank them for helping her succeed.

I saw her a while later and she had passed her training. "Hey, that 11:11 thing really works," she told me.

Several times while at work, something would draw my attention to these numbers. I often had people from other police or fire agencies calling to ask the date or time of a call or when their medics or police officers arrived on the scene. One day I looked up a call and burst out laughing when I saw the time, 11:11:11. The date was 11/11.

Even though I see these numbers several times a day, I am always surprised and delighted by them. I reward the angels by doing a little dance. I whirl around, blowing kisses at the ceiling, followed by deep bows, as if I had just played a piano recital at Carnegie Hall, and curtsies as if I've just danced the lead in Swan Lake. I frequently hear my sister laughing. "Why are you bowing and curtsying? You didn't do it; the angels did."

"Hey, it takes two to tango," I tell her.

If I was worrying about a work situation or a family problem, I would invariably look at the clock or see a license plate that read 222, which means to have faith because the situation would be resolved. In every case, the situation did resolve itself.

My friend Amy had a similar experience with 222. She was miserable at her job so she decided she was going to quit. She went to bed very worried about the situation. In the middle of the night something woke her up. She started thinking about Cathy and suddenly she heard a whirring noise. She realized that the clock was resetting itself. It stopped at 2:22 a.m. as if to tell her, "Don't worry, have faith, everything will work out."

Recently I started noticing other numbers on license plates. At first I ignored them because I didn't think they had any significance, but I heard someone say, "If you notice them, they mean something."

I decided to look up the meanings of 113, 513, and 913, which I had just seen on license plates. I was surprised when each number gave similar messages regarding the ascended masters. The numbers meant that the goddesses or female ascended masters were guiding me to positive thoughts and outcomes.

I had been thinking about how little most people know about the female ascended masters. I felt sure that there were female masters guiding me, but I wasn't sure who they were.

Virtue explained in *Archangels and Ascended Masters* that many of the deities who were worshipped in ancient times really do exist and many are ascended masters.

Virtue said that today we do not worship ascended masters, angels, or other divine beings. We merely appreciate them. Virtue calls the male ascended masters *gods* and the females *goddesses*, with a small g to show that they are part of God with a capital G. Virtue said that the many divinities listed in her book represent the many traits, personalities, and facets of God. So in asking these deities for help, we are not worshipping multiple gods but simply asking for guidance and expertise, which God has asked them to provide. After all, every ascended master has conquered life on earth. Who better to give us guidance?

In his book *The Spontaneous Fulfillment of Desire*, Deepak Chopra called these spiritual entities Archetypes. The ancient themes that represent our heroes and heroines exist at the level of the collective consciousness and have been with us forever. Chopra wrote that archetypes are enacted in modern movies and television shows any time we see a character that is larger than life. We are hardwired at the soul level to emulate archetypal characters. It is irrelevant whether we believe that these figures are real or mythical. What is important is that we recognize which archetypes are reflected in our own personalities. This will assist us in moving toward our soul's ultimate destiny.

I read in *Archangels and Ascended Masters* about some of the female ascended masters and felt that there were many who were offering me their assistance. For example, I learned that Brigit, also known as St. Brigid, is the female version of the Archangel Michael. She helps people with divine guidance, life purpose, and prophetic information. Like my sister and me, her purpose is to help blur the lines and boundaries that human beings have created in order to promote unity.

Kuan Yin is a popular Eastern master. She is the Chinese goddess of mercy and compassion and the Eastern counterpart to Mother Mary. She encourages people to allow all opportunities to flow to them without struggle and promotes spiritual enlightenment and clairvoyance. I feel a strong pull toward Eastern philosophies, as Cathy did. I believe that Kuan Yin's advice regarding the natural flow of events has been helping me to have patience in the long process of writing a book.

Cordelia is an instrument of contradiction. She represents the opposites of the earth and sky, hot and cold, sunrise and sunset, day and night, the physical body and the spirit. She advises people to release earthly concerns and learn to walk on middle ground between the earth and the stars. I felt she was helping with the writing of *Twin Souls* because of its main theme of uniting opposites.

Kali is a Hindu goddess from India. Her purpose is to guide people through the ending of one life cycle into the next. She encourages people to transform their lives by letting go of the old and allowing in the new. This resonated with me because I felt that I was moving away from my old fearful views to a new, enlightened spiritual path. And I realized that this was a parallel to what was happening in the world.

I also liked the way Virtue described her personality. Kali is feisty and wants people to stop dilly-dallying and move with single-minded passion toward their life's mission. Both my sister and I feel the same impatience in wanting to change the world.

I knew that the angels were calling my attention to these numbers so that I would realize the enormous amount of support and guidance I had been given.

I felt especially connected to Athena. I read that she is known as one of the great protectors of the world. She is dedicated to spreading wisdom, knowledge, and truth. When I got Eleanor's reading I knew why I was so attracted to the archetype of Athena because like Cathy and me, she is a spiritual warrior who wants to destroy ignorance and promote enlightened thinking.

## A Wave of Light

According to Virtue in *Healing with the Angels*, more and more people are having encounters with non-physical divinities and angelic beings. As we move further into the new millennium, there will be more angels and spirits guiding us than ever before.

It is truly an amazing time to be alive. Angels described to Virtue how souls are actually standing in line to come to a life on our planet. There are more souls who want to come to a life on earth than there are bodies to accommodate them.

Spiritual teacher Orin told Sanaya Roman in *Spiritual Growth* that it is a dramatic time for our planet. He said that a wave of energy is passing through our galaxy that is changing everything it touches. According to Orin, ancient prophets foretold of this wave. He said that the idea of major transformation was planted into our collective consciousness before we got here. The change affects the energy of the entire planet and causes all matter to move to higher vibrations. This increased energy is bringing us more spiritual experiences and is causing human beings to feel a deeper desire to find their life purposes.

Some have said that this time will be marked by great upheaval. But Orin said that the turmoil does not have to continue if we allow the attitudes of our lower nature to be replaced by those of a higher nature. According to Orin, many have come to assist us during this special time. Our angels and spirit guides are playing a crucial role in helping us become a part of this wave of light. If we pay attention, they will lead us away from spiritual ignorance and into the light of love and unity.

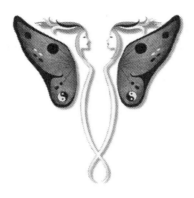

## Chapter Seventeen:
## What Is God?

### Redefining God

All our lives, Cathy and I have been known for saying things directly and without mincing words.

"Tell us how you really feel, Betsy," my friends and co-workers say.

"Don't sugarcoat it, Cathy," people would tell my sister.

So here it is the straight talk about God. Cathy and I believe that humanity's spiritual ignorance begins and ends with our definition of God and our concept of who we are in relation to God. If our goal is to move away from religious dogma and toward unity and universal truth, it is in our best interest to redefine God.

It is not the essence of God that will change but our understanding of God. What people believe about God is important because our theological ideas influence everything including our laws, customs, and social norms. Our current views have created escalating violence, intolerance, and hatred on a worldwide scale.

We have developed the view that God is separate from us, watching from above. These ideas are further confused by the fact that every religious group has a different name for God: Jehovah, Brahman, Yahweh, Allah, God, etc. Each group believes that its God is the real God, which not only promotes separation from God but from one another.

We cannot continue to believe in a God who is angry, vengeful, jealous, needy, and petty. We have created this God, who is more like a dictator than an all-powerful, all-loving Creator.

Neale Donald Walsch learned in *Tomorrow's God* that the deity that humanity has invented is an illusion and has nothing to do with reality. We believe in a completely contradictory God, and unfortunately we act on these beliefs. We love and hate in God's name, we create and destroy on behalf of God, and we accept some people while rejecting others in the name of God. As long as we hold this view of a two-faced God, we will continue to experience joy and terror side by side. It cannot be otherwise.

It is not appropriate in our society to question these beliefs because they are part of the world's religious scriptures and are therefore considered sacred and off-limits. Anyone who does challenge them is ridiculed or persecuted.

With these facts in mind I asked my sister, "How on earth do I write a chapter about such a sacred subject as God?"

"Ask God," Cathy said.

"Oh yeah, that's probably a good idea." I laughed. "Okay, God, here's the thing. I'm going out on a limb here and telling people that our ideas about God need to be redefined, so I could sure use Your help." I didn't hear the answer right away. I had been writing for many hours and was distracted and tired. I decided to put everything away and sleep on it.

The next morning I went downstairs to my office and asked again for God's guidance. I had index cards with quotes from several books spread out all over my desk and felt a little overwhelmed.

Suddenly I picked up my pen and wrote: "What God Is Not." After that, the ideas continued to flow, and all the sections of the chapter came immediately to my mind: *What God Is Not, What God Is, Experiencing God, Our Relationship with God, The Myth of Separation*, and finally, *Be the Light.*

"Cool," I thought. "When you ask God for help, you get it."

What you read about God in this chapter may cause you to feel relief, wonder, and joy. It might surprise you, disturb you, or even offend you. But Cathy and I believe it is time to say, "Will the real God please stand up!"

## What God Is Not

One of the first fallacies about God, according to Doreen Virtue in *Divine Guidance*, is that God is not a super-being residing somewhere in the universe. Many people view God like Santa Claus, an elderly man who is far away from us and doles out favors and punishment at His whim.

This is a traditional Western view of God called *dualism*, in which God is separate from man and merely a bigger version of a human being. But haven't we always said that humans are made in the image and likeness of God?

Second, God is not a male. I have used *He* throughout this book when referring to God to avoid awkward he-she-it phrases, but in reality God has no gender.

The view that God is male has caused people to believe that males are superior to females in almost every country in the world. Some of the worst atrocities have occurred against women because of this misguided belief.

According to Virtue, early versions of the Bible spoke about God as Mother and Father. Many theologians support the view that God is a male by pointing to the fact that Jesus used the term "Our Father," when talking about God. But in *The Messengers* Nick Bunick remembered that Jesus referred to God as "Father" because he knew his words would be better received at that time in history if he used masculine terminology.

In his book *The Isaiah Effect*, author Gregg Braden explained that because the Western Bible has undergone so many translations from various original biblical languages, it does not necessarily reflect the original intent of the authors. The first line of the Lord's Prayer, "Our Father who art in Heaven," does not represent an actual translation of the ancient text because there are no exact English words for the original Aramaic. A closer approximation of the meaning does not include a gender when speaking to God: "O thou! The Breathing Life of all," or "Radiant One: You shine within us."

Third, God is not temperamental or angry, as human beings often are. These emotions are based in the human ego, which has been defined in earlier chapters as the lower self, which is separate from God. The idea that God can become angry is very prevalent in many religions.

For example, one night during Mass, our priest was explaining one of the readings, which described the story of Moses and the Ten Commandments. He said that when Moses came back from receiving the Ten Commandments he found the Israelites partying and worshipping animals and other idols. The priest exclaimed, "Moses knew that God was simply furious!" My husband shot me a dirty look as I stifled a laugh. It just sounded so absurd to me. To believe that God experiences fury or any other lower human emotion is not to understand God.

Our religions have taught that God is a loving God. But they have also taught that God will love us only if humans do as God wants and in the exact matter in which God wants it or He will be angry. Yet the true definition of love is that which is unconditional.

## What God Is

God is the essence of life itself. God is love. God is creativity and freedom. God is all things and nothing, the Alpha and the Omega. God is male and female, yet God has no gender. God is an energy force that we are all part of.

Because God is everything, God can be anything. God can take on the form of someone with whom we can have a conversation. God will communicate with us through a song on the radio, a card in a bookstore, a field full of flowers, or a bird flying overhead or through animals. If we believe that God shows up in only one way we will be looking right at God all our lives and never seeing God.

According to Virtue in *Divine Guidance*, God is always talking with us and everyone can have a conversation with God. Not only can we talk with God, we can also laugh with God.

I found out that God really does have a great sense of humor. In March of 2005, I had just read a few of the *Conversations with God* books and was astounded by the profound spiritual information within them. I suddenly felt like my sister, running around telling everyone they needed to read *Conversations with God*.

One day I was at work and was listening to the radio between 911 calls. I used to be an avid listener of the conservative political talk show host Rush Limbaugh. It just so happened that the radio station was tuned to Rush that day. I heard him mention Brian Nichols, the convict who killed several people, escaped from an Atlanta courtroom, and then held Ashley Smith hostage for seven hours. Smith read to Nichols from *A Purpose-Driven* Life by Rick Warren and by doing so, she was able to persuade Nichols to let her go and turn himself in.

I heard Rush say, "I believe God was in that room that day." He told everyone not to email him to ask why God was not in the room with the other people who were killed. What he meant to convey was that God was within

Ashley Smith and this helped her survive. Then I heard him say, "If you want to know more about that, you can read *Conversations with God* by Neale Donald Walsch."

I almost fell out of my chair. I didn't view Rush Limbaugh as a spokesperson for spiritual topics, or the most likely advocate for a book like *Conversations with God*.

When I met Walsch in person, I made a point of telling him what Limbaugh had said on the air about his books. He was as shocked as I was until we both remembered that messages come from unlikely messengers.

The morning after I'd heard the radio broadcast, I was out jogging and said to God, "I liked the Rush Limbaugh touch. Very clever."

To my surprise, I heard God respond, "Thank you, thank you very much," a la Elvis. "Did you like that?"

"Yes, I did. You are brilliant."

"I am, aren't I? But if I am brilliant, then you are brilliant, too."

"Oh, you're right, I am brilliant."

I understood His reference to the *Conversations with God* theme that we are one with God and that God is within each of us. I laughed all the way through my jog.

### Experiencing God

God is experienced in every moment of our lives through anything that brings us peace and joy. Yogananda said in *The Second Coming of Christ* that God can be found in a temple or outdoors in nature, but to truly experience God one must turn his or her attention inward.

We experience God through our sixth sense. Unfortunately, most people only know God through the five senses. People have incorrectly been told that God is outside of themselves and therefore everything to be learned about God should come from what other people tell them. This has prevented people from truly experiencing God.

Famous nineteenth-century clairvoyant and healer Edgar Cayce said that it was man's attempt to connect with the spirit world that initially led man to religion.

According to Harmon H. Bro, in his book *Edgar Cayce on Religion and Psychic Experience*, Cayce said that while the myths, dogmas, and symbols of religion have been clumsy at best, man came up with these rituals to help find a connection with his inner Source. Cayce, who was a devout Christian, explained that the processions, sacraments, and commandments were all developed to help people align their inner energy with God. Cayce said that every soul has been given a sixth sense and, by developing this sense, humans can experience a feeling of unity with God. Our intuition is our direct link to God and we receive divine guidance through our sixth sense. Prayer is simply mind-to-mind communication with God.

Yogananda wrote in *The Second Coming of Christ*, "Intuition is the father of all reason." He said that reason is limited by the five senses, but those who have developed spiritual intuition can access unlimited power through direct contact with God.

## Our Relationship with God

Virtue wrote in *Divine Guidance* that God would prefer that people talk with Him more. Most people only talk to God while they are rushed and they often condense their communication into one hour per week. But God told Virtue that instead of talking with Him once per week or only during times of trouble, it is better and more rewarding to talk with God on a continual basis.

Somehow we have developed the notion that God has an agenda. I was reminded of this one night at a hospice training class. I was talking to a woman sitting next to me about my patient, Lois. I told the woman that Lois was not supposed to have lived more than six months, and that diagnosis had been given in 2003. Three years later, in 2006, she was still alive and feisty at the age of 91.

"I guess she hasn't made the decision that it is her time to go yet. She must have something more to do," I said. A smiling little man in front of me turned around.

"It is up to the Big Guy upstairs when she dies," he said.

"Well, I believe that on a soul level we actually make that decision with God's help," I countered.

"It's up to the Big Guy," he insisted, pointing to the ceiling.

Remembering Cathy's statement that it is not my job to try to persuade people, I smiled at the man and continued the conversation with the woman next to me.

I hear many people use the term *God's will*. But if God wants or needs nothing, then what kind of elaborate plan would God have for us? Our higher selves are one with God so God's will is the same as our will. Our soul's plan is God's plan. If we want to answer the question, "what is God's will?" I believe we merely have to look within ourselves in quiet contemplation and the answers will come.

Humanity's group purpose is to evolve to a higher level of spiritual maturity, realize our own divinity, and create our own reality. Anything we desire to be, do, or have can be ours. This is what Jesus meant when he said, "Ask and you shall receive."

I was telling a friend about *The Last Hours of Ancient Sunlight* by Thom Hartmann and how Cathy was leaving it everywhere, hoping people would read it. I told him that one of Cathy's messages to the world was that the planet is in trouble because of the man-made Armageddon we have created. My friend, a lifelong Catholic, immediately said, "Oh, I'm not worried. God will step in. He won't let that happen."

Free will allows human beings to make choices, decisions, and mistakes without God's interference. God will never impose on us with help or guidance unless we ask. When we do ask, it is given freely and immediately. If we follow our inner guidance, we will find solutions, but I do not believe that God will "step in." If God intervened in our creative process that would violate our free will.

We are much more powerful beings than we have given ourselves credit for. Once we realize our true divinity and our co-creative abilities, we will remember who we really are, and we will experience a rewarding relationship with God.

## The Myth of Separation

Cathy and I have said that spiritual ignorance is the root cause of what ails the world. One of the main components of this spiritual sickness is the myth of separation. Many of the terrible things we see happening in the world today stem from the idea of a separation between humanity and God, and among one another. We can only allow these things to happen because we do not see God in ourselves and other people.

One of the important concepts that Jesus relayed to the authors of *The Course In Miracles* is that all minds are really only one mind, the Universal Mind. In *Conversations with God*, Walsch learned that there really is only one soul. Most people view the soul as being within the body, but in actuality the soul contains the body and holds it together. And likewise, God's soul contains the universe and holds it together. Walsch was stunned to learn that there really is no place where one soul ends and another begins and that there is no place where human beings end and God begins. We quite literally are all one. The one soul or one essence that makes up everything is God. God is all-that-is.

This is a very difficult concept to grasp. I have always seen myself as completely separate from others, especially because I have worked in law enforcement. People who call the police are generally operating out of their lower selves. After ten hours of dealing with people on this level,

273

it is very difficult not to judge them. It is no wonder that I often left work feeling angry and frustrated.

I have always thought that judgment was a necessary part of life. But in a higher spiritual sense, it is not appropriate to judge another because when we judge another person, we are actually judging ourselves.

This concept really was driven home to me one night when my husband and I witnessed two fourteen-year-old kids rob another young man of his bicycle. My husband and I were on the way to church when the crime occurred right in front of us. My husband immediately jumped into action. He leaped out the car, chased down the two suspects while I called for backup. My husband exhibits a ferocious demeanor when dealing with criminals because of his experiences with gangsters. He has always said that gang members only understand the language of intimidation and violence.

The two boys were unrepentant, but my husband put such fear into them that they finally cooperated. The boys had taken the bike away from the other boy by telling him that they were in a gang and he had better give up his bike or they were going to shoot him.

Even though the suspects had committed a felony crime and an egregious act, it was not a gratifying sight for me to see two young kids, dressed completely in red, the colors worn by Blood gang members, being handcuffed and put into the back of a police car, especially since it was obvious they had been through the routine before.

As we drove away, my husband said, "Well, we won't make it to church, but I guess I did my good deed for the day." Three years earlier, I would have agreed with him. I had a deep hatred for criminals. I thought they were worthless human beings and could be lined up and shot for all I cared. But I realized that night that I felt compassion for the two young men who had committed the crime. Even though I knew that a criminal act had been stopped, I still couldn't reconcile what I had just

274

witnessed with goodness. My husband didn't understand my dilemma, saying, "They're just two dirtbags."

When we met our friends from church for dinner, their responses to story of the robbery were similar to my husband's. They said it was great that the scumbags would be put in jail. "They'll get what they deserve," they said. Again I felt a pull of sadness inside of me.

I asked my sister what had changed in me that I saw things so differently. I heard her say, "You are seeing through spiritual eyes."

I told my husband that he had done a good thing by stopping a crime in progress and preventing someone from being victimized. My objection was his lack of compassion and his judgment of the suspects.

I think he understood on a deeper level because while we were at the restaurant, he bought dinner for a homeless man who was huddled at a table drinking coffee, trying to stay warm.

"Earlier you were doing your job. What you just did was your good deed for the week," I told him.

A few days later, a friend of mine who had first directed me to Yogananda's work left me a message saying that he had a book for me to read. Curious, I went and picked it up. The book was called *The Gospel: Explained by the Spiritist Doctrine* by Alan Kardec. I found out that Alan Kardec was the pen name of a nineteenth-century French educator and philosopher. Kardec had compiled a large number of notebooks and journals containing transcripts written by highly evolved spirits through a variety of mediums. The book was part of a set of four books called the *Spiritist Doctrine*. It examined the writings of the New Testament from the viewpoint of those who had crossed over into the higher spiritual realm.

I randomly opened the book to a section entitled *Love Toward Criminals*. Kardec's spirits had a lot to say on the subject. They explained that when Jesus reminded his followers to "love thy neighbor as thyself," or when he said to "turn the other cheek," he was not advocating lawlessness or weakness. What he was saying was that it is not appropriate to judge another, and, even more important, one should not seek revenge against another.

The spirits explained that people are under the false notion that there is some kind of honor in getting revenge against one's enemies. They believe mistakenly that this is justice. But in reality, it is simply a sign that most people cannot rise above their earthy passions. What most of us fail to understand that it takes more courage to rise above an insult than to avenge it.

The spirits said that one should always feel compassion for others because compassion is the biggest element in spiritual growth and it puts us in the company of angels. They said that now is the time for true brotherhood to reign on earth and warned that we should not discriminate against the less fortunate because we do not see their path and we are all equal in the eyes of God. The spirits said that the presence of criminals among us is meant to be a learning experience for us all.

Our only desire should be to help people who have chosen a life of crime and that a criminal is as much our neighbor as the more upstanding members of society. His soul may have strayed but was created for the same reason as ours—to evolve and experience his own divinity. We must not hate him because wrongdoing is never a permanent character trait.

I finally understood the statement Cathy had made about the job she was doing at the Border Patrol and law enforcement in general. In an e-mail dated Wednesday, September 18, 2002, Cathy wrote to Tom, "What law enforcement does is try to solve a negative problem with a negative solution, which doesn't work in the long run." I thought back to one of my math classes and remembered that a negative plus a negative always equals a negative. In the bigger scheme of things, applying a negative solution to a negative problem simply brings more of the same.

276

I heard my sister say, "It's a circular problem." I understood that the more a person feels separate, alone, and judged, the more that person feels justified in committing criminal acts. The more criminal acts a person commits, the more separation others feel toward him or her. The cycle must be broken, and it begins with each person understanding who he or she really is.

Many people have told me that they don't see how the world can be changed. They say that things have just gone too far. "How can we change other people's actions?" they ask. It is difficult to apply these spiritual principles when we see increasing crime and violence.

But I believe it is actually quite simple. We must start by feeling compassion for the other person, regardless of who that person is. Once that is accomplished, we should seek to see God in ourselves and others.

## Be the Light

Walsch learned that almost every culture has its own creation myth that features an angry God who has separated Himself from humans because of something God wanted that He did not get.

This is an illusion that must be dispelled if we want to move forward. In *A Course in Miracles* it says that we have paid dearly for our illusions and that nothing we have paid for has brought us the peace that we seek.

We must *be* that which we want to see in the world. If we want peace, we must be peaceful; if we want love, we must be loving. If we want compassion, we must be compassionate. We are not merely reflections of God's the light. We *are* the light.

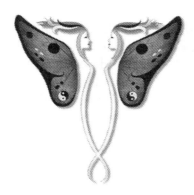

## Chapter Eighteen:
## What Is Life?

What is life? Why are we here? What is our purpose? These are the questions that plagued me after Cathy died. I was surprised when many answers came to me.

I learned that we are all part of the eternal cycle of life and death. Or, more accurately stated, we are all part of a giant circle of life in spiritual form and life in physical form. Life is a process; each soul is at a different stage in the process, and each segment of the process is equally important for the growth of the soul.

### Journey of Souls

One of Cathy's favorite books was *Journey of Souls* by Michael Newton, Ph.D. She had written her name and the date—October 2002—on the front cover of *Journey of Souls* and the follow-up book, *Destiny of Souls*. I knew that she had purchased the books sometime earlier in the year because I found a letter she had written to Michael Newton in September of 2002, saying that she had read both books and she described how intrigued she was by them. But something had possessed her to write the month and year that she died in both books.

When I found *Journey of Souls* and *Destiny of Souls* among her things I didn't think much about them until I saw the dates written inside. It took me a while to comprehend the magnitude of the information contained in Newton's books. Newton was a traditional hypnotherapist who was extremely skeptical of using hypnosis for metaphysical purposes.

He considered himself very conservative and old-school, and was not comfortable with what he considered "New Age" philosophies. But like Dr. Brian Weiss, he inadvertently opened the gateway to the past lives of his hypnosis subjects. He was stunned by the revelation of past lifetimes and their therapeutic effect on his patients.

He was even less prepared for what happened next. A patient came to him because she felt profound sadness and couldn't pinpoint its cause. While under hypnosis she viewed herself in the spirit world between lives and began to sob uncontrollably, saying she was so lonely on earth and that she missed her friends in her group. When Newton inquired which group of friends she was referring to, she said, "Here in my permanent home."

Newton found that it was even more meaningful for his clients to view their lives in the spirit world than experiencing their past lives. By seeing themselves in spirit, they remembered their true identity by connecting with their higher selves.

Cathy wrote to Tom about *Journey of Souls* and *Destiny of Souls*, "I know this might sound crazy to you but when I read this information I had a very strong feeling that it is true...I can't wait to know the truth. I think the truth is much better than most people have imagined."

Newton learned that most of his clients were initially apprehensive about discussing the spiritual world while under hypnosis. But with the help of his subjects' spirit guides, Newton found specific triggers that put his clients at ease and enabled them to recount details about the spiritual dimension.

Newton perfected the technique, which allowed him to follow his clients into their lives in the spirit world, and began collecting detailed information about life on the other side. Remarkably, he was able to go far beyond the point where most near-death experiences end.

Newton was profoundly amazed by the synchronicity of the information he had collected. The race, age, gender, cultural background, or religion of the subject didn't appear to matter; each gave a remarkable similar account of the journey back to his or her real home and the long preparation for the next life on earth.

*Journey of Souls* and *Destiny of Souls* represent a ten-year collection of individual case studies that give explicit details on life after death and, more important for this chapter, information on how we prepare to transition from our life in spirit to physical form.

## The Soul

I often wondered what the difference was between the spirit and the soul. According to Nick Bunick in *In God's Truth*, the spirit is the part of us that is one with God and is immortal and unchanging. The soul is also one with God and is immortal, but it is also our personality, intellect, and character. The soul changes, grows, and evolves with every human experience and lifetime. A soul chooses to leave the spirit world and take on the challenge of a human body because it yearns to experience itself in the physical sense.

According to Gary Zukav in *The Seat of the Soul*, God takes on physical form through each individual soul. As the soul increases its understanding of itself, it becomes larger and more godlike. This is the mastery that each soul seeks.

The first thing that Newton's hypnosis subjects learned was that the soul was their true identity. Under deep hypnosis, subjects described the soul as a powerful, non-physical force, a pinpoint of white radiating energy.

Newton's subjects realized that their bodies and their personalities were temporary and artificial aspects of their souls. They also learned that the soul does not have any gender. They saw that they had experienced lifetimes as both males and females. However, they said that most souls tend to gravitate toward one particular gender, both in physical form and in spirit.

Zukav said that once people see themselves as multisensory beings instead of five-sensory beings, they feel more radiant and alive because they are more fully connected to their higher selves. In *Destiny of Souls*, Newton's subjects were in awe when they saw the power and magnificence of their souls and they knew that the soul was their true identity.

## Karma

"Your karma is moving toward you in this lifetime," said Portia, the psychic I visited after the baseball game with my husband. I didn't fully understand what karma was at that time. I used to think that karma was just some silly idea conjured up by Eastern mystics to encourage people to be good. But according to Zukav in *The Seat of the Soul*, karma operates outside our physical reality and is the universal law of motion: for every action, there is an equal and opposite reaction. The basis for karma is the golden rule. We receive what we give. We reap what we sow.

Contrary to what many people believe, karma has nothing to do with morality, judgment, or punishment. These are ideas created by human beings. Karma is merely a balancing of energy that serves as a universal system of justice. Zukav says that karma allows us to see what needs to be corrected without the negative emotion of judgment.

Many people ask the question, "How can there be justice without judgment?" But souls create their own justice and rid themselves of intense negativity through the laws of karma.

I believe that one of the most important things we should understand is that when we judge others and even ourselves, we always create negative karma that we will have to be balanced later in our current life or in a future lifetime.

Zukav goes as far as suggesting that we should even avoid judging what seems tragic to us, like the loss of a child or a person who is injured and bound to a wheelchair because we do not know what is being healed within the souls of the people taking on these challenges. When we see these things, we should respond with compassion, not judgment.

According to Zukav, it is vitally important to understand that every action has far-reaching implications. If we participate in a particular action, whether it is positive or negative, it is impossible for us not to experience the effect of this action.

Newton's hypnosis subjects said that karma played a pivotal role in their choices to come to a new life on earth. The purpose of every lifetime is to have experiences that will balance positive and negative energy created by the soul in past lives.

## The Process of Life

The process of life on earth begins long before physical birth. People under hypnosis said that before a soul comes to a new life, there are elaborate planning and role-playing sessions with spirit guides, soul groups, and other groups who will be involved the upcoming life. Souls realize that what they are about to experience on earth is really just a giant play with each actor playing his or her part.

Before we come into our new lives, we make agreements with our guides that we will not remember our past lives or lives in spirit. The amnesia helps the soul and human body to merge, and it is better for the growth of the soul to start with a blank slate.

According to Newton, the restrictions on amnesia are being loosened a little because we have gotten to a point where we have completely forgotten who we are. Cathy believed this also. She wrote to Tom on October 15, 2002, "I believe that most information is deliberately blocked from us. However, the beings upstairs are starting to allow more to come through recently because the world is in trouble and they are trying to help us." I also believe that we are learning more about past lives and the spirit world because we are moving into higher consciousness.

According to Newton's subjects, the decision to make a journey back to earth is not an easy one. Souls must leave a world of freedom, love, wisdom, and order to enter one of chaos, fear, anger, and uncertainty. However, most souls expressed nostalgia and excitement about returning to the physical world. They welcomed the opportunity to take on the challenge of life on earth again.

Hypnosis subjects said that every soul must answer the following questions before embarking on his or her journey back to earth: 1. Am I ready for physical life? 2. What experiences do I want to have in order to advance my development and evolution? 3. Where should I go and who should I be to best facilitate these goals?

The first phase of planning for a new life is to choose a time and place. Then souls choose who they will be and, finally, they make agreements with the souls who will be their parents and the other people who will influence them.

I often hear people say, "You don't choose your family." But Newton's subjects say that we actually do pick our family members, and the relationships we choose always enhance our identities as souls in some way.

Newton learned that no condition, including illness or bodily injury, happens by accident. Newton's subjects said that dealing with a handicap greatly accelerates a soul's growth, and it is always the choice of the soul to take on these challenges.

284

Hypnosis subjects in *Journey of Souls* described situations in which groups of souls planned a tragic family event such as the loss of a child. These events always involved a large number of karmic issues and were usually related to the karma of the parents. This does not imply that the parents did something wrong but that they wanted to have this experience for a certain reason. Newton's subjects also said that many times the soul of the child lost decides to come back to the parents in another child, either by birth or by adoption.

According to Zukav in *The Seat of the Soul*, our close friends often agree to play difficult, adversarial roles, which push us toward our goals. Zukav said that some of the most difficult times we experience in life offer us "doorways to awareness."

### Birth

Newton's subjects said that the initial stages of conception felt like going down a long dark tube into their mother's womb. Many said that they believed this tunnel was the same one seen at the time of death. I remembered Kim explaining that my daughter was waiting to go down a long chute but had to wait to see if conditions were optimal for her to come.

A soul's job is to integrate with the mind and body of the baby. Newton's subjects described the nine-month period as boring and a little confining, but they were able to travel out of the womb to visit other souls who were also waiting to be born. Interestingly, Newton's hypnosis subjects said that the shock of physical birth was much greater than that of death.

### Advancement of Souls

Although a soul has no beginning or end, we often hear the term *old soul*. In *Conversations with God*, Walsch learned that all souls as individual segments of energy were created at the same time. But certain souls have been reincarnating for a longer period of time, and some souls progress faster than others.

Newton was shocked when he hypnotically regressed one advanced soul who had been reincarnating for 130,000 years. Her level of understanding was clearly much greater than souls who had only been reincarnating for a few thousand years.

According to Zukav in *The Seat of the Soul*, the path of spiritual growth is a vertical path. A person who wants to advance spiritually develops a connection with his or her higher self and non-physical entities. Zukav wrote that the vertical path is one of great wisdom and clarity. In contrast, a horizontal path is one in which a person sees things only from an earthly perspective and does not spend much time thinking about things larger than the self.

Newton believes that three quarters of all souls currently inhabiting the earth are in relatively early stages of their development. Yet, I believe that there has recently been an influx of higher-level souls to help the world with the transition to higher consciousness.

Newton's subjects said that the most advanced souls do not continue to reincarnate on earth except for a few, called "sages," who are dedicated to the earth. Newton learned that most people would not recognize these advanced beings because they usually choose quiet unassuming lives. Newton's subjects said that these sages were great prophets from earlier times who have come back to assist the earth and its inhabitants.

According to Newton in *Journey of Souls*, the mark of an advanced soul is someone who has great patience, and composure, and who exhibits extraordinary coping skills. Newton discovered that higher-level souls are often involved in the helping professions or they spend time combating social injustices in some fashion. As souls advance, they usually become teachers and mentors to other, younger souls, both on earth and in spirit.

286

Advanced souls like Mother Teresa come to earth to lead by example. They show humanity the higher spiritual qualities of selflessness, love, compassion, and an amazing dedication to helping others.

I asked how one might become this type of advanced soul. I heard someone answer, "Masters do not attempt to persuade others to follow them; they inspire others to follow by their example."

## Why Do We Choose Life?

One day I was having a conversation with one of my friends about spiritual matters. She said that she didn't believe in reincarnation because she couldn't understand why anyone would deliberately volunteer to leave a world of great peace and joy to take on such difficulties more than one time.

Newton's subjects explained that while in the spirit world, our souls are unencumbered by the human mind and body and have a much larger perspective. Souls want the chance to address karmic issues from their past lives.

A soul understands that the purpose of incarnation is not to experience only love and joy, as it does in the spirit world. The soul could never appreciate positive feelings without experiencing hardships or difficulties.

Newton's subjects said that one of the most important qualities for a soul to possess when coming to a life on earth is the ability to adapt and change. Souls are most successful in their life journey when they can accept change and welcome challenges as a part of their lives. Walsch learned that every tough choice is an announcement from our soul that we are about to experience an enormous breakthrough. Challenges offer us rare opportunities to accelerate our spiritual growth.

## Life Purpose

Having a purpose in life is what keeps us connected to our higher selves. Every person makes a sacred contract to perform certain tasks while on earth, and we feel great joy when we accomplish our purpose.

The tasks can be anything from raising a family to changing the consciousness of the world. Zukav said that although we all take on specific tasks, there are many paths we can take to accomplish our missions. Every decision leads to many more options, so our free will is always in play.

I recommended Kim to Cathy's friend Jackie after Jackie lost her own sister to cancer. As the reading began, Kim told Jackie that her spirit guide had come to her before the reading, saying that Jackie was not just coming to learn about her sister. Jackie's guide wanted to remind Jackie of her life purpose.

Kim told Jackie that her sister was fine but not ready to come forward yet. She had lived a difficult life and was still in the process of reviewing things. All Jackie's sister had to say about her death was that it was "anti-climactic."

Jackie's spirit guide said that Jackie was very different from her immediate family and that she should not feel discouraged about the fact that she had nothing in common with them. She had only selected them so that she could get to earth in physical form.

Kim said that Jackie's primary life purpose was to lay a clear foundation for her children to accomplish their own life purposes. Her secondary purpose was to learn how to "be." Kim explained that anyone can stay focused in the present moment under calm circumstances, but it was Jackie's choice to have a busy and active mind and at the same time learn to stay calm and focused in the present. Kim said that Jackie's life would always be challenging and busy, so she would find it difficult to quiet her mind.

This resonated with Jackie because she was always racing around, constantly planning, and thinking ahead. Kim said that she had chosen to learn "being while she was doing."

Souls take great pleasure in helping one another, and I believe that many choose life purposes that will help set up another person's life purpose. I think that my mother chose to die a rather difficult death by cancer so that I would be drawn to volunteer for hospice, which would help me understand more about death, thus setting up my own life mission.

## Cathy's Life Purpose

Cathy thought she had finally found her mission when she discovered her love of working with underprivileged and at-risk youth. However, I believe the purpose for everything she did, including counseling young people, was to set the stage for the story that would unfold after her death.

It is interesting to look back now and see that all of her struggles and experiences had meaning. Everything was leading her to the time when she would fulfill her life mission by leaving the world to be part of something even bigger than she had imagined.

Shortly before Cathy died, she wrote a letter to Michael Newton asking to be hypnotized. She described the anxiety attacks she was having and how she woke up feeling as if she were suffocating. She explained that she believed her night terrors were caused by some experience from a past life. She wanted to be hypnotized into the superconscious state so that she could better understand her struggles and her life purpose.

Cathy seemed to have great clarity that monumental changes were under way, not only in her own life but also for the planet as a whole. This understanding is evident in the following excerpt from her letter, dated September 29, 2002:

"I have always had the feeling that I am on earth to do something very important. I am just not sure what. I have an identical twin sister and we almost died at birth...but we both lived, and my mother always told me that we lived for a reason. I think she was right.

"I believe that this is a very important and pivotal time in history. I believe that the decisions we make now will decide the future and the survival of the human race. I have been planning to go back to school to study something, but I have vacillated back and forth on what would be the best thing for me to focus on. So the world and I are at a critical turning point..."

Less than a month later, she died. I believe she did have an important purpose on earth. Her struggles, experiences, and even her death were intertwined with my own life purpose.

## My Life Purpose

Zukav wrote that when a soul incarnates, it usually has only a dim awareness of its purpose. The ideas lie dormant until an experience triggers the memory of the contract we made before taking on physical form.

I was shown many road signs throughout my life regarding my life purpose, but it wasn't until my sister died and I wrote a long letter to my brother explaining my experiences that I truly remembered what I'd come to do. I believe that every person has both an inner and outer purpose. Some describe it as a primary and secondary purpose.

## Outer Purpose

My primary and outer life purpose is to write *Twin Souls* and many other books with the help of my sister and others in spirit. I also learned that my communication with the world would take many different forms including one-on-one counseling, radio, and television. As *Twin Souls* began to take shape, I understood intuitively that it had all the makings of a poignant and compelling story.

I knew that the human-interest factor of twin sisters, struggling with opposing political and spiritual ideologies,

290

and finally finding unity in death, would propel our story into the mainstream spotlight.

To some, the information in this book is common knowledge. But Cathy conveyed to me that the purpose of *Twin Souls* is to reach many people who have not heard of or contemplated these spiritual ideas.

I reasoned that some people would not be open to reading a book called *Conversations with God* or *Many Lives, Many Masters*, but they might read a book called *Twin Souls*. The general public has a fascination with twins and their inner connection to each other. I knew that I could reach people who have doubts and fears about life after death because it would be easier for them to believe that the spiritual bond between twins continues after death.

Thus, the *Twin Souls* message would be widely read and would help expand the positive spiritual changes taking place around the world. As my friend Sonia predicted, "This will break things wide open!"

### Secondary Purpose

I learned from a variety of sources that my inner or secondary life purpose is to accept situations and people as they are.

At first these two purposes seemed contradictory. How could I write a book like *Twin Souls*, which advocates big changes in the world, while at the same time accept things and people the way they are? Had I set up a dichotomy for myself?

Walsch learned in *Conversations with God* that a divine dichotomy occurs when two seemingly contradictory truths exist simultaneously in the same space at the same time.

For example, the idea that we are all individual expressions of God, yet we are really all one soul, is a divine dichotomy. Walsh learned that divine dichotomies are part of life and that one cannot live gracefully without accepting this truth.

Cathy wrote to Tom about this idea on October 15, 2002, ten days before she died: "I read that two seemingly opposite situations can exist at the same time. Everything depends on how you look at it. I don't think there is anything illogical going on in the universe. But based on our limited view, it can seem that way, but everything is really very logical from a higher perspective."

I learned that large changes are not made through large actions. Great changes happen through transforming the self, not in attempting to change others.

It is human nature to believe that our way is the right way, but in a larger spiritual sense, there is no right way or wrong way. Differences between people are a very necessary part of life. I learned that uniting opposites does not mean that we must change the other's point of view. It means allowing opposing views to exist simultaneously, and often it means seeking to see the best in both ideas.

Walsch wrote in *Conversations with God* that the biggest mistake people make is focusing on what others are doing instead of focusing on their own actions. One day I heard someone say, "You are holding yourself back by worrying about everyone else."

It was true. I constantly worried about friends or family members. One day I pondered my reasons for taking on everyone else's problems. I got an intuitive picture of myself taking care of my mother while she was sick. Then I saw myself after my sister died, running around preparing for her funeral, sending letters to her creditors, and working on getting her life insurance company information so that my father could receive his benefit.

During my angel reading with Helle, she helped me to see that I was carrying a lot of anger because not only had I experienced significant losses like everyone else, but I was also the one who picked up the pieces and moved everyone forward. I somehow felt responsible for everyone's happiness.

The role that I had taken on was in itself a dichotomy because I needed to take on a leadership role for karmic reasons, but also I allowed my frustration with the role to hold me back.

My biggest challenge is to understand that I can't save other people from suffering. I must accept that they have chosen to experience certain struggles that cannot be circumvented.

"You're not the happiness police," my sister told me one day while I was out walking.

"I know, but how can I be happy when other people are suffering?" I had a sudden memory of how I had agonized constantly about my sister. I worried nonstop about her lack of happiness. She showed me that my worrying had brought me nothing but unnecessary heartbreak.

I realized that Cathy now had everything she wanted, and according to Kim, the part she played in life was exactly the role she came to play.

## Trip to Sedona

My husband and I decided to drive to Sedona, Arizona, for our fifth wedding anniversary in December of 2005. I wanted to see Sedona because I had heard it was a world-renowned spiritual center. My husband would have preferred to have gone somewhere else but agreed to go because I felt strongly that there was a reason I had to go there.

Every time my husband and I got ready to do something that was outside our ordinary routine, his meticulous personality went into overdrive. Everything got on his nerves. Our trip to Sedona was no exception. He wanted to control the situation and make it as orderly as possible. And, as usual, I was driving him crazy by running around at the last minute throwing things in my suitcase.

The first hour in the car was spent arguing about everything from my disorganization to the control of the air conditioner and radio.

Most of our disagreements stemmed from my inability to be as efficient as my husband wanted me to be. In the larger sense, our arguments reflected our differing views of the world.

When we arrived in Sedona, our bickering had subsided and we were eager to check into our hotel. I asked the woman at the front desk about Sedona's famous energy vortexes, which are said to emanate heightened earth energy, causing feelings of rejuvenation. I asked if she had actually felt a shift in energy while visiting the sites. She said that she had experienced heightened energy and she suggested that we go there with positive emotions because whatever emotion we were experiencing at the time would be magnified.

The next day we drove around the town admiring Sedona's stunningly beautiful red rocks. I must have still been harboring some anger toward my husband because when we visited the energy vortexes, my breathing tightened and I felt somewhat agitated, not refreshed or uplifted.

Sedona has a large community of spiritual healers, mediums, psychics, and angel therapists. I decided that I would see a medium who specialized in healing and energy work to see if I could get to the root of my breathing problem.

I looked through the brochures and selected a woman named Lynn, who advertised herself as a healer, spiritual teacher, a channel for angels, spirit guides, and ascended masters. She was an ordinary, kind-looking woman in her thirties.

She brought me to a small room with a table and a few chairs. She asked me what I wanted to focus on. I told her that I was having a problem with my breathing. She suggested that she do some energy work with me. She stood behind me and seemed to be feeling my aura and channeling messages about me.

"Tell me what is going on," she said.

"I just can't feel complete happiness," I told her, breaking down into tears.

"What is stopping you?" Lynn asked.

"I feel as though I can't be who I came to be." I told Lynn about the differences between my husband and me and how frustrated I was in trying to deal with them.

I explained to Lynn, "My husband always tells me that I am not efficient and organized like him. But I feel that his desire for control stems from fear. He doesn't see the bigger picture, and I think his spiritual views are inefficient."

The energy in the room intensified as Lynn said, "Your spirit guides are asking, 'Are you going to choose fear or are you going to choose love?'

"You have chosen a difficult journey in this lifetime. Not only are you on the path of ascension, but you have also chosen to teach other people about the spiritual path.

"But you must learn to accept that there are those who see things differently, and they are not wrong. Every person has chosen a specific life experience, and it is not up to you to try to change it."

"Whew! That was a tall order," I thought. I told Lynn that I felt bad because my husband was Catholic and that I had begun our marriage as a Catholic but had taken a turn away from the church after my sister died. Lynn just shook her head. "That was part of the plan."

I expressed my frustration over religion and how I saw very little truth in religious teachings. I described how I felt the same negative energy during the Catholic Mass that I did while answering 911 calls for the police department. She asked why I went to Mass if I was uncomfortable with it. I told her that I wanted to support my husband. I could see that it brought him a great deal of peace.

"One person's discomfort is another person's peace," Lynn said. She explained that it was her own experience in the Catholic Church that led her to become a spiritual healer.

"The Mass is energy, and it is not necessarily positive energy. The discomfort that you feel is the long history of fear and oppression that the Mass represents. Your guides and angels are saying that if you are going to go to Mass, you should visualize yourself surrounded in brilliant white light to counteract this negative energy and that you should allow yourself to view it as a time for research. You are seeing firsthand the manifestations of fear and separation."

I told Lynn that I believed I had a much clearer view of spiritual issues than my husband and that I wanted him to see the truth. I was under the assumption that he would read my book and would immediately change his point of view. But Lynn said that was a false assumption.

"He will certainly expand his views, but I do not see a significant change as far as his religious beliefs. Your husband is not in touch with his true self in this lifetime."

"I knew it!" I said. "I knew he was not seeing the whole picture."

"Well, don't jump to conclusions. This was intentional on his part. You are meant to be opposites. You are on the inner path, and he is on the outer path. This was by no means an accident.

"Your guides are saying that you are going to have to face your biggest fear, the fear that you will have to leave your husband so that both of you can make progress with your own life missions.

"I see you wondering how you will make these opposing ideologies fit together. The answer is, you won't. Stop asking 'why' or 'how' and accept things as they are or move on. No matter whether you stay or go, if you choose love over fear you will always be making the highest choice." I sat there stunned. She had hit on my deepest fears about having to let go of my husband.

Lynn asked me to close my eyes to see if I could sense any energy cords that ran between my husband and me. I had read in Doreen Virtue's *Angel Medicine* that energy cords develop between people in relationships. These invisible cords deplete our energy and often leave us feeling out of control and powerless, as if someone else is in charge of our thoughts and feelings. Virtue says that the cords look like surgical tubing and they grow larger based on the length and intensity of a relationship.

I told Lynn that I saw in my mind's eye a very large tube extending from my solar plexus to my husband's solar plexus.

"Yes, I can see a lot of doubt and fear going back and forth between you as well as a struggle for power and control. You both need to lovingly cut this energy cord, and each of you should be the individuals that you came to be."

This made sense because I read that the solar plexus chakra is the main power center in the body. In martial arts, the solar plexus area is the center of ch'i, also called life-force energy. A dancer concentrates on the mid-section in order to gain control and balance.

A person experiencing problems with the solar plexus chakra is usually having difficulty maintaining personal power. I remembered Kim saying that I had this very strong energy clinging to me and that I was having a difficult time moving through life because of it. She could see that my husband had a tendency to allow fears and doubts to dictate his actions, and he often extended this energy to me. I had a strong intuition that this was not the first lifetime in which we had struggled with these issues.

## Another Loss

I began to see that my husband and I were moving away from each other instead of coming together. I knew it was happening, but I felt powerless to stop it. In March of 2006, I attended a seminar put on by Helle and Lisa, which I will describe in greater detail in the last chapter.

During the seminar, they told the participants that we might experience strong emotions as we did certain meditations to clear away negative energy that we were holding onto. I have always been a strong person and I pride myself on maintaining control over my emotions. I have even felt disdain for others who cannot control their emotions. So of course I was the one who became incredibly emotional for several hours during the cleansing part of the seminar.

I felt angry with everyone: my father, my brother, Cathy, my mother, and especially my husband. It was as if someone had turned on a faucet of tears, and I did not have access to the shut-off valve. As Lisa led us through several deep meditations the realization came to me that my husband and I had completed what we came to do together, and if we stayed in the marriage we would both be miserable.

I remembered Portia's statement that my husband and I were not soulmates but we came to go through certain things together. I thought about Kim's comment during our second reading when I had asked about my husband and his life purpose. She was silent for a while and then she said, "He will have his dream, but it will not play out like he thinks." I understood that it was time for him to let go of the balloon string and let me soar away.

After the seminar, I contacted Lisa for a reading. She told me that my guides were telling her that I was judging myself for wanting to leave my husband and that I shouldn't because we had planned everything that was taking place before we came to this lifetime. Lisa saw that our combined energy was not very compatible. She laughed because she was being shown two porcupines. "You are basically carrying him and his fear on your back.

It is holding you back spiritually. Your souls have already separated. Do you feel that way?"

"Yes, I do." I sighed.

"Why are you making a judgment about it? This was predetermined by both of you," Lisa explained. "You had an agreement to go only so far and then go your separate ways." Lisa said that we would both find soulmates if we chose to let each other go.

"Your sister is saying that you are almost out of the tunnel. I see you have had many struggles. The point was to discover who you really are and it has helped you to determine what you really want."

I couldn't help feeling devastated and guilty about wanting to leave my husband. How could I give up this man whom I loved so much? A man who would put his life on the line for another person and who loved Christmas more than any other person I knew? I cried and cried and even screamed at Cathy, "How can I face another loss in my life?"

"It won't be a loss in the end," she told me.

I began to see new numbers everywhere. Instead of seeing 3s and 4s, I was now seeing 5s, 8s, and 2s. The number 5 relates to change. The number 8 has to do with prosperity, and 2 is a reminder for us to have faith.

For example, several times I saw 582. According to Doreen Virtue and Lynnette Brown in *Angel Numbers*, 582 means, "Have faith in the changes you are making, as they are bringing you abundance in all ways. Keep your heart filled with gratitude, and release all worries to heaven."

## Spiritual Partnership

I learned in *Conversations with God* that the institution of marriage is no longer working for humanity anymore. It was originally invented for security and safety, but it no longer serves that purpose. Unfortunately, many people stay in miserable relationships rather than take the risk of being alone and starting over again. I believe that this is

299

often just what many of us need to release negative energy, find our purpose, and begin the fresh and vibrant lives that we planned for ourselves before we got here.

Zukav wrote in *The Seat of the Soul* that in the future, people will have to look at marriage as a *spiritual partnership*. We have evolved too much for people to stay in a marriage out of the need for security. Unlike the institution of marriage, a spiritual partnership is not based in fear. Two people come together to assist each other with spiritual growth. Both partners are equal in the relationship, and they can truly discuss issues in a less emotional manner than people in traditional married relationships because they see the bigger picture. I knew that was what I wanted.

Eleanor told me that ultimately it would be in my best interest to find someone who was not a protector like my husband. She said that I am attracted to this type of person because I have the same protective energy within myself, but combining the two doesn't work for very long.

"Because you have all the water signs in your chart, you tend to bend to what others want and adapt yourself to fit other people's realities. Water is very yielding yes, but it is also strong enough to wear stones away. So you have to balance your desire to accommodate others with your very strong side that knows exactly who you are and what you want. In order to do what you came to do, you need to be with a man who is your equal and spiritual partner."

## My Decision

I thought about Walsch's statement in *Tomorrow's God* that every tough decision is an announcement from our soul that we are about to experience great spiritual growth. And I knew that one of the most challenging aspects of life is our relationship with others.

I had learned that we make agreements with other souls to share certain experiences and then go our separate ways. Our closest friends often play roles that push us and

300

challenge us. And it is often these difficulties that cause us to remember our purpose. My husband and I were playing these roles for each other.

I had always thought that I was more of a teacher for my husband than the other way around. But Eleanor explained that because of the oppositions in my astrological chart, I was attracting my teachers. Most of them are men who I perceive to have more power or authority than me. Starting with my father and then my husband, my teachers have been hitting me over the head trying to get me to trust my own instincts and stand up for myself. Eleanor said that I experienced huge emotional upheaval to help me let go of old habitual patterns that no longer served me.

I was at a crossroads in my life, and I knew the path that my soul wanted to take was leading me away from my husband. Eleanor added additional clarity when she explained to me that I had just completed what is known as the *Uranus Opposition*. It is a time when huge shifts happen in our lives. Many call it a mid-life crisis, and everyone goes through it in some form or another. She said that I had been through a complete breaking up of my foundation, which allowed me to move ahead in my journey. Divorces often occur during this time because one person grows faster than the other or the two go in opposite directions.

Eleanor said that if a person does not leave a marriage when he or she needs to, chronic illness can set in because there is too much energy being stifled. This described my feelings perfectly. My spirit felt stifled. No one was to blame. We simply had reached the end of our mutual journey in this lifetime. I had made my decision, and as difficult as it was, I knew that it was made out of love and not fear.

## Humanity's Decision

In *Journey of Souls*, Newton's hypnosis subjects remembered their friends in the spirit world laughing and teasing one another about how overly dramatic they had been while on earth. They told Newton that we all take life too seriously and that life is just one big stage play.

I believe that the most important way we can expand our views about life is to remember that we are all playing a role that we chose before we got here. We are active participants in our lives, not just onlookers. We always have many choices available to us, both in spirit in physical form.

Zukav wrote in *The Seat of the Soul* that the Garden of Eden story in Genesis describes the beginning of the human experience. The most fundamental decision for our species remains the same: Are we going to choose doubt, shame, and fear, or are we going to choose knowledge, wisdom, and love?

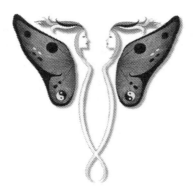

## Chapter Nineteen:
## What Is Death?

"Oh my God! I'm not really dead...I can look down and see my body lying flat in the hospital bed...I'm supposed to be dead, but I'm alive," exclaimed one of Michael Newton's hypnosis subjects in *Journey of Souls* as he witnessed his death in a past life.

It seems strange to me to call what I am about to discuss "death" because I know that death doesn't exist. In fact, the thing we call death is really a reawakening, a return to our natural state. Walsch learned in *The New Revelations* that there is no such thing as a dead thing. Everything in the universe is alive and constantly moving, just vibrating at different speeds. We see that even a rock is alive and moving when viewed under a microscope. All things are made up of life-force energy. The Western religious view that we die and are later resurrected to life is contrary to the laws of nature. Our energy never dies. It simply changes form. We began as spirit, and when it is time for us to relinquish our bodies, we return to spirit. This is the cycle of eternal life of which we are all a part.

## Tragedy or Triumph?

In *Journey of Souls*, Newton hypnotically regressed patients through their own deaths in past lives so that they would no longer fear death and would instead embrace life. Newton said that every subject expressed great awe and excitement at re-experiencing the freedom of separating from his or her body. Newton never tired of watching the look of wonder on his clients' faces as they witnessed their own immortality. Newton's subjects realized that their lives in spirit were more real than the lives they had left on earth.

The advanced spiritual beings in Alan Kardec's *The Gospel: Explained by the Spiritist Doctrine,* said that human beings are under the mistaken notion that a death can be untimely.

A good friend of my sister's had a very difficult time with her death. She insisted that if Cathy had not joined the Border Patrol she would not have died. She felt strongly that Cathy had so much more to contribute to the world and that her life was cut short. This is an understandable reaction and a common human perspective on death. But the fact is that she died when she was supposed to die, in the manner in which she had chosen before she came to this life. This is something that I know at the core of my being.

When people learn of my sister's death, they look at me with such pity. "I am so sorry about your sister," they say. While I appreciate their sympathy and kindness, I always feel very awkward because I want to tell them that she is not dead. She is full of life, feisty as ever, and she is still my twin sister. The only sadness that I feel is when I realize that I won't completely be with her again for many years. But I also know that I have a full life ahead of me and that time is inconsequential to her, and so I am overjoyed with the path we have chosen. I know that Cathy will contribute far more to this world by dying than she ever could have alive.

304

In May of 2006, I was thrilled when I saw that the book on dying that Walsch had told me about during his seminar was finally available. When I read *Home with God: In a Life That Never Ends*, I was amazed because I had already written this chapter on death, and the information contained in Walsch's new book was extraordinarily similar and confirmed everything I had written on the subject.

Walsch learned that every death brings messages to those of us left behind on earth. It is up to us to decide what the deaths on 9/11 meant or what the message was from the tsunami or from any other death. The purpose of death is what we demonstrate it to be through living our lives.

Kardec's spirits explained that our limited vision prevents us from seeing that our souls live more fully while in spirit. They suggested that we expand our viewpoint to see that our lives are just a speck of time in the infinite journey of our souls. There is no tragedy in death, only triumph.

## What Is Heaven Like?

In *Journey of Souls*, subjects reported that they ascended through layers of opalescent light, which the Indian Vedas and other Eastern writings have called the *astral planes*.

Newton's subjects said that these astral planes reside very near the physical world. Many people have experienced these astral planes during near-death experiences, meditation, under hypnosis, or during out-of-body experiences. The consensus is that the planes grow lighter and brighter the farther one moves away from the earth.

Newton's subjects felt a sense of great peace and love as they were pulled through a gateway or portal into the spiritual dimension.

In *Heaven and Earth*, James Van Praagh wrote that Heaven is not really a separate place but a different dimension, with no physical borders. Van Praagh learned from spiritual entities that the other side has different levels of vibrating light; the higher the frequency, the brighter and purer the light. Highly evolved beings gravitate to the higher etheric frequencies.

In *Journey of Souls*, subjects described the spirit world as a space of pure thought. Everything is guided by a powerful mental force that is directing everything in unbelievable harmony. The idea of pure thought is difficult to comprehend on an earthly level, but souls say they have mental contact with everyone and can visit with anyone simply by thinking of the soul they want to communicate with.

Newton asked one of his advanced clients if God resided somewhere in a central space in the spirit world. The soul was rather confused by the question and said that the concept of God had been misused. She explained that the Source *is* the spirit world.

Many view Heaven as a place where people float around aimlessly. But Newton's subjects described the spirit world as one of perfect order. Every soul has a specific space within this heavenly realm. When Newton's subjects reached their final destinations, they realized that they had forgotten the indescribable peace of their true home.

## Where Is Hell?

In the West, our religions teach of a place of eternal punishment and torment called Hell. Some religions say that people may also go to Purgatory, a lonely place where souls are trapped between Heaven and Hell.

According to Michael Newton in *Destiny of Souls*, Eastern religions have their own mix of superstitions and tales about lower astral planes and spiritual prisons. The doctrine of transmigration has been used in India to control bad behavior. People are told that as a punishment, they will reincarnate in a subhuman life form.

According to Yogananda in *The Second Coming of Christ*, seventh-century Buddhists corrupted the teachings of the Buddha and developed the hellish doctrine of annihilation as the ultimate end of life. This arose out of a misinterpretation of the word *Nirvana*, which stated that at the time of death, the ego, and therefore all human consciousness, ceased to be.

On July 28, 1999, Pope John Paul II told his papal audience, "Damnation cannot be attributed to an initiative of God because in His merciful love He cannot want anything but the salvation of the beings He created." The Pope announced to a stunned world that Hell does not exist as a place but as a situation in which people find themselves when they freely choose to withdraw from God's love and light.

The Pope went on to say that people must be very careful in interpreting biblical descriptions of Hell because they were meant to be symbolic and metaphorical. The pictures and descriptions of fire and torment are meant to "indicate the complete frustration and vacuity of a life without God."

In *Home with God* Walsch learned that whatever state of mind people have when they leave their bodies will be what they initially experience as they cross over into death. People who believe they will go to Hell will temporarily see themselves in their version of Hell. However, they will only see themselves in a hellish condition but will not experience any suffering because there is no negativity or suffering in the spirit world. As soon as souls realize this they give up their ideas of Hell and move onto happier, more loving experiences.

According to Newton in *Journey of Souls*, in his ten years of working with souls, he had never run into a physical place of torment and condemnation other than the discord subjects experienced on earth. Newton's subjects said that all souls go to one spirit world after death and that every soul is treated with love, kindness, and patience.

## Displaced Souls

Newton learned that a small percentage of souls lose their way and become attached to the earth's lower astral planes after death. These disturbed spirits are often younger souls who are angry and feel that they have been treated unjustly. If they continue to cling to the earth, some will become ghosts. Newton said in *Journey of Souls* that this category of displaced souls has been largely overblown by television and movies. Usually the immature soul feels he or she has unfinished business and refuses to leave the earth's plane. Often these souls have obsessive attachments to certain places or people and simply refuse to let them go. Essentially, ghosts are trapped in a no-man's land between the lower astral planes that surround the earth and the higher spiritual world.

Newton says that these souls are not demonic; they just have a high level of discontent. Many people believe that when someone's life is taken the soul remains near the earth's plane, angry and bitter. Many say that these disgruntled souls roam around the earth looking for weaker souls to influence.

Eventually these displaced entities are persuaded by their spirit guides and other special caretakers to make their transition into the spirit world.

Newton learned that some souls who commit very violent acts on earth are separated upon return to the spirit world. Some will go into seclusion for quite a while. Newton found that souls who have committed the most heinous of acts are sent to what could be described as an intensive care unit where they are rejuvenated with light and energy. The purpose of separating the soul is not punishment but rehabilitation.

Ultimately the soul goes back to his or her soul group under intense supervision. The point is to help the soul gain more self-awareness so that the soul will treat others better.

308

Newton found that as souls progress, they move out of their soul groups and move into new groups with other souls who are also advancing. Some of Newton's subjects who were having great difficulty on earth had remained in their initial soul groups for as long as 50,000 years before moving on to the next spiritual level.

## Suicide

Kardec's spirits said that it is a lack of connection to one's inner being that causes a person to commit suicide. They said that a spirit-centered view of life brings confidence and serenity when facing trials and challenges. Most suicides come from inner discontentment and skepticism about the future. The spirits pointed out that scientists of great stature have argued that nothing exists after death. By doing this, they have led humanity to conclude that there is no hope. Without a sense of hope, people believe that killing themselves will stop their pain and will save them from having to suffer more later.

According to Newton in *Destiny of Souls*, some of his subjects had a difficult time merging with their host bodies, and some souls took on new lives too quickly, before they were ready. Because they were ill-adjusted, they felt alone and confused, and this can lead a soul to want to commit suicide. Newton found that abnormal brain chemistry or hormonal imbalances also influence the soul to feel a pull toward suicide.

According to Newton's hypnosis subjects, souls who commit suicide due to mental illness or severe debilitating diseases are treated differently in the spirit world than those who had healthy minds and bodies. Souls did not express any guilt when they were involved with a mercy death. They told Newton that when we are subject to unendurable physical suffering, we have the right to be released from the unending pain and indignity.

When Newton worked with clients who committed suicide in past lives, the first thing they often said after viewing their death was, "Oh my God, how could I have been so stupid?" Healthy individuals who committed suicide to avoid life's challenges said that they felt they were somewhat diminished in the eyes of their guides and peer groups because they had broken their covenant to fulfill their life missions.

Souls knew immediately after committing suicide that it did not ultimately relieve them from facing the earthly burdens they sought to avoid. They knew that they would have to face these same trials again in another life.

Newton discovered that one of two things happen to souls who commit suicide while in healthy bodies. If they do not show a pattern of killing themselves during multiple lives, they are often sent back to a new life rather quickly, at their own request, to try to make up lost time. This could happen as soon as five years after their death.

Those who do have a habit of committing suicide over several lifetimes face some difficult and rigorous rehabilitation. Newton's subjects who committed suicide said that they were not sent to some dark place or lower spiritual region. But some were sent to a world with trees and water but no people. The souls were to reflect on why they were having such difficulties while in physical form. They expressed feelings of frustration with being left out. While their friends were taking on new challenges and growing spiritually, they were standing still.

One young soul remembered killing herself in several lifetimes. When she returned to the spirit world, she was taken to a library where she was to look at her life books. She saw an elderly man coming toward her, muttering and shaking his head. He brought her a stack of scrolls and charts.

"You're early," he said simply. The soul reviewed her "chart" and was shown many alternatives she could have chosen besides suicide.

Newton learned that many souls enter lifetimes with a high probability of dying young. But suicide is never a preplanned karmic option for anyone.

Even though suicide is highly discouraged, a soul is never subjected to punishment or eternal damnation, as some religions teach. No great torture is visited upon them save their own feelings of guilt and shame. In every case, the souls are their own worst critics.

Newton learned that a soul has the free will to make a decision to die when there is a very low quality of life and there is no possibility of recovery. Our souls know when it is time to go, and each individual soul has the right to make that decision.

## The Process of Death

Hospice nurses and doctors notice that people become peaceful and somewhat detached from their loved ones shortly before death. According to Newton in *Journey of Souls*, this happens because souls become more strongly connected with their higher consciousness.

After my sister died, I realized that she had been preparing for death for several months. I have spoken to many other people who had the same observation about their loved ones before they died. This included people who died in "accidents."

Cathy had always been very feisty and intense. But thinking back now about the months before she died, I realized that she had become much more peaceful and calm.

"Of course," my friend Lena said as I described Cathy's change in demeanor, "she was closer to the light."

According to Yogananda in *The Second Coming of Christ*, a person's life-force energy withdraws from the spine and exits the body through the medulla oblongata at the base of the skull. Some of Newton's hypnosis subjects felt their energy release through the top of their head.

People who are sensitive to energy can feel the life energy leaving the body of a dying person. Famous medium Edgar Cayce was said to have gotten onto an elevator, only to promptly get off at the next floor even though that was not his destination. He could feel that there was very little life-force energy in that elevator. Immediately after he got off, the elevator plunged several stories, killing everyone.

## Leaving the Body

Newton's subjects in *Journey of Souls* universally reported a sudden release of energy and the feeling of floating above their lifeless bodies. They realized that they were dead but they did not feel any sadness about their death. In fact, most expressed a euphoric feeling of weightlessness, freedom, and joy and did not want to return to their bodies.

Many said they felt frustrated because of their inability to comfort their loved ones. They often attempted to convey loving thoughts, but because their family members were so overcome with grief they are not able to reach them. Newly departed souls do not feel the devastation that we on earth feel because they are able to see a larger picture. They understand that their family members will be okay. They also know that they will see them again in the spirit world and probably in later lives as well.

Souls report a gentle pulling sensation away from the earth. Many also hear a buzzing or humming sound that they attribute to increased energy. At this point, some souls are met by their spirit guides, while others report meeting them after leaving the earth's plane. Occasionally a soul wants to linger for a few days to witness his or her funeral, but most choose to move on rather quickly. I believe it is important for people to understand that souls have little interest in what happens to their bodies after death.

My sister and I had a terrible dispute with our grandfather when my grandmother died. My grandmother had said for many years that she did not want to be cremated due to her religious beliefs. After her death, my grandfather insisted on cremating her. Cathy and I sought out a friend who was an attorney and asked her to put a cease and desist order on the burial. The dispute went on for several weeks until the stress of the situation became overwhelming. Finally we decided to relinquish the body. Neither Cathy nor I ever visited my grandmother's grave.

This type of anguish can be avoided if people understood that their deceased loved ones see their body as a shell they have shed and no longer need.

### The Tunnel

Souls describe the portal to the spiritual world as a dense black tunnel with a dim circle of light at the end. Even though the souls are in darkness, they do not express any fear. The feeling is familiar, and they sense other souls traveling home through the same tunnel.

At the moment of death, some of Newton's subjects saw the opening to the tunnel right next to them while others saw it higher above the earth.

The farther the soul moved through the tunnel, the brighter the light appeared at the other end. Subjects reported that the earth felt close by, but they knew they were moving into another dimension.

Another strong sensation that souls experienced is the power of their own thoughts. They realized that as soon as they thought something, it materialized.

Newton said that because souls have different thoughts about heaven and life after death, every soul experiences the entry into the spirit world a little differently. Some examples of heavenly visions were castles, brightly lit buildings, fields full of flowers, a white sandy beach, or a bridge over a river.

313

Newton's subjects and those who have had near-death or out-of-body experiences describe a feeling of vastness. They see huge magnificent spaces that shimmer with multicolored lights, and they have a feeling that the space is infinite.

### Reuniting with Loved Ones

Some people report seeing their deceased loved ones at their bedside right before death, but more often a soul is met by family, friends, and spirit guides after he or she moves through the tunnel. Sometimes guides will hang back and wait until the returning soul has reunited with his or her loved ones before coming forward. But our guides are always nearby and they are responsible for orchestrating our reunions.

One of Newton's subjects became ecstatic when she was met by a member of her soul group. She remembered him as her husband in three of her past lives. Newton watched as tears of joy streamed down his client's face as she reunited with her soulmate. Then the subject was overjoyed as she described seeing her brother, who died when he was young, as well as her aunt and her mother.

According to Newton, as souls move to the end of the tunnel, they hear vibratory sounds similar to bells or chimes. They describe these sounds as incredibly soothing and peaceful. This description resonated with me because I immediately feel a sense of tranquility when I hear wind chimes or bells of any kind.

Once souls have passed through the tunnel, they realize they have gone through the initial gateway into the spirit world. Newton found that the farther souls moved into the spirit world, the more uniform their visions became.

The most common feelings expressed by Newton's subjects as they moved into the spiritual realm were relief and joy. They expressed how grateful they were to be away from the stress of the earth and they felt as if they were floating in beautiful, peaceful light.

I remembered the words my sister spoke to me in a dream: "It's not scary at all. I am so happy here. It is so beautiful. I am in my favorite place."

## Counseling

Newton's subjects said that the next step is counseling and a life review. The amount of counseling depends on the soul's level of advancement. Younger souls are given special attention because they have not yet adjusted to the abrupt transition from the physical to the non-physical.

Souls and their guides go to the council of ascended masters for a life review. Newton's subjects say that these masters are familiar to them and that it is not an interrogation but a discussion.

Newton's subjects said that the life review begins the long process of self-evaluation. During the review, we are able to see our actions from the point of view of others. Souls feel both the positive and negative emotions that they caused in other people.

In *Conversations with God,* Walsch learned that at this stage in our death journey we are given this opportunity to look at our lives in a nonjudgmental way to determine if we accomplished what we set out to do. We also evaluate how well our thoughts, words, and actions served us and the other people in our lives.

## Final Destination

After a soul finishes a life review, it is time to go home. Although Newton's subjects described the spirit world as vast and endless, they knew they were going to a specific space and they experienced a peaceful journey toward their final destination.

Every soul is part of a specific group of three to fifteen entities who match the soul's maturity level. Newton learned that the friends and family members who initially meet us upon our arrival in the spirit world might not be part of our soul group because the souls with whom we share our lives on earth are at differing spiritual levels. Souls do not express distress at this; in fact, they are happy to be back with their own groups.

This is often one of Newton's favorite parts of the hypnosis journey, as his subjects approach their true homes and begin to recognize people from their soul groups.

In *Destiny of Souls*, Newton learned that souls are welcomed home with hugs, cheers, and laughter. Often elaborate homecomings are planned. One soul told Newton that her group organized a classical Roman festival with an enormous marble hall, togas, singing, dancing, and wine. The subject said that she and members of her group had spent many lifetimes together in the ancient world and the party was intended to recreate the bonds they felt during those lifetimes.

I have always been bothered by the term "rest in peace." While our souls do rest after death, they are also quite active with academics, research, recreation, and grand celebrations. After years of studying life in the spirit world, Newton concluded that the afterlife is very busy. In fact, there is no such thing as sleep in the spirit world.

Newton learned in *Journey of Souls* that our time in the spirit world is for rejuvenation, relaxation, and review of past lives and karmic issues. Souls described a classroom-like setting where groups gather to discuss and dissect their past lives. The groups compare and study their decisions and actions and even engage in role-playing to help one another gain greater self-awareness and understanding.

After a period of time that can equal hundreds of years on Earth, souls begin to yearn for the challenge of a new life, and the complex preparations of a new incarnation begin once again.

316

## Culture of Failure

God told Walsch in *Conversations with God* that our medical professionals are trained to keep people alive at any cost instead of making them comfortable and allowing them to die with dignity. Doctors are trained to see death as failure. Because death represents a doctor's inability to help a patient, it is viewed with great trepidation and even disdain in the medical community.

## Near-Death Experiences

Since the 1970s, large amounts of data have been collected on near-death experiences (NDEs), as well as other compelling information related to life after death. Yet the medical community has largely ignored this information, writing it off as hallucinations or wishful thinking.

Dr. Brian Weiss wrote in *Through Time Into Healing* about a Gallup survey that indicated that more than eight million Americans have had near-death experiences and that many were young children. The accounts of these NDEs are startlingly consistent and very well documented.

A near-death experience can occur when a person is declared clinically dead. At that point people become detached from their bodies and watch medical personnel attempting to resuscitate them.

Almost every person is drawn away from the earth and into a tunnel with a bright, white light at the end. Most people report seeing spiritual figures and deceased family members who have come to greet them. Almost everyone describes a feeling of freedom, peace, and joy, and many marvel at their complete lack of pain. Inevitably people are told that it is not their time to go, and they are returned to their bodies.

In 1982, a twenty-seven-year-old pediatric intern named Melvin Morse witnessed the miraculous recovery of a seven-year-old girl who had been in a coma after spending twenty minutes at the bottom of a swimming pool.

According to the February 2006 *Reader's Digest* article "Spirited Away," the girl's CAT scan showed massive swelling of the brain, and she was unable to breathe on her own. Dr. Morse believed that death was imminent. But three days later, the girl emerged from the coma with her brain functions completely intact. The girl proceeded to describe to Dr. Morse the medical procedures that had been performed on her, and she was able to describe the appearances of the different doctors and nurses who had attempted to revive her.

Melvin Morse began researching NDEs in children. Over the course of a ten-year study, Morse discovered that the children gave eerily similar accounts of their "deaths." Morse compared his findings to an earlier groundbreaking book called *Life After Life*, written in 1975 by medical student Raymond Moody, and found that Moody's findings were virtually identical.

Morse proved in each case that the children's experiences were not due to hallucinations, anesthesia, low oxygen levels, or sleep deprivation, as many physicians speculated.

According to the *Reader's Digest* article, Morse was scorned instead of hailed for what he thought was a major breakthrough. Morse was criticized because he had blurred the lines between science and spirituality. But Morse believes that the medical community simply does not want to portray death in a positive light. Morse said that doctors are afraid that patients might not fight to avoid death if death is not seen as a negative outcome. I believe that the skeptical views about death and the afterlife in the scientific and medical communities have had far-reaching, detrimental effects on our society.

## Hospice

Hospice is a beacon of light in our terminally ill medical system. It is not until a patient has been given six months to live and has chosen hospice care that he or she will be treated as a whole person with important emotional and spiritual issues to deal with.

Contrary to what many people believe, hospice is not just a place but also a philosophy. The hospice philosophy is that every stage of life is important. The last days of life can often be full of revelations, contemplation, and healing for everyone involved. The goal of hospice is to make a person as comfortable as possible and to allow the person to spend the last days of life relatively pain free, at home in the company of loved ones. Not only does hospice focus on the patient, but it also extends support and guidance to the family members of the dying person.

When I began volunteering at San Diego Hospice and Palliative Care, one of the largest home hospice programs in the country, I was amazed at how fast the system sprung into action to help a dying patient. When the hospice received a call for help, it made every attempt to visit the patient that same day.

Once a person was brought onto the hospice service, he or she was assigned a doctor, a nurse, a pharmacist, a home health aide, a social worker, a volunteer, a chaplain who was trained in his or her particular spiritual beliefs, and even a homemaker who helped with cleaning and cooking.

Because of the negative views surrounding death in the mainstream medical community, hospice social workers and caseworkers often have to fight doctors to allow their patients to choose hospice care. Even though it is quite clear that people know when they are going to die, many physicians see a patient's choice for hospice as an indication of giving up hope, and they often fight this decision.

By refusing to refer patients to hospice or by fighting a patient's request for hospice care, a physician is denying his or her patients the right to die in the familiar and peaceful setting of their own home versus the chaotic and antiseptic atmosphere of a hospital.

During my first reading with Kim, she said that she saw me working in a hospice someday. In my mind's eye I can see myself in a beautiful building on the top of a hill with skylights, hardwood floors, fireplaces, waterfalls, fountains, trees, and flowers. Patients will be taught to die with joy, expectation, dignity, and understanding.

In the future I believe that patients will know that death is as natural as birth, yet far more peaceful. I envision spiritual teachers and healers coming from all over the world to hospices to help prepare and guide people into what should be one of the most profoundly important times of their lives.

## Beyond Words

St. Paul was known to have said, "I die daily," meaning that his spirit left his body every day during deep prayer and meditation. The same thing occurs while we are asleep. Newton's subjects confirmed that during sleep we are free to leave our bodies to travel in the spirit world. When the subjects witnessed their deaths, they realized they felt no fear because they had done it many times before in past lives and while sleeping.

While on earth we often experience sadness due to our subconscious desire to return to spirit. But we also know on a higher level that we have chosen our lives for a specific purpose, and we are thrilled at the opportunities and challenges of experiencing life in physical form.

In *Reaching to Heaven*, medium James Van Praagh asked many spirits what death was like. Van Praagh learned that although there are many similarities in the death experience, death is really beyond the scope of human intelligence.

Walsch learned in *Conversations with God* that there really are no words that can adequately describe the splendor of the transition that we call death. I remembered Cathy's message, "*No hay palabras*": there are no words to describe the beauty of where she is.

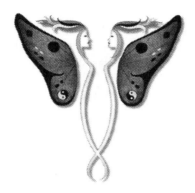

## Chapter Twenty:
## It's the Thought That Counts

This is one of the most important chapters in this
book. We cannot move forward as a species without a
clear understanding of how our thoughts impact our
reality. Our beliefs are creating behaviors, which are
creating our experiences. Our future depends on what we
think, say, and do.

### Forgotten Power

I was browsing through the spiritual section of the
bookstore and came across a book by Gregg Braden called
*The Isaiah Effect*. I learned that Braden is a lecturer, earth
scientist, and leading authority on ancient prophecies,
sacred sites, and spiritual practices around the world. I had
no idea whether Cathy had ever read *The Isaiah Effect*, but I
suddenly felt compelled to buy the book. I later found out
through our friend Amy that Cathy had read Braden's
book and had been enthralled with it.

Braden explains that 2,500-year-old manuscripts found
in 1946, known as the Dead Sea Scrolls, reveal an ancient
inner science that was lost to the West 1,700 years ago.
One of the most remarkable finds was a complete text
written by the prophet Isaiah.

Isaiah, and many other ancient sages, said that human beings possess a God-given inner power that allows us to transcend war, destruction, and suffering. Braden learned that this lost inner science was shared openly in past societies.

According to Dr. Wayne Dyer in *The Power of Intention*, an invisible energy field permeates everything and extends to both the physical and non-physical worlds. The human body, mind, and spirit are all part of this pervasive universal energy force. Dyer explained that the only way to deactivate this all-powerful force is to believe that we are separate from it. This is exactly what most of our world has done.

How have we lost our knowledge of this inner power? Braden says we must look again to the fourth-century council at Nicea. The council disallowed forty-one gospels and other texts that spoke of this inner power. Braden believes that the council's motives were not necessarily sinister. They may have intended to put together a collection of writings that would reach a wider audience then decided that some of the esoteric traditions would not be understood by the masses.

According to Braden, the church leaders could not have foreseen the far-reaching implications of their censorship. They had no way of knowing that their sanctioned writings would one day become the Holy Bible, the basis for the largest and most powerful religion in the world.

Unfortunately, the council decided to remove all documents that spoke of mankind's inherent power and relegated them to elite priesthoods and seminaries. There is evidence that a group of Essenes, the Carmelites of Mount Carmel (many believed that Jesus lived in this community when he was a child), hid copies of their most sacred writings in remote places around the world because of the corruption of the texts after the time of Jesus. Stories passed down by Native American tribal leaders tell of emissaries bringing Essene traditions to North America as far back as 2,000 years ago. Manuscripts were also stashed in remote monasteries in Tibet and other locations in Asia and the Middle East.

Braden believes that these omissions altered the course of history on our planet because we learned to view ourselves as observers instead of co-creators. The loss of this ancient wisdom has caused us to forget our true relationship with God, the cosmos, and one another.

## Thoughts Are Energy

According to Gary Zukav in *The Seat of the Soul*, we are not static beings. Instead, we are dynamic entities made of pure light. Energy enters our bodies at the tops of our heads and is continuously flowing through us. We are able to shape this light-energy through our thoughts. So the way we think about something actually changes our experience.

The first thing hypnosis subjects discovered in *Journey of Souls* after crossing over to the other side was the overriding power of their thoughts. In her book *Embraced by The Light*, Betty J. Eadie wrote that during her near-death experience she was shown how powerful human beings truly are. She said that if we only knew how important our thoughts were in shaping our reality, we would guard them very carefully and avoid all negative thinking.

Dr. Wayne Dyer explained in *The Power of Intention* that there are five levels of energy. The first level is the material world. Physical form vibrates as such a slow level that it appears to be solid. When souls incarnate they go through a massive reduction of energy to infuse into matter. The energy is calibrated to such a level that the soul can experience itself in physical form.

The second level of energy is sound. In *Journey of Souls*, subjects who experienced themselves leaving their bodies described a soothing, vibratory sound. Some have heard this same sound under general anesthesia. Newton explained that this vibratory sound is universal life-force energy that permeates everything. In Eastern traditions, the sound "om" or "ah" is chanted to raise one's vibrational level to match the frequency of this universal energy.

The third level is light. Light moves faster than the material world and faster than the speed of sound. Dyer said that there are no actual particles that form light. When we see different colors, we are actually seeing pulsating energy. Every color vibrates at different frequency. Violet vibrates at an extremely rapid level and is considered the highest spiritual color. Violet or purple corresponds to the crown chakra at the top of the head, which is connected to the Universal Mind.

The fourth level of energy is thought. Thoughts move faster than the speed of sound and light. David R. Hawkins, M.D., Ph.D., has shown in his book *Power vs. Force* that the frequency of thoughts can be measured. Emotions such as fear and anger vibrate at a much lower rate of speed than compassion, joy, and love.

Neale Donald Walsch learned in *Conversations with God* that it is extremely difficult to reverse the effects of negative thinking once they have taken on physical form. Walsch wrote that when we make our minds up about something we set the universe in motion. Forces that are more subtle and complex than we can comprehend are in play, and we are actually shifting the intricate web of energies that make up life itself.

The fifth and highest level of energy is spirit. The energy of the spirit is vibrating at such a supersonic rate that manifestations of disharmony, disease, or pain are impossible. According to Dyer, thoughts, emotions, and actions of kindness, love, and peacefulness vibrate at the same level as the spirit world. By focusing on these higher emotions, we are actually matching ourselves energetically to the spiritual realm. The physical and emotional healing can be astounding.

## Law of Attraction

During our trip to Sedona, I walked into one of the many metaphysical shops in the area. I looked around at the gemstones, crystals, and cards. Suddenly my eyes were drawn to a display of blue glass butterflies. I was thinking about buying one when I noticed a book next to the display called *Ask and It Is Given* by Jerry and Esther Hicks, and I saw that Dr. Wayne Dyer had written the forward. I admired Dyer's work so I contemplated purchasing the book. But I decided that I had too many other books at home that I still needed to read and walked away.

But my mind was continually drawn back to the blue butterflies and the book. "Okay, I'll go buy it," I told Cathy. I knew that she was trying to get my attention with the blue butterfly display.

When I got home I began reading it. I read solidly for two days until I had finished it. I learned that Esther Hicks had first discovered her ability to communicate with spiritual entities in the middle of her life when she visited a trance medium at the urging of her husband, Jerry. The medium's spirit guide came through and told Esther that she would be able to interact with highly evolved spirits and that she would write many books with the help of her spirit guide. The medium told Esther that she needed to learn to meditate.

Esther could hardly believe what she had heard. She had never meditated before, but when she got home she sat quietly and focused on her breathing. Soon she was receiving messages from the spirits the medium had spoken about. She was given the name "Abraham" for her spiritual guide. Esther learned that Abraham was actually a collective consciousness speaking with one voice.

This group of multidimensional beings transmitted blocks of thought in the form of vibrations similar to radio signals. Esther was able to receive and translate the signals into words. Abraham described itself as a family of non-physical beings whose purpose was to remind humanity of the universal laws that govern everything and to let us know that we truly are extensions of God.

Esther began translating while Jerry wrote the information down. They discovered that at the heart of Abraham's teachings was the powerful, universal law of attraction. Hicks learned that every thought vibrates and radiates a signal. Then that thought attracts back to itself a matching signal of the same frequency.

The law of attraction dictates that we draw to ourselves whatever we are predominantly thinking about. Whether we are thinking about what we want or what we don't want, the law of attraction is neutral and will bring us exactly what we are sending out. According to Abraham, there are no exceptions to this rule, so it is extremely simple to understand.

Walsch learned in *Conversations with God* that the universe is like a giant Xerox machine. Whatever we are focusing our attention on, the universe will bring us an exact replica of those thoughts. When we think about something enough, the energies "clump" together, the vibrations become heavier and slow down to the point where they become matter. Our thoughts are so powerful that they actually create physical form.

Abraham explained to Esther that although our thoughts are magnetic, they are not like loaded guns, instantly creating whatever we are thinking about. There is a time period that acts as a buffer between what we have been thinking about and the actual manifesting of the thoughts. This gives us time to examine our thoughts and decide whether we want to manifest what we have been focusing on.

328

The minute we realize we have been thinking negative or low-energy thoughts, we should immediately find less resistant, higher frequency thoughts. Interestingly, even a small shift in a positive direction will make a significant difference.

Abraham told Esther that the majority of people on the planet believe that they have no control over what they think and that they are simply observing and evaluation what is going on around. If we focus on what has always been or what we believe is the "truth," the universe will deliver exactly that—what has always been. Abraham said that something only becomes truth because someone thought about it and others focused on it enough that it became reality.

My husband often used this line of reasoning. Because he is a police officer, he reviews all possible scenarios before making a decision on something. Often he talked for prolonged periods of time about possible negative outcomes. When I told him to stop focusing on something he didn't want, he became indignant and explained to me that he was simply being realistic, smart, and open-minded by taking into account all possibilities.

"You don't understand how the universe works," I told him.

His response was always the same: "You are telling me, a veteran cop of twenty-two years, how the universe works? I have seen it all; I know how the universe works." And we were back to square one.

I understand how my husband developed this worldview. He was raised in a religion that teaches of an unpredictable God, who is loving and vengeful at the same time. He has learned that he is separate from other people and from God. He works in an occupation where at any given moment some unforeseen negative event could occur. He believes that his survival depends on his ability to anticipate and analyze these unwanted events.

Although things appear to happen to us in random fashion, this is actually a fallacy. In the next chapter, Science and Spirituality Meet, I will discuss how modern science has now proven that the act of focusing our attention on something actually alters the outcome of events.

## The Art of Allowing

Of all the books I have read, *Ask and It Is Given* offers the most simple and straightforward explanation of why it seems as if we do not get what we ask for and why unwanted things come into our lives.

Abraham told Hicks that the process of creating our reality involves three steps:

1. Ask. This is our job. According to Abraham, we are asking for what we want constantly via our thoughts and feelings.
2. The answer is given. This is not our work. God and the universal law of attraction will automatically give us what we are asking for, whether it is wanted or unwanted. It is not our job to make something happen. The powerful universal forces that are in place will take care of that. We simply have to determine what we want.
3. We allow ourselves to receive what has been given.

According to Abraham, what most of us fail to comprehend is that every subject is really two subjects. There is that which we desire and the lack of the thing we want. Often we think we are focusing our thoughts on what we want but in actuality we are focusing on the lack of the thing. For example, if we want more money, we should focus on the wonderful feeling of freedom we will experience when we have more money. Instead we are focusing on the negative idea that we are lacking in money or that we do not have enough. The universe automatically brings us more of what we are focusing on—the lack of money. If we want to lose weight, most of us focus on how bad we look or our inability to lose the weight instead of imagining the way we will feel and look when we reach our desired weight loss goal. In order to allow ourselves to receive what we really want, we must change our thought pattern to focus on what Abraham calls pure desire.

Hicks learned that it is not necessary for us to understand the complex forces of the universe in order to reap the benefits. My sister used to always say, "There is no lack of anything in the world." I thought she was off her rocker, but now I understand that there is no such thing as scarcity or shortages, only low-energy thoughts, which hold us apart from what we want.

### Emotions

I noticed that my brother often seemed to be facing some kind of obstacle. I had been told many times that the people around me were experiencing struggles for their own personal growth and I couldn't stop them from suffering. But I knew that he was struggling partly because he was attracting unwanted things into his life because of his thought process.

I decided to take a chance and send him a copy of *Ask and It Is Given*. I explained the story of how the book came to me and told him that I really hoped he would read it because it would change his life. I waited, hoping that he might take some of it to heart.

He called me after receiving the book. "This is the biggest bunch of crap I have ever read. I don't have a Source, and I sure as hell am not vibrating!"

I tried to explain to him that the ideas only seemed absurd to him because he had never heard them before and that the word *Source* was simply a universal word for God.

"And what is this thing about emotions and desires? That's for women!" He laughed.

"Why did I bother?" I thought.

"You have emotions," I told my brother. "You don't think anger is an emotion?"

But I understood his sentiment regarding emotions. I also used to scoff at anything emotional. In fact, during my training as a 911 dispatcher, I was marked down on my evaluations because of my intolerance for hysterical callers, especially females. Whenever I got a call from a female who was out of control, it made my skin crawl, and I instantly became impatient and angry, telling her to "get a grip." It took a lot of effort to change my outlook and gain more compassion. I still have a bias against people who are out of control emotionally.

It is very common, especially among conservative thinkers, to associate emotions with irrational behavior. But now I understand that when people are hysterical or out of control, they are simply allowing themselves to experience emotions without any thought. I also think that it is a very dangerous idea to believe that emotions are only for women. This misguided notion has cut half of our society off from their inner intuition and higher spiritual emotions.

According to Abraham in *Ask and it is Given*, our emotions are actually very sophisticated translators of our vibrational patterns. Our emotions help us to define our experiences and are intricately connected to our intuition and sixth sense. If we feel a strong emotion about something, our thoughts help us to understand why we are having the negative emotion, and our intuition will help us make appropriate decisions about the situation. People who use their gut instincts to make decisions are actually operating at a higher level than someone who only uses his or her rational intellect.

According to Gregg Braden in *The Isaiah Effect*, ancient manuscripts described only two basic emotions: love and fear. Hicks wrote that the highest emotions associated with love are: joy, knowledge, empowerment, freedom,

332

appreciation, passion, and enthusiasm. As one moves down the frequency range toward fear, a person may feel blame, anger, insecurity, guilt, unworthiness, despair, powerlessness, and depression. By understanding the way we feel, we can determine how closely connected we are to the Universal Source of well-being.

Many believe that the most powerful people are those who feel and show no emotion. But this relates only to outward power. According to Braden, the ancient Essenes understood that our emotions are our direct link to true inner power and that our thoughts have no creative power without emotions.

## Money Is Energy

Jesus said, "It is easier to pass through the eye of a needle than for a rich man to enter the Kingdom of Heaven." Many have said that Jesus meant to imply that money was the root of all evil. But according to Doreen Virtue in *Healing with the Angels*, Jesus was indicating that an *obsession* with money is a block to happiness.

Someone who has an obsession with money worries chronically that he or she won't have enough money, or he or she has enough but hoards it for fear of losing it. Both ideas are rooted in deep insecurity and fear.

I believe it is extremely important for people to understand that prosperity is our natural state and that there is nothing inherently wrong with money or financial success.

In *The Abundance Book*, John Randolph Price wrote that the idea of prosperity as a natural human condition was a central building block to all philosophical and religious systems until the second century A.D., when Price says that the war on self-knowledge and self-reliance began.

Ancient prophets taught that through meditation one could come to understand God as being one with the self. By going within and experiencing this truth, divine energy is released and transmutes all ignorance into wisdom and lack into abundance.

People were taught that money was a symbol of appreciation for one's service to others. The core of this teaching was that when a person embodied love, peace, gratitude, and harmlessness, wealth of every kind would pour forth into his or her life.

Even after 2,000 years of censoring and editing, the idea that abundance and wealth is our God-given right is evident in the Bible. Randolph quoted several passages that indicate this truth:

"Beloved. I wish above all things that thou mayest prosper."

"Prove me now herewith, said the Lord of hosts, if I will not open you the windows of heaven and pour you out a blessing that there shall not be room enough to receive it."

"Let the lord be magnified which hath pleasure in the prosperity of his servant."

"All things whatsoever ye pray and ask for, believe that ye have received them and ye shall have them."

Price said that we should avoid worshiping money but see it for what it really is—merely a symbol of the divine flow of well-being that exists in the universe, which we are all a part of and have access to simply by being aware of our inherent power.

Abraham told Esther in *Ask and It Is Given* that there is no source of poverty or lack of money in the world. The idea of scarcity is a man-made idea. We can block our financial flow by focusing on lack.

In order to attract the energy associated with wealth and money, we must *feel* financially secure. It is the feeling of knowing that we are secure, that attracts financial success and other types of abundance.

My husband always had a strong fear of not having enough money. He learned a lesson about money and security when his father was diagnosed with multiple sclerosis and had to retire from his job while he was still in high school. His mother had never worked outside the home, so Jack believed that his family would have had difficulty making ends meet if his father hadn't had the foresight to save half of everything he had ever earned throughout his career.

I learned that my husband had also struggled with financial worries in at least one of our other past lives together. Whenever the issue of money came up, he got a terrified deer-in-the-headlights look in his eyes.

He was constantly lecturing me about financial issues and was always talking about how we had to save more money. He could not stop worrying about the possibility of somehow losing his savings or his retirement.

I don't believe that it is a coincidence that he was with someone like me, who doesn't worry about money. One time I allowed one of our accounts to become overdrawn because I wasn't really paying attention and didn't balance the checkbook. I thought my poor husband was going to blow a gasket while I was trying to stop myself from laughing at his overly dramatic reaction.

I teased him because when he got his bills in the mail, he practically ran to pay them, and then raced them to the mailbox so they would go out the same day. My bills, on the other hand, would lie on the counter for several days.

"I am with you in this lifetime to help you lose your fears about money," I told him.

"How do you know that you are not with me to learn to be more financially savvy?" he always asked.

"Because you are the one with the fear" was my standard answer.

I tried to tell my husband that by focusing on his fears and insecurities about money he was actually attracting a shortage of money into his life. But somehow the conversation always turned into a discussion about my inability to save money.

After one such conversation, I went out jogging to try to release my frustration.

"I understand the principles of abundance, Cathy, but what if I am living with someone who doesn't get it and insists we hoard more and more money?"

"Oh, just humor him," she answered. "He isn't going to get it for a long time."

Eleanor told me that because of my particular astrological chart, money would never be an issue for me and I would always have enough. I was surprised at how accurately she described my views about money.

"When you have money, you don't hold onto it very tightly. If you see something you want you buy it. The money comes in and goes out so there is a flow. You are also very open and generous, which attracts prosperity and wealth."

According to Dyer in *The Power of Intention*, there is no exception to our ability to attract financial abundance into our lives. We are all connected to the same Universal Source, so what works for one person will work for everyone.

When we go to buy something, our only concern should be whether we want to buy it, not whether we can afford it. This kind of thinking takes an enormous leap of faith that most people are not prepared to make. But Dyer said that there is a ceaseless flow of unlimited supply that is readily available to all of us. All that is necessary is to remove doubt.

## Prayer

According to Braden in *The Isaiah Effect*, the scholars at ancient Qumran who wrote and compiled the Dead Sea Scrolls gave us a glimpse of the powerful science of prayer that allows us to change the chemistry in our own bodies by our thoughts and emotions. In fact, our thoughts and emotions are a form of prayer because they emit powerful signals, which let the universe know what we want.

336

Braden wrote that prayer is often thought of as a passive act and is used as a last resort. But he showed in *The Isaiah Effect* that modern science and ancient prophecy have proven that prayer and meditation offer us the single most sophisticated and powerful force that we have ever known.

According to Braden, our religions have encouraged us to make prayer a part of our lives, yet they have not shown us how. Braden lamented that the instructions given have been vague and imprecise. Texts that predate modern history reveal the true power of prayer was lost to us long ago.

### Feeling

In *The Isaiah Effect*, Braden described his journey in 1998 to an isolated monastery in the highlands of Tibet. Braden was fortunate enough to gain an audience with the abbot of the monastery. It was obvious to Braden that the man was a highly advanced spiritual master.

Braden asked the holy man through a translator about the purpose of the repeated mantras and chanting. The abbot answered simply, "Feeling." He explained that the outward movements and sounds are used to achieve an inner feeling. Braden was ecstatic. The abbot had confirmed what had been written 2,500 years ago in the Dead Sea Scrolls. To gain a feeling of bliss and heightened consciousness wasn't just a factor in prayer; it was the actual purpose of prayer.

Braden believes that many people have lost faith in the power of prayer because they do not understand that the secret of prayer lies beyond the words. The authors of the Dead Sea Scrolls explained that prayer cannot be explained in the written word. It is the feeling behind the prayer that opens the door to the powerful universal force we are all a part of.

## Knowing

In most Western religions, we are taught to ask for an outcome that we want, such as peace in the world. But according to Braden in *The Isaiah Effect*, the act of asking acknowledges the lack of what we want and therefore actually reinforces the state of non-peace.

Translations of Aramaic manuscripts show that the idea of asking and receiving is actually a mistranslation. According to Braden, the original intent of prayer was to *know* that what we have asked for already exists. It is just a matter of attracting it to ourselves.

Jesus fully understood this spiritual principle. Before every miracle, he thanked God in advance for it. It never would have crossed his mind that what he had asked for would not happen. Many believe that Jesus' entire purpose was to show that everyone has the same power as he did. It is just a matter of having enough faith to know that what we are asking for, we have already received.

## Gratitude

Another element that is often missing is gratitude. A Native American friend of Braden's explained that every prayer must begin with a feeling of authentic gratitude for what is. Once we realize that every situation is perfect and we show gratitude for what we currently have, then we will be able to choose something new.

Braden wrote that in conventional prayer we ask for intervention from a higher power like God or Jesus to change the situation for us. Instead we should acknowledge that we have been given the power to change our world and feel deep gratitude for this ability. Dyer wrote in *The Power of Intention* that the Universal Source that surrounds us and is within us responds to appreciation and gratitude like a magnet.

338

## Non-Judgment

Another important element that has been left out of our current understanding of prayer is non-judgment. We should witness events around us without attaching a right or wrong value to them. Although it is difficult, it is important to see every situation as perfect even if on a human level, something seems like a tragedy. Ancient and native peoples prayed without conditions or judgment, and they had great faith in the goodness of God and the universe.

## Faith

Jesus said, "Faith of a mustard seed moves mountains." If we really think about that statement, it is rather extraordinary. It means we do not need the faith that Jesus had; we only need a fraction of his faith to make changes in our world.

For the ancient and indigenous cultures, faith meant the acceptance of their own inner power. They understood that prayer was about new possibilities, and they trusted that the right thing would happen.

Many people feel helpless in the face of what appear to be huge obstacles, such as poverty, natural disasters, war, and terrorism. But according to Braden in *The Isaiah Effect*, our ancient ancestors left us a form of active prayer that unites the mind, body, and spirit and allows us to direct non-physical forces around and within us. Through our own will and conscious intent we have been given the power to move mountains.

## The Secret

In December of 2006 a friend gave me a copy of a book written by author Rhonda Byrne. I learned that she had experienced great loss in her life, as I had, and she felt as though her whole world was falling apart. And also like me, she had received a book that changed her view of the world, and suddenly her worst tragedies became the

339

catalyst for her life purpose. She wrote a book and produced a movie called *The Secret,* which combines the teachings of the world's most prominent leaders, philosophers, inventors, theologians, and scientists who all understood the power of our thoughts. As you read earlier in this chapter, the idea that human beings possess innate power, has been hidden and suppressed throughout history. But Byrne was able to find and interview people alive today who understand and practice the secret.

I was thrilled that someone had finally made a movie that taught the general public about the power of thought. I bought several DVDs and gave them to everyone I know. In February of 2007, I was even more ecstatic when I learned that *The Secret* was going to be featured on Oprah. I knew that if anyone could spread this all-important idea, it would be Oprah. Sure enough, the response to her show was huge. I couldn't believe when I heard morning DJs talking about *The Secret* and the law of attraction.

The following is a list of some of my favorite ideas and teachings from *The Secret*:

> All people work with one universal power.
> Every thought has a frequency and the thoughts we are sending out are magnetic energy signals.
> Whatever we are feeling is a reflection of what is in the process of manifesting.
> The universe will re-arrange itself based on our thoughts, feelings, and desires to bring us what we want.
> *How* it will happen is the domain of the universe.
> Visualization is how we rehearse our future.
> A positive thought has far more power than a negative thought.
> It is important to decide what we want, believe we can have it, believe we deserve it, and know that it is possible.

340

➢ We are here to create the world around us and we must allow others to see the world the way they want to see it.

➢ There is more than enough love, joy, and wealth to go around.

➢ When we receive our guidance from within more often than from outside sources, we have mastered our lives.

➢ The next frontier is not space but our minds.

## Beyond The Secret

I have had many life experiences that have led me to understand that the law of attraction is only a part of a complete spiritual outlook. Some things that are not emphasized in *The Secret,* which I believe have a significant impact on our ability to manifest our desires are: meditation, karma, surrender, and intuition.

As mentioned previously, in March of 2007 I went to see Siva Baba—an Indian master who is best known for his mentorship of Wayne Dyer. He gave Dyer the ancient teachings of the master Patangeli and his *japa* meditation, which will be discussed in the next chapter. During his seminar called "Beyond The Secret," Siva Baba explained that human beings do not always have the power to attract what they want because of past life karma. In order to move past any negative karma, it is important to learn to make contact with the divine through inner stillness and meditation.

In November of 2006 I met a talented medium named Betty. During a reading she drew a diagram given to her by those in Spirit regarding my ability to manifest my desires. On the left side of the diagram was a box labeled "Desire." The middle box said "Be still." The box on the right said "Allowing." Spirit said that I was getting an A+ in letting the universe know my desires. But I was not able to move my desires to the "Allowing" box because I was skipping the middle box—"Be still." Spirit told Betty that

I was unable to "hear" answers that were coming to me because I wasn't still enough to receive the communication.

It is also necessary to differentiate between the desires and goals of our egos and the desires of our souls. My ego may want to be wealthy, drive an expensive car, and live in a large home, but if my soul has not chosen these experiences, all the visualization in the world will not bring them into form.

Once we have made our desires clear it is time to surrender and release them to the universe. In her book *Quantum Success,* Sandra Anne Taylor explained that the needier we are about our goals, the more we will push them away. Taylor wrote that desperation is very low energy and should be avoided as much as possible. The best approach is calm but continuous action.

Our angels and guides are always gently nudging us toward our true life purpose. I have found that when I make a decision that isn't in my highest interest, I experience a great deal of stress about it.

Once our intuition lets us know what is right for us, then we simply have to visualize it, meditate on it, feel as if we have it, have faith that it is already so, and then surrender it to the universe. Through our positive intentions, we truly do have the power to live the life we want. According to Bob Proctor in *The Secret*, life should be phenomenal, and it will be when we discover the power of our thoughts.

## Conscious Change

A renowned lecturer and expert on mental processes, Dr. David Hawkins has studied the power of human thought for more than thirty years. Through precise kinesiological testing, Hawkins has been able to measure energy levels and found that a large majority of humans currently calibrate at a very low level.

Hawkins reported in his book *The Eye of the I* that a single person who vibrates on a higher energy level by practicing optimism and non-judgment can counterbalance the negativity of 90,000 lower-energy individuals.

A person who resonates on a level of pure love and reverence for all life can counterbalance the negativity of 750,000 people.

One individual who focuses only on joy and infinite peace can counterbalance the lower-level energy of 10 million people. Hawkins said that there are approximately 22 such high-level masters alive today.

One single avatar such as Jesus, Krishna, or Buddha counterbalances the negativity of the entire population on the earth. According to Hawkins, the human population would self-destruct if it were not for the balancing effects of these high-level individuals who operate completely outside the human ego.

Zukav wrote in *The Seat of the Soul* that many human beings are now beginning to evolve into whole and conscious individuals. We are becoming aware of our true nature as beings of light, and we are reawakening to the idea that we can shape the energy that exists within all things by focusing on the outcome that we desire.

Ancient prophecies and modern science point to this moment in history as an unparalleled opportunity to transcend all suffering by remembering the divine force that resides within each of us. Through conscious intent, we will choose our destiny.

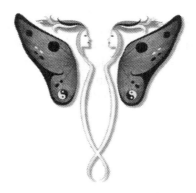

## Chapter Twenty-One:
## Science and Spirituality Meet

Cathy e-mailed Tom on October 15, 2002: "It is fascinating to me that science fiction is now becoming reality. What is even more interesting is that our spirituality is coming closer and closer to our scientific theories. Eventually they will merge and become one."

Yogananda wrote in *The Second Coming of Christ* that scientists and the majority of the world have believed for centuries that the processes of nature are the mechanical workings of blind forces. But Yogananda pointed out that we only have to observe the harmony in nature, the continual change of seasons, the mathematical precision of planetary order, and the miracle of life itself to see a powerful universal intelligence that permeates everything. Yogananda said that only an obstinate rationalist would ascribe to chance the miraculous symmetry and order seen in all forms of life.

Unfortunately, some scientists, like many in the clergy, have locked themselves in a conservative prison. If data is presented that goes against established beliefs, the information is swept under the rug or blocked from being published.

Co-creators of the movie *What the Bleep Do We Know!?* William Arntz, Betsy Chasse, and Mark Vincente wrote in their book of the same name that elements in our society are fiercely opposing new scientific information that proves that science and spirituality are coming together. Established science, *and the religious orthodoxy*, (emphasis mine) have become deeply entrenched and are completely opposed to change. Ironically, many scientists, who are supposed to see the world objectively, have been afraid to let new ideas emerge. The two groups that are supposedly searching for the truth have shut down and have refused to continue an honest search for answers.

## Looking Back

In October of 1987, Jeremy W. Hayward, Ph.D., and Francisco J. Varela, Ph.D., met with a group of scientists and the Dalai Lama in Tibet to discuss the converging relationship between science and spirituality. The conference's purpose was to specifically talk about the similarities between Western science and Eastern philosophies, especially Buddhism. Hayward and Varela published the transcript of the proceedings in a book called *Gentile Bridges*.

Hayward opened the conference with a look back at the history of scientific discovery. According to Hayward, people had an extremely negative view of the world between the fourth and tenth centuries, known as the Dark Ages. The Christian point of view at that time was that the world was a terrible place, and people were told to spend their lives reaching for another, better place called Heaven.

The Middle Ages began with the discovery of ancient Greek texts, particularly those written by Aristotle, who taught that nature was its own reality with its own predictable modes of functioning that could be learned through study and observation. A duality was formed between the heavenly realm, known only through faith and

346

written scriptures, and the earthly realm, known through the five senses and rational thought.

In the thirteenth century, St. Thomas Aquinas was able to bring together the Christian religious viewpoint and the ideas within the Greek writings that had captivated the Middle Ages. Aquinas declared that the earth was the center of the universe. He believed that there were nine spheres surrounding the earth. The outermost and tenth sphere was the place where God resided. The view at that time was that all knowledge came from previously written texts given to humanity by God. Human experience and observation were not allowed.

In the sixteenth century, Galileo argued that one should actually observe how things are in order to decide which writings were correct. One of Galileo's discoveries was that all objects fall at the same rate of speed. This opposed Aristotle's view that heavier things would fall faster because they were moving toward the earth, which was at the center of the universe.

The prevailing view at that time was that all things were stationary and that the cosmos was not in motion. Psalm 93 states, "The earth is set firmly in place and cannot be moved." Galileo had the audacity to suggest that the earth did move. Not only did the earth move, but it also revolved around the sun, not the other way around. He was suggesting that the earth was not the center of the universe, as the Church had been teaching. Galileo was captured during the Inquisition and threatened with death if he did not recant his views. (The Catholic Church only recently pardoned Galileo in 1992.)

In 1642 Galileo died and Sir Isaac Newton was born. Newton is the person most associated with our current scientific worldview. Newton saw the world as a giant machine. There was very little place for God or the soul in Newtonian science. The planets moved automatically, without any intelligent intervention.

According to Lynne McTaggart in *The Field*, Newton described a material world in which particles of matter followed the law of motion through space and time. I believe that many of our religions followed suit, no longer allowing spirituality to be part of the equation. Like science, religion became about laws, rules, and rituals. Even our bodies were seen as well-oiled machines.

McTaggart said that these beliefs basically took the heart and soul out of the universe. And things only got worse with Charles Darwin's theory of evolution. Life was seen as random and purposeless, and only the strong survived. Human beings were nothing more than an evolutionary accident. McTaggart called it "genetic terrorism." To Darwin, life was not about cooperation or interdependence but about winning. People were forced to choose between religion and science.

Clearly these ideas are counter to any higher spiritual teachings. We now have evidence that those who appear the most weak in society, with physical or mental disabilities, are often the most highly advanced souls among us.

According to Hayward in *Gentile Bridges*, by the end of the nineteenth century, this mechanical system of science became the dominant Western view. Great debates ensued between Christianity—in which God was the creator—and the so-called scientific viewpoint, which had diminished the role of God. Newtonian physics had shown that the planets moved around by themselves automatically, and Darwin said that organisms, including human beings, evolved mechanically. In this view, all scientific processes were independent of any human observation in a world that exists separately from humanity. Free will was thrown out, and everything was believed to be predetermined.

Hayward said in *Gentile Bridges* that this very simplistic model of science has still prevailed within the mainstream public as well as with many scientists who are not allowing themselves any deeper reflection.

## Moving Forward

According to Russell Targ in his book *Limitless Mind*, ancient Eastern philosophies say that our consciousness has always existed. This idea is finding acceptance in an unlikely place: Western science.

In *Tomorrow's God*, Neale Donald Walsch learned that the universe is a living system. Everything is interdependent, like a giant matrix; waves of vibrating energy are creating our physical reality. Human consciousness is eternally intertwined with this life-force energy.

In his book, *The Self-Aware Universe*, physicist Amit Goswani wrote that consciousness, not matter, is the foundation of all life. Yogananda said in *The Second Coming of Christ* that modern science is now proving that the universe is more of a giant thought than a giant machine, as previously believed.

God told Walsch in *The New Revelations* that science and spirituality are coming together. Soon it will become known that they were always the same thing, only each was seen from different a perspective.

In *The Field*, McTaggart wrote that the world is on the brink of a scientific revolution as bold and profound as Einstein's discovery of relativity. Science has begun to develop new ideas that challenge everything we believe and is now proving what spirituality has been saying all along—human beings are much more extraordinary than we thought.

## The New Science

Cathy wrote to Tom, "I think that if more people were educated in the physics of what actually makes the universe work, there would be an amazing transformation in the way that human beings view life."

In his book *The Dancing Wu Li Masters*, Gary Zukav described his participation in a scientific conference. Zukav had never had any connection to the scientific community before so he was surprised that their conversations sounded more like theological discussions than scientific inquiry. He was amazed to learn that physics was not tedious, as he had imagined, but quite profound and multifaceted. Zukav's book *The Dancing Wu Li Masters* was based on the Chinese word for physics—*wu li*, meaning the study of "patterns of organic energy," or the study of "universal order." Zukav said that the founders of Western science would not have comprehended or appreciated this definition of physics, but everything in modern science is now pointing to this meaning.

Hayward wrote in *Gentile Bridges* that by the early 1900s the Newtonian viewpoint began to break down. Einstein's theory of relativity and physicist Max Planck's idea that everything in the universe is made up of tiny packets of light called *quanta* radically changed the traditional scientific view of the world as a mechanical machine.

Physicists Niels Bohr, Werner Heisenburg, and Albert Einstein, in the 1920s, established the principles of what is now called quantum physics or quantum mechanics. Nothing in science was certain anymore. Researchers found that on a microscopic level, an atom might suddenly transmit from one energy state to another.

Scientists were baffled as they examined what they thought was a subatomic particle and found out that it showed up as either a particle or a wave and only possible outcomes could be predicted. Most astounding of all, the new physics proved that at the subatomic level, there is no such thing as solid matter.

According to Dr. Wayne Dyer in his book *The Power of Intention*, scientists have been able to work backward from creation, using supercomputers, to look at molecules, atoms, electrons, and subatomic particles. When scientists put subatomic quantum particles into a particle accelerator searching for the source of life, they learned that the source is pure energy, vibrating so fast that it defies measurement. Dyer said that the discovery of this energy source at the core of our being further proves the unity theories taught by spiritual masters throughout the ages.

*The New Physics and Cosmology: Dialogues with the Dalai Lama*, edited by Arthur Zajonc, presents another conference held in Tibet during the 1990s between Western scientists and the Dalai Lama. Scientists from the world's most prestigious institutions attended the conference, including The Princeton Institute for Advanced Study, Harvard University, Stanford University, and Cambridge University. The participants came to the conclusion that new developments in physics have called into question the basis for all scientific disciplines.

According to McTaggart, in *The Field*, scientists have found that empty space does not really exist. In what appears to be a void between objects is a hive of subatomic activity. According to the uncertainty principle developed by Werner Heisenburg, one of the chief architects of quantum theory, no particle ever stays completely at rest but is continually moving due to this field of energy. What we have believed to be a stable, mechanical universe is actually a seething mass of subatomic particles in constant motion.

According to Zukav in *The Dancing Wu Li Masters*, science has traditionally been anchored in the idea that there is an absolute truth out there somewhere, completely independent of human existence. But with the new physics, scientists are being forced to acknowledge that there is no separate reality outside the consciousness of humanity.

In her book *The Quantum Self*, Danah Zohar wrote that the fundamental theory in quantum mechanics is the principle of complementarity. Whether a quantum entity manifests as a wave or a particle, one always complements

351

the other. The whole picture emerges from the unity of both. Zohar wrote that there is a very ethereal quality to this new science. Zohar likened the wave and the particle to the right and left hemispheres of the brain—each supplies information that the other side lacks. According to Zohar, the basics of modern physics is parallel to the idea of male and female, yin and yang, and the unity of opposites. To understand a quantum entity as both a wave and a particle, or "wave packet," is what Zohar calls the quantum mystery.

### Spiritual Unity Theory Proven

In 1964, physicist John Bell mathematically proved the spiritual principle that all things are interconnected. Bell repeatedly sent out two quanta of light in opposite directions. Each time the particles maintained their connection with each other. The distance between the two particles did not change their ability to communicate.

Einstein was not thrilled about this new discovery called non-locality, which he called "spooky action at a distance." He was baffled by the idea that two separate entities could communicate with each other across large distances, even though no exchange of energy had taken place. But Bell's theorem has been proven over and over again in the lab and has shown that all things are intimately linked on a level beyond time and space. Many physicists believe that Bell's theorem is the most profound scientific discovery ever made.

Scientists have even begrudgingly admitted that Bell's theory also sheds light on telepathy and other psychic phenomena. Interestingly, identical twins have been used often in non-locality and telepathy experiments. According to Guy Lyon Playfair in *Twin Telepathy*, studies have shown that because twins have such a strong emotional bond, they have a remarkable ability to communicate with each other and often experience the same emotions and physical sensations even though they are separated.

Playfair wrote that this phenomenon can only be explained by quantum physics. Modern science has shown that all people have the ability to communicate telepathically. It is a skill that simply needs to be developed.

David Bohm, professor of physics at the University of London, wrote in his textbook *The Undivided Universe* that at the most basic level, there is an unbroken wholeness that he calls *that-which-is*.

Bohm explained that like a hologram, each region of space and time contains information about every other point in space and time. He believes that there is a collective consciousness that transcends all boundaries.

According to Zukav in *The Dancing Wu Li Masters*, enlightenment means casting off the veils of ignorance so that one may perceive the unity of all things. Zukav said that to the unenlightened, the world seems like a group of many separate parts. But spiritual traditions throughout the world and modern science have shown that individual parts are merely manifestations of the whole. Quantum physics has proven what once was relegated to mystics and the occult.

### Role of the Observer

The experimenter in classic physics has always been seen as a separate entity, a silent observer watching a universe that was operating on its own regardless of whether it was being observed or not. But in quantum physics, scientists made a startling discovery. They found that unobserved electrons behaved as waves. As soon as they were subject to observation, they "collapsed" into particles and could be physically located.

These experiments tell us that we cannot observe something without altering it. The observer and the observed are interrelated. These astonishing findings have earth-shattering consequences on how we view our world. According to Dyer in *The Power of Intention*, when we look at this discovery on a much larger scale, we can see how our attention to something alters it and therefore affects our reality.

Mountains of data and scientific evidence have forced physicists to sound more like mystics than scientists. Quantum physics has given human consciousness a much more central role in the universe than anyone could have imagined. These findings caused Einstein to say, "The more I study physics, the more I am drawn to metaphysics."

## Remote Viewing

Braden wrote in *The Isaiah Effect* that the word prophet, or the more modern word psychic, conjures up visions of men draped in hooded robes or women wearing turbans on their heads. However, Braden says that the science of prophecy has a new updated name—remote viewing. A remote viewer can, in a relaxed state, receive impressions of things occurring in other places and even other time frames. According to Braden, remote viewers are rigorously trained to accept and record these impressions without bias.

Jean Houston wrote in her forward for Russell Targ's *Limitless Mind* that remote viewing is based on cutting-edge physics and is done by accessing a giant matrix made of higher light vibrations that hold all information and knowledge. Psychic phenomenon is simply a by-product of this all-encompassing force field.

*Limitless Mind* presents three decades of research on remote viewing. Targ was one of the founders of the Stanford Research Institute in California. He wrote that despite repeated corroboration of our natural psychic abilities, mainstream science has not accepted it as real.

Targ said that offering scientific opinion contrary to the prevailing paradigm has put him and his colleagues in a similar position to scientists such as Galileo who were persecuted heavily for going against the accepted ideas of his time.

According to Targ, there is a skeptical element within the scientific community that is working to "save" science from frauds and charlatans. But Targ believes it is just as serious an error to ignore real but unexpected data as it is to accept false data.

A 2001 Gallup poll showed that more than half the U.S. population has had psychic experiences. But these experiences are strongly repressed so many of them are never revealed.

As I was preparing to write this chapter, I heard remote viewer and retired U.S. Army intelligence officer Major Ed Dames on a radio program talking about his long history of "psychic spying" for the United States military.

Shortly after I heard the radio broadcast, I picked up a March 2006 *Reader's Digest* and was amazed when I opened it to an article entitled "The Most Secret Agent." I have often found that *Reader's Digest* prints cutting-edge information that other mainstream sources are not willing to report.

The article was about Paul Smith, an Army intelligence officer working with Ed Dames as a remote viewer on the government's super-secret Star Gate program.

Smith began one of his remote viewing sessions by relaxing his mind into a meditative state. He began to get impressions of a tall gray structure with angular projections. He heard a clanging sound and realized that what he perceived was an American destroyer warship. Suddenly, he heard a loud noise and saw a glare and a metal cylinder. The vessel shook, and Smith saw smoke and metal debris and heard frantic voices.

After about an hour, Dames seemed disappointed and told Smith they would try again the next day. Smith figured that whatever they were looking for, the vessel he had seen wasn't it. But Monday morning Smith got an excited phone call from one of his co-workers about a story on the front page of the paper.

Smith's vision had been amazingly precise. An American frigate, the U.S.S. Stark, had been hit by two Iraqi missiles while patrolling the Persian Gulf.

According to Targ, remote viewing is not a spiritual path but the ability to awaken our consciousness to a higher level. He believes that remote viewing shows us beyond any doubt that our minds are limitless and that they function beyond time and space.

## The Power of the Gap

According to Braden in *The Isaiah Effect*, the ancient Essenes wrote in the Gospel of Peace that it is between our breaths that all mysteries of creation are hidden.

Scientists now believe that everything is made up of short bursts of vibrating light. Braden said that it is in the moment between the pulses that we can take a quantum leap to another outcome.

Yogananda taught a special chanting technique to his Self-Realization Fellowship students that prolongs the gaps between breaths and between heartbeats. I found the meditation to be amazingly refreshing. After several minutes, long pauses occur between my breaths, and my heart rate is almost imperceptible. When the mediation is over, I feel as though I have just had a massage and a deep, relaxing sleep. This form of "following the breath" is also taught in Deepak Chopra's book, *The Spontaneous Fulfillment of Desire* in Chapter Seven, "Meditation and Mantras."

Wayne Dyer teaches an ancient form of mediation described in his book *Getting in the Gap*, where one focuses on the gaps between thoughts. Dyer wrote that focusing on the gap for even a moment will reinvigorate the soul because the silence between words and thoughts is where God resides. Dyer says that silence is something that can never be divided and is where all creation begins.

Scientists have discovered the Zero Point Field, a mass of energy that connects all things like a giant web. Human beings are made of the same essence, so focusing on this powerful energy source is highly beneficial.

Dyer learned of a special technique called *japa* meditation in which the sound "ah" is chanted along with the visualization of being in the gap. According to Dyer the sound "ah" is the name of God. By chanting this mantra we are connected to God at the highest level of consciousness.

I noticed an interesting phenomenon while doing japa meditation. While I was chanting the "ah" sound it seemed as though my voice was not the only one making the sound. It wasn't exactly an echo but it seemed as though the sound was reverberating from somewhere else and I was chanting along with it.

Dyer wrote that the gap is a place where miracles occur, a place where the higher human dimensions of creativity, insight, and intuition are activated. Dyer calls this "making conscious contact with God." By meditating on the gap between our thoughts, we are joining forces with our own internal energy source and tapping into the infinite abundance of the universe.

## Effects of Consciousness

According to Braden, during the last quarter of the twentieth century and into the twenty-first century, scientists have documented unprecedented catastrophic events that have exceeded all previous measurements.

In December of 1997, astronomers detected an explosion at the edge of the universe that was second only to the primordial Big Bang. Cal Institute of Technology documented the blast as lasting two seconds with a force equal to the energy force of the entire known universe.

In June of 1998, scientists witnessed two comets slamming into the sun, an event that had never been seen before. According to Braden, studies released in 1998 showed that for the first time, the temperature in the northern hemisphere climbed higher than in any other time in the past 600 years. Scientists were alarmed by the discovery that errors in satellite data had masked the signs of the rising temperatures.

Braden said that many researchers are baffled by the recent geophysical changes because they have no frame of reference in Western science to explain them. Many scientists look at these events as their Newtonian training has taught them, as random, mysterious, unrelated events.

But for ancient traditional cultures such as the Tibetans, Native Americans, and the Essenes, there is a frame of reference in which these events make sense. These cultures have always taught that our bodies are made up of the same materials of the earth. Ancient teachings, along with modern science, show that catastrophic events are mirroring our collective negative beliefs. According to Braden, destructive weather patterns reflect the chaotic consciousness of the world.

What most people do not understand is that even small changes in consciousness can lead to large changes in later outcomes, hence the saying: "If a butterfly flaps its wings over the Pacific Ocean, it can cause a hurricane in the Atlantic."

According to Thom Hartmann in *The Prophet's Way*, our world is incredibly complex. Ancient spiritual teachings and now science show that changing our course of action in often very small ways, can change the course of our entire future.

The Essenes understood that imbalances imposed upon the earth would be mirrored in our bodies, and vice versa. According to Braden, conditions such as cancer and other diseases are breakdowns in our immune system and are due to our malfunctioning collective consciousness.

An interesting example of the effect of consciousness on our environment is a book by Dr. Masaru Emoto, translated by David A. Thayne, called *The Hidden Messages in Water*. Emoto conducted remarkable experiments that showed the effects of positive and negative thoughts on water. He marked water bottles with signs, some saying positive things such as "love" or "thank you." Others were negative such as "I will kill you," or "hate." The water with positive messages formed beautiful complex snowflake-like crystals. The water with negative messages became malformed and ugly. Emoto's experiments show how water is deeply connected to human consciousness. Because the earth and human bodies are made up of seventy percent water, Emoto believes that we can heal our planet by consciously sending out thoughts of love and peace.

This was shown in an astounding way when a one-hour prayer and meditation service was held at the Fujiwara Dam in Gumma, Japan. Before the service, samples of the water were dark and without any form. After the prayer service the molecular structure of the water became clear, bright, and looked like a hexagonal crystal. The water was visibly more beautiful and even the pollution levels decreased significantly.

## Prophecies and Possibilities

When I read *The Isaiah Effect*, I felt déjà vu when Gregg Braden described how he felt listening to a radio program with a well-respected author talking about all the converging disasters that humanity has created. He felt great frustration, as I did, knowing that this is not the way it has to be.

### Prophecies

In *The Isaiah Effect*, Braden reviewed many of the ancient prophecies, including those of Isaiah, Daniel, Matthew, John, the Book of Revelation, the Hopi Indians and other native tribes, the Bible Code, Nostradamus, and Edgar Cayce. At first glance, these prophecies appear to contradict themselves. Each predicts a time period of horrendous destruction, loss of life, natural disasters, government breakdowns, wars, and religious conflicts, followed abruptly by visions of great renewal, hope, and joy. Modern science has now proven that these predictions are not actually contradictions but choices that humanity will have to make.

## Possibilities

According to Braden, twentieth-century physics and ancient prophecies indicate that our future actually unfolds in possibilities.

In their book *What the Bleep Do We Know!?* Artnz, Chasse, and Vincente quoted physicist Hugh Everett, who explained that when a quantum measurement is performed, every possible outcome is actualized and the universe splits into as many versions of itself as needed to accommodate all possible measurements.

This is similar to the mystical notion of numerous parallel universes in which all quantum possibilities play out. Braden said that while this might seem impossible, scientists have been able to use supercomputers to retrace creation back to the Big Bang and have found an interesting coincidence: At the time of creation, 90 percent of the universe disappeared and only 10 percent remains in our current models. Studies have shown that human beings only use 10% of the capacity of their minds, while 90 percent lies dormant.

According to Braden, many researchers now believe that after creation, the universe was expanding so rapidly that its vibration could no longer remain within the laws of our three-dimensional world. The lost 90 percent of the Universe was vibrating at such a speed that they moved into a higher state of existence. Braden believes that it is within this realm where parallel universes and quantum theory exist.

Braden explained that within the world of possibilities something has to trigger a certain outcome. By placing our attention on something, we start a chain reaction that will bring into existence that which we are focusing on.

Prophets of the Dead Sea Scrolls suggested that to change a prophecy in the future, we must change our actions in the present moment. It is this concept of selecting outcomes, given by the ancient prophets and modern science that will allow us to redirect the catastrophes that are currently developing.

Quantum physics can now explain the multiple prophecies, both old and new, that predict war, death, and destruction followed immediately by a time of peace and great renewal. It is clear that both events will not happen. Only one will happen, depending on humanity's collective choices.

## Crossroads

We are at a crossroads at which science, philosophy, and spirituality are melting into one, and at the center is human consciousness. The language of Western scientists and Eastern philosophers are beginning to sound very similar. In *The Isaiah Effect*, Braden wrote that science has now given us the concepts of time waves, particles, quantum outcomes, and choice points, which describe exactly how prophecy and psychic prediction work. It is now possible for us to determine our future.

Unfortunately, in the West we have been taught that science and religion are opposite of each other. In his book *Original Blessing*, Matthew Fox wrote that it is time for a truce in the West in which common exploration for knowledge and understanding by both spiritual seekers and scientists is encouraged. Both science and spirituality offer wisdom that, when combined, is very powerful.

In the East science and spirituality is intertwined. Yogananda wrote in *The Second Coming of Christ* that to doubt and to question is what keeps religion free of dogma and superstition. In Hinduism and Buddhism and other Eastern philosophies, religion is treated like a science because it is important that religious doctrine be subjected to the test of experience.

Zukav wrote in *The Dancing Wu Li Masters* that we have given traditional science enormous power, and I add that we have given traditional religion vast power as well. Both have been telling us to believe in something that is impossible. Each has taught that there is nothing more to learn, and each sees the world as a separate mechanical entity, devoid of life.

He says that we have, for centuries, relinquished our part in the universe. We took on mindless living and allowed the scientists to do all the wondering about creation, truth, and death. And I believe we have allowed our religions to tell us about the divine instead of experiencing it.

Braden wrote in *The Isaiah Effect* that the melting ice caps, rising sea levels, increasing earthquakes, and other natural disasters, along with escalating war and violence are all signs that we are in the beginning stages of the destruction prophecies. But Braden says we still have time to make another choice. The sooner we recognize our relationship with the earth and the important role we play in saving it, the sooner we can, as individuals and collectively, choose the prophecy of healing, renewal, and peace.

Daya Mata, longtime assistant and successor to Yogananda, described on the Self-Realization Web site (www.yogananda-srf.org) her journey to visit the great Mahavatar Babaji in the Himalaya Mountains, more than thirty years ago.

While deep in mediation one night, she had a terrifying vision. She saw that the world was going to face a very difficult time, a period of great turmoil and unrest. She saw a huge black cloud descending on the universe. But suddenly she saw an immense, loving white light pushing back the waves of darkness.

She was shown that the dark cloud would be pushed away by the spirit of God, manifested through vast numbers of individuals who would remember their true

362

spiritual natures. She saw that, although our world would experience strife due to our spiritual ignorance, we would subsequently become part of a wave of light moving across the Earth, cleansing everything in its path.

Mata said that this would take place because each individual, and humanity as a whole, will consciously choose a higher spiritual path. We are about to witness a quantum leap in human evolution.

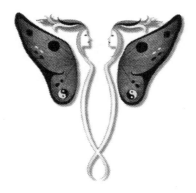

## Chapter Twenty-Two:
## The Ying and Yang of Politics

In an e-mail dated September 24, 2002, Cathy wrote to Tom, "The things I have seen with the Border Patrol and the things I have seen in South America have disturbed me. When I saw homeless children on the streets of San Diego it made me realize that we are at a critical turning point in the world. We either need to start addressing these problems or eventually we will completely destroy our society. I know this sounds like a bunch of liberal BS, as my sister would say, but it has come from my experiences and the things I have read and not just what other people have told me. Besides, I don't think the issues facing our world today are even political issues anymore...Okay, I will get off my soap box now."

Before Cathy died, she and I had been exchanging angry e-mails about politics, one of our constant sources of conflict. After she e-mailed me, she would then e-mail her friend Tom to complain about how stubborn and wrong I was.

She had been pushing me to read a book called *Healing the Soul of America* by Marianne Williamson. But I flat-out refused to read anything she recommended, especially if it had to do with politics. After she died I felt as though she was still pushing me to read the book. I knew that the issues Cathy and I fought about most of our lives were relevant to the struggles taking place in the world. Some of the clearest messages I received from Cathy and others were in regard to political issues. As I thought about our opposing views, I kept envisioning the yin-and-yang symbol.

Something kept bringing me back to the idea of the unity of opposites. The message she gave me on the Capitol lawn in May of 2003 reverberated in my head: "There is no bigger fallacy than to believe that one way is right and another way is wrong."

Finally I gave in and opened *Healing the Soul of America* to the first page of the introduction. I laughed when I read the first paragraph, which began with a description of the principle of yin and yang. According to Williamson, the Chinese believe that there are opposing forces in the universe, and when they are brought together, they create a balance or unified whole that is necessary for harmony in the world. The yin-and-yang manifest as male and female, night and day, darkness and light, heart and head, and inner and outer. According to Williamson, the yin and yang come from a universal force that the Chinese call Tao, a space where infinite possibilities exit. Like the body and soul, our spiritual and political evolution is intimately linked.

## Spiritual Politics

In *Conversations with God, Book Two* Neale Donald Walsch had a dialogue with God about politics. When the book was published, many people were angry. They believed that God might give advice about personal relationships, but they had difficulty believing that God would have opinions about political issues. But God explained to Walsch that people have been asking for centuries what has gone wrong and have continually been asking for guidance. Walsch learned that God has no preferences or opinions, but, given the direction the human race has said it wants to go, we are going in the wrong direction. We have said that we want to move toward harmony and peace, but instead we are continually creating more separation and violence.

Walsch wrote in *Tomorrow's God* that one of the most dysfunctional ideas that human beings have ever invented is the idea that politics and spirituality should be separated. One of the first things American children are taught in school is that our forefathers came to this country to escape religious persecution. Religion and government were prohibited from interfering with each other but this was in no way meant to be an impediment for the search for higher truth. While our founders whole-heartedly embraced God, they did not acknowledge any specific religion. Williamson pointed out that unlike religion, spirituality unites us by reminding us of our oneness.

The Pennsylvania Quakers, who had great influence on the earliest versions of the United States Constitution, had very profound spiritual views. They had no ministers or priests, and they believed that God was within each person. The Quakers always espoused looking inward for the "inner light," and they cherished their God-given right of individual freedom.

Williamson wrote that spirituality is not a compartment of our lives but is something that is all-inclusive. It is inconceivable that we can speak of a God who is all-loving and yet not love and respect one another.

She believes that we should follow the lead of people throughout history who have personified a balance of spirituality and political intelligence, like Martin Luther King, Jr., Abraham Lincoln, and Mahatma Gandhi.

Dr. King said that humanity should have tough minds and tender hearts. Williamson wrote that many tough-minded thinkers seem to lack heart and that those who are soft-hearted do not spend time doing much critical thinking regarding political issues. King's concept of a tough mind and kind heart described my sister perfectly. Cathy was feisty and tough and was always reading and thinking about the issues facing the world. Yet she had a huge heart and always felt compassion for others. If we strive to bring both heart and head into politics, we can transcend the angry, low-energy bickering that goes on in political circles today.

## Politics As Usual

Walsch learned that the biggest barrier to our enlightenment is our refusal to see other people's points of view. Anything that doesn't fit into our picture of life is immediately rejected. It takes an enormous amount of maturity to see that all points of view can exist simultaneously without any one of them being wrong.

In the fall of 2004, I learned a lesson about one-sided politics in an unlikely place—a Spanish class. I took an immediate disliking to the professor because she took every opportunity to talk politics, and let's just say her views were the opposite of my own. I am sure that she could tell by the look on my face that I was not a fan of her political discussions. As the 2004 elections approached, it became almost unbearable to be in her class. I knew that I needed to finish the class so that I could complete my long-awaited degree, but I felt so much anger and frustration that I was exhausted all the time.

The day of the election came and I prayed fervently that President Bush would win or there was no way I could not go back to my Spanish class. I was so worked up over it that Cathy literally screamed at me: "Beeeeeeeeetsy, he is going to win!" That day, while driving in my car, I glanced at the clock, it read 4:44 pm. The numbers 444 comprise a universal symbol that reminds us that there are thousands of angels surrounding us.

When I returned to my Spanish class after the election there was an air of defeat and anger in the room. The instructor ranted on and on about what a sad day it was for America because Bush had won. I could barely contain my glee.

But after it was all over, I asked Cathy what the point of the experience was. She conveyed that one-sided politics don't work, regardless of which side one is on. I no longer see myself as being affiliated with one political party and even registered as an independent. I realized that seeing the world from only one point of view is too limited, and I know that neither political party embraces even the most basic spiritual principles. More and more, politics is about separation, not solutions.

Williamson wrote in *Healing the Soul of America* that both major political parties in the United States are steering the discussion away from what truly ails us because they have no spiritual frame of reference that would lead to a higher discussion.

I sat and thought about America's two political parties, pondering their core beliefs and how both had gone off track. The Republican Party is about rugged individualism and entrepreneurship. Conservatives want less government, and they believe in hard work and creativity, all very noble pursuits. But rugged individualism has become an every-man-for-himself mentality. Every person has to pull him-or-herself up by the bootstraps, and if he or she does not, then it is assumed that it is due to pure laziness and incompetence. Compassion has been lost, and power has become the name of the game.

Historically Democrats have believed that government should extend a helping hand to the needy and less fortunate. They represent the common man and worker's rights. But now helping people has become secondary to gaining voters by creating dependency on government. They too have entered the political power-grabbing game.

## Rebellion Needed

Thomas Jefferson wrote to James Madison in 1787 that rebellion is as necessary in the political world as

369

storms are in the physical world. Jefferson wrote that without a taste for rebellion, there is no taste for freedom. Williamson said that we, the citizens of the most powerful nation on earth, have lost our sense of rebellion, and we had better get it back.

Throughout human history, from Jesus to Galileo to the founding fathers of America, great leaders have never embraced the status quo. Williamson believes that to solve our current problems, we must go beyond what exists now and look within ourselves for true spiritual power.

Cathy wrote to Tom, "Many people have started to question the status quo in their lives. 9/11 has helped that along and maybe that was the point of it all, I don't know. We have to continue to change our own lives and eventually others will follow in our footsteps."

## For or Against

Mother Theresa was once asked if she would join a march against the Vietnam War. She said that she would not protest against anything and that she would only come when there was a march for peace. To change the status quo in politics, we should focus on what we want, not what we don't want. In *The Secret* Hale Dwoskin said that instead of being *against* a particular candidate it would more productive to be *for* his opponent.

In *Tomorrow's God*, Walsch wrote that when we eliminate the idea of separateness, political campaigns will also change. There will be no more attack ads or character assassinations. It will no longer be appropriate to vilify one's opponent.

## Bias and Blame

An issue that we must tackle in our society is bias. It is very easy to fall back on our learned biases, but in reality they are nothing more than judgments.

One day, I was working out at my gym, which involves following a circuit of weights and cardio machines.

Starting at different points in the room is encouraged, so I began my workout in the middle of the room. Although I tried to go with the flow, somehow I always found myself going the opposite direction of everyone else (the story of my life). A dark-haired woman and I came to a machine at the same time. I simply went around her to the next machine and continued to work out.

"You're going the wrong way," she told me.

"There is no wrong way," I said, letting my annoyance show. Then I saw the t-shirt she was wearing: "John Kerry for President."

"Oh, of course," I thought, "she would be worrying about what doesn't concern her," and I started giving her dirty looks.

Suddenly I heard my sister say, "I thought you said there is no wrong way."

Well, she had me there. I started to try to justify my actions, but I knew she had caught me.

"Okay, okay," I said sheepishly.

Needless to say, I stopped giving the woman dirty looks and finished my workout. As I got in my car, I laughed. "That wasn't fair; I was framed!" As I drove out of the parking lot, two vehicles drove by with 444 on the license plate. I knew it was just a little reminder for me to remember to let love lead the way.

We all are guilty of bias, and even with the best of intentions, we allow ourselves to fall into the trap of making judgments based on pre-conceived notions without putting much thought into it. Many of my conservative friends roll their eyes any time someone mentions the dire state of the environment, and they immediately call the person an "environmentalist wacko." Or, if someone mentions their desire for peace, many conservatives have a knee-jerk reaction, calling the person a "bleeding-heart liberal," something I called my sister many times.

There is also a bias against conservatives in the spiritual community. When I attended a spiritual seminar, I made the mistake of telling some of the attendees that I was a Republican and that my sister had been a Democrat and that we had always fought about our views. I might as well have said that I was a Martian. I felt shunned and very out of place, as if I had hit on some hidden taboo.

Another issue holding the world back is blame. I have noticed that many people have jumped on the bandwagon in blaming others for what ails the world. Modern science and ancient spiritual teachings have come together to show that all human beings are interconnected at an energetic level. When we point a finger at someone else we are actually placing the blame squarely on ourselves.

It is much easier to find a scapegoat than to face the fact that the problems we are dealing with are due to the collective consciousness of not only those of us who are alive today but many thousands of years' worth of negative emotions and acts of violence.

"All blame is misguided," Cathy told me. She wanted me to understand that blame and peace cannot co-exist simultaneously.

As we saw in previous chapters, the conditions existing on earth today have been predicted for thousands of years. Cathy and I believe that if we really want to bring the world together and help people to see that we are all one, each of us must move beyond our biases, blame, and judgments. When we speak, and act with our higher selves, and allow everyone to come to the table, only then will we have the spiritual renewal that we have been seeking.

## Circles

Although there were some people who did not like *Conversations with God, Book Two* because of its political nature, I was fascinated by it. I even bought the original manuscript in a silent auction held at Walsch's seminar. As I read, I was more and more intrigued by the fact that the concepts being presented seemed to be diametrically opposed in a political sense. He wrote that the role of government should be limited. And he warned that governments should help the weak, not make them weaker. Walsch learned that nothing serves people more than allowing them to govern themselves.

He also learned that help should only be offered to people in the way that they feel they need to be helped. This reminded me of Cathy's work with StandUp For Kids. The organization's mission is to find homeless kids on the street and ask them what kind of help they want and only offer them what they ask for. Cathy said that some kids just wanted a pair of socks and food. Others wanted help getting off the streets, and some wanted to go home. Cathy was thrilled with the idea of empowering kids by allowing them the freedom to decide what they wanted.

Abruptly, Walsch's conversation with God turned from limited government to communism. He wrote that whenever someone talks about the "common good," everyone starts yelling "communism." But God said that communism was a noble and beautiful idea. "From each according to his ability, to each according to his need" was just another way of saying, "I am my brother's keeper."

God explained to Walsch that communism failed because it was robbed of its nobility when it was ruthlessly enforced. Brotherhood is an idea that can only occur voluntarily, through greater spiritual understanding.

According to Thom Hartmann in *The Prophet's Way*, communism broke people's spirits and completely destroyed their work ethic because there was no room for individual pride and freedom. It was the implementation of communism that didn't work.

One day I was out walking during a break from work. I silently asked: "Why do these ideas seem so far apart? It's as if they are on completely opposite ends of the political spectrum."

Very clearly I heard someone say, "You people think everything is linear, when in fact everything is actually circular. If you take a line and put the two opposite ends together, what do you get?"

"A circle," I answered immediately. And as I pictured it in my head, I realized that the two ideas that seemed so far apart would actually be right next to each other at the top of the circle. "Wow," I thought, "that was rather profound."

I had what was called an "a-ha moment." I remembered reading in *Conversations with God* that everything in life is a circle.

"So," I said, "you are talking about the unity of opposites?"

"Yes."

"I get it! If we as a society could take what we think are opposing ideas, analyze them, decide what works and what does not work, and put the two together, we would really have something, right?"

I heard, "Yes, you would."

The conversation ended at that point, and I had to go back to work. I was thrilled by what I had just learned. I had a vision of people from opposing parties getting together. Each side would present what it felt were its best ideas and the other side would listen with complete openness. Then the other side would have its turn. Afterward, there would be a discussion on how the two sides could come together. Many people have told me that this is impossible. But it is only impossible because we do not see each other from a spiritual perspective. We cannot create the society we have always wanted unless we have the courage to change our way of thinking.

Williamson said that the difficulties facing America and the world are not partisan issues. Cathy and I believe that the struggles of our time—such as the crisis in our environment, poverty, oppression, and war—cannot be

374

seen in terms of politics and political parties. These are the world's issues, and we are all citizens of the world.

## Choosing Peace

Cathy wrote to Tom, "I think that those who are peacemakers in the world are in line with the Divine Powers of the universe and therefore have the momentum to succeed."

Gandhi said, "There is no way to peace. Peace is the way." Deepak Chopra wrote in his book *Peace Is the Way* that peace is love in action. And when enough people in the world transform themselves into peacemakers, war will end. There is nothing we have to do. We simply have to *be* the peace we want to see in the world. Gandhi believed that peace must exist in the hearts of people before it can exist in the world.

According to Chopra, the way of peace that Gandhi spoke of isn't based in religion or morality, and it doesn't even require us to renounce our desire for revenge. To truly have peace, we merely need to consciously choose it.

## The War Mentality

My husband printed an e-mail that someone sent him called "Wolves, Sheep, and Sheepdogs," and he insisted that I listen while he read the article because he thought that I might somehow use the information in my book. The excerpt was taken from a book written by Lt. Col Dave Grossman (RET) called *On Killing*. Grossman quoted from a speech that William Bennett gave at the U.S. Naval Academy in 1997. Bennett told the story of a conversation he had with an old Vietnam War veteran and retired colonel. The colonel told Bennett that society is made up of three kinds of people: wolves, sheep, and sheepdogs. The wolves are the evil people in the world that want nothing more than to harm the sheep. The sheep are those who walk around in denial, not wanting to believe there is evil in the world. The sheepdogs are the warriors, soldiers, and police officers who protect the sheep from the wolves. My husband told me that he was one of the sheepdogs that kept the wolves from the sheep.

"Okay, I'll use the information, but not how you think," I told him.

Not long ago I would have agreed with him and the article. I understand the argument for force very well because I used it many times while trying to persuade my sister it was the only way. Even Cathy would have agreed with it earlier in her life.

But now we both see the truth. As we move closer to the light by raising our spiritual consciousness, we will see that we have outgrown the idea that there are evil people in the world.

I have the greatest respect for those who are willing to put their lives on the line for others, but I believe it is time that we realize that spending billions of dollars for military operations that protect against the evil in the world doesn't work. It is time that we see that that the idea of "us vs. them" is an illusion created by our own beliefs. Braden wrote in *The Isaiah Effect* that military force served us in the past but now we have a much more efficient way to bring peace to the world. We simply have to re-focus our thoughts on peace as if we already have it and the results will be astonishing.

While we move out of the old energy of scarcity and competition and into the new age of cooperation, compassion, and unity we will see a change in the occupations of many of our world's warriors.

As billions of dollars are redirected away from weapons and military power, one might wonder what will become of the many noble people who have joined the armed forces to defend others.

It is no coincidence that Cathy and I both have worked in law enforcement. I remembered in Eleanor's astrology reading her statement that we came into this world with an amazing gift. We embodied the energy of soldiers, warriors, and generals and at the same time we had a strong pull toward spirituality and selfless service. Eleanor said that, at its lowest, this warrior energy could be one of rage and violence. But at its highest it is the energy signature of the sacred warrior and social change agent.

As we move into higher consciousness and shift away from the futile acts of war, fighting terrorism, and guarding our borders, soldiers and law enforcement officers can use their incredible warrior spirits to move mankind forward through humanitarian work as Cathy and I have been called upon to do. After all, soldiers and police officers have taken these jobs because they want to protect and serve others and so they are familiar with the role of selfless service.

Chopra wrote that if we want to end war, we have to realize that war has become a habit and that the act of war now comes naturally to us. According to Gregg Braden in *The Isaiah Effect*, quantum physics shows us that the war-like mentality between individuals is causing the same thing to happen on a global scale. If we treat other people rudely and insensitively, or look down on others in lower social positions, or judge and criticize others for the decisions they have made, we are promoting war.

Cathy wrote to Tom, "I have noticed that people are getting worse and worse as far as manners are concerned. People cut you off in their cars without even looking at you. They will be damned if they're going to let you over. This is the mentality that has lead to the majority of the world's problems."

I told Cathy that I envisioned war in our society as a huge mountain and peace as a green valley below. "We can't get to peace from where we are," I complained.

Cathy reminded me, "Faith of a mustard seed moves mountains." I understood her meaning—we can have peace by striving for the highest vision of ourselves and by having faith that we have the power to change our conditions on earth.

## Terrorism

According to Chopra in *Peace Is the Way*, the conflict between terrorism and love is the most critical issue facing the world today. From an earthly perspective, terrorism appears so strong that opposing it with equal force and intolerance seems like the only way to stop it. But Williamson wrote in *Healing the Soul of America* that terrorism is an internal disease that mirrors our collective consciousness.

There is no political or military solution to terrorism. Chopra said that standing up against terrorism is basically a police action. But a police action is only effective when the criminal would rather give up than die. Gary Zukav wrote in *The Seat of the Soul* that a person who is full of hatred is without light and in deep pain. Hating that person in return only brings more pain to him or her, and inevitably the pain comes back to us. Based on the law of attraction, fighting a negative problem with a negative solution actually creates the exact situation that we seek to avoid.

To cure terrorism, we need the most powerful spiritual forces in the universe—love, compassion, and forgiveness. Terrorism would whither and die in a world led by higher consciousness.

## Power

Martin Luther King, Jr., said "We have in our hearts a power more powerful than bullets." But we have for centuries attempted to gain external power rather than the much more effective internal source of power.

Zukav said that external power is about fear. It is represented by outward symbols of control such as boots, guns, and badges. All great masters like Jesus, Krishna, and Buddha have possessed the ultimate internal power

378

and have changed the world without ever hating or
harming anyone.

## Non-Violence

In Eastern philosophy the highest spiritual principal is
called *ahimsa,* a Sanskrit word that literally means to avoid
violence. The ancient Indian master Patanjali said, "When
a person is established in non-violence, those in his
vicinity cease to feel hostility."

Many of us in the West have been taught about the
power of love and non-violence when we learned about
the life of Jesus Christ. Unfortunately, our religions have
lost most of the true wisdom that Jesus brought to the
world. Martin Luther King, Jr., said that Gandhi was the
first person to actually put Jesus' teachings of non-
violence and love into action. Gandhi said that to refrain
from fighting back in the face of an attack requires much
more discipline and courage than lashing out in anger.
Many might scoff at this idea, as I did not long ago. But
the form of love that Gandhi taught is a force more
powerful than the human mind can conceive.

Hartmann wrote in *The Prophet's Way* that forgiveness
is the key. Forgiveness and compassion have farther-
reaching consequences than we can imagine. According to
Dyer in *The Power of Intention,* if we react toward lower
energy with love and compassion, the lower energy will
automatically gravitate toward us and will transform into
higher energy. Dyer once broke up a fight between two
angry young men by walking between them humming
Amazing Grace.

## Freedom

Hartmann wrote in *What Would Jefferson Do?* that
freedom is a method of non-violence. It is clear that the
most peaceful nations are those that are free. I believe that
the idea of countering oppression and tyranny by
spreading freedom is a valid concept. I think it is

disingenuous to say that people in other countries do not really want to be free. I have been bothered by the fact that the Iraqi elections and formation of a constitution has been largely ignored. I asked Cathy about it. "It should not be ignored," she responded.

The issue of the war aside, it is remarkable that Iraq is a free nation for the first time in history. There will always be those who fight these types of changes. Often when we attract something we want into our lives, initially we will also attract the opposite condition, but we should know that the opposition will pass.

The day I saw the Iraqi people holding up ink-stained fingers showing that they had voted, it sent chills all over my body. It was an amazing testament to the human spirit that they were willing to put their lives on the line just to go vote. They wanted to be part of their own destiny at any cost.

## Democracy

According to Williamson, democracy is a force of consciousness, not a political process. It is the force of freedom, love, and the belief in the inherent goodness of humanity. She believes that democracy is profoundly relevant to the evolution of humanity and can create miracles in many places around the world. Some are put off by the word *democracy* because it sounds too political, but it is actually an expression of our divine natural state of true freedom.

Hartmann wrote in *What Would Jefferson Do?* that the idea that people have the right to govern themselves did not begin with America. Prehistoric tribes organized themselves in a democratic fashion and were the model for ancient Athens. Many indigenous tribal cultures around the world today still maintain a democratic form of government. America's founding fathers modeled the U.S. Constitution on ideas that came from the Native American Iroquois confederacy of tribes.

Hartmann explained that democratic societies have no mass poverty and less internal violence and political strife. Democracies are the most efficient at producing wealth and are more stable than non-democracies. Researchers have found that no two democracies have ever gone to war against each other and no democracy has ever sponsored a terrorist act.

According to Hartmann, scientists have found that democracy is the natural state of all mammals and is deeply ingrained in the human spirit.

## A United World

One day I thought about Lena's statement, "How your sister died will become important." Ironically, Cathy was killed on the exact spot where the extension of the border barrier fence between the United States and Mexico is being debated in Congress.

My sister saw the futility of putting up fences and sitting in a vehicle for ten hours a day watching a desolate stretch of land where one impoverished country ends and another prosperous nation begins.

Cathy and I believe that regardless of the numbers of agents stationed along the American borders, the issue will still exist because we are attempting to solve a negative problem with a negative solution. People are screaming more and more loudly about immigration issues, yet I believe there is an answer that would cause these problems to simply fade away.

Walsch wrote in *Conversations with God* that we currently see the world as a collection of separate nations. Any internal problems within a nation are not the rest of the world's problems. If we want peace and prosperity, we must start seeing other people's problems as our own. Walsch learned that it would be in humanity's best interest to create a new world government based on the spiritual idea that "we are all one." This would allow all the people of the world to share in our planet's abundance of resources. It is clear that even the ancient Mayan calendar predicted this shift would begin to happen at this time in history.

Walsch was exhilarated by this idea, but he lamented that the people of the world would probably not agree to it. But then God reminded him that there is a great experiment going on in our world with just this exact scenario called the United States of America.

When America began, it was a loose confederation of states like the nations of the world are now. Initially the individual states protested against coming together, because they feared losing their individual power and identity. But eventually they agreed, and the unity provided even greater security and prosperity for all the states.

The world government could be modeled after the United States, with a congress of nations with two representatives from every nation and an assembly proportioned to the population of each nation. The balance of powers would be built into the world constitution just like the U.S. Constitution, with an executive, legislative, and judicial branch.

For those of you who are choking on your Cheerios while reading this, I ask you to hear it with your higher selves. Feel it in your soul. See the possibilities for creativity and prosperity. Cathy and I believe that as we move into higher consciousness, many solutions will come to us that we could never have imagined, and we should not disregard them out of fear.

"The United States of the World," I said out loud. "Where have I heard that before?" Then I realized that Yogananda had written something similar. I was utterly amazed when I went directly to Yogananda's *Man's Eternal Quest* and opened it to the exact page that I was looking for. I read this quote:

*"When many devotees follow the path to Him, there will arise a United States of the World...As the individual states of America maintain independence and yet are united in common ideals and*

*goals, so if God's Kingdom is to come on earth, the various countries of the world must similarly unite in a bond of harmonious cooperation and brotherhood."*

## Transformation

The call for transformation is not new. In the 1960s, Martin Luther King, Jr., said that the challenge of our time is to rise above narrow individualistic concerns and expand our views to include all of humanity. In the new millennium, this call has reached a feverish pitch.

Cathy and I believe that humanity would benefit greatly by allowing spirituality and politics to come together. Unity is needed at this time in our evolution to create the whole and peaceful world we have been seeking.

What is this magic bullet that would annihilate immigration issues and bring peace to the world? After Cathy died, I found her tattered Border Patrol notepad. She had jotted down her ideas, and it seemed as if she had been writing to someone. Then I realized that she had been writing to me. An excerpt from her notebook gives us the answer:

> *When making decisions, we should always ask the question: "Is this who I really am?" And we should ask, "What would love (Jesus) do now?" Then we should let go and let God. The truth will speak for itself. The right and just cause will always prevail. These concepts are higher and bigger ideas than what liberals or conservatives think. These are bigger concepts than the war on terror. It is always about what will work and what won't work. It is always about remembering who and what we really are and why we are here—to evolve as spiritual beings and to share our love with others.*

## Chapter Twenty-Three:
## A Return to Ancient Wisdom

In the Book of Proverbs, wisdom is portrayed as an independent aspect of God. Wisdom comes to the world in feminine form and attempts to spread her knowledge but laments her inability to communicate with humanity.

"Listen! Wisdom is calling out in the streets and marketplaces, calling loudly at the city gates and wherever people come together.

"'Foolish people! How long will you enjoy making fun of knowledge? Will you never learn? Listen when I reprimand you; I will give you good advice and share my knowledge with you. I have been calling you, inviting you to come but you would not listen.'" (Proverbs 1:20-24).

In *The Prophet's Way*, Thom Hartmann wrote that the loss of wisdom has caused huge suffering on our planet and has set the world up for severe difficulties. The wisdom we need lies within us. We simply need to remember old truths and recreate the ancient wisdom of our ancestors.

### Tribal Cultures

According to Gregg Braden in *The Isaiah Effect*, tribal cultures as far back as the ancient Essenes knew that our relationship with the world goes far beyond the role of passive observer. Braden said that universally, ancient and indigenous cultures saw the connection between our everyday outer world and the world of our inner consciousness.

In *The Prophet's Way*, Hartmann wrote that native cultures understand the basic spiritual principles that make our lives rich and fulfilling. They understand the importance of knowing our life's purpose. They know that living in a strong community is the key to security and prosperity. They understand that being grounded and connected with nature gives human beings a feeling of unity with our souls, our higher selves, and the universe.

According to Hartmann in *The Last Hours of Ancient Sunlight*, older cultures did not face the cycles of crisis that we do because they focused on the inherent goodness of human beings. They emphasized healing rather than punishment. Tribal cultures have remained stable for thousands of years because they have developed economic, cultural, and religious systems that preserve the abundance of the earth's natural resources.

Modern societies might view these cultures as being materially poor. But according to Hartmann, our Western culture is extraordinarily poor in spirit, time, and security, and indigenous cultures have a lot to teach the modern world about true wealth.

Hartmann learned that tribal societies typically spend only a few hours a day working together to insure the necessities of life such as food, shelter, and clothing. The rest of their time is spent in recreational activities and the pursuit of spiritual enlightenment. Most people in our modern culture spend a minimum of forty hours per week working in order to meet the needs of their families.

In evolved societies such as Native American cultures, every member of the community is valued. The elderly and the young live together. Elders are seen as highly valued for their wisdom and experience. Hartmann believes that we have lost the influence of our elders by shuffling them off to nursing homes.

Everyone is taken care of in tribal communities. If someone is sick, the community will care for him or her. If someone is hungry, the community will make sure that person is fed. In native cultures, there is no greater affront to God than eating while another person starves.

Walsch learned in *Conversations with God* that the modern world sees the simplicity of ancient cultures as unsophisticated. But God told Walsh that the mark of a primitive, unsophisticated culture is the belief that simplicity is barbaric and complexity is advanced. Those who are highly evolved know that it is the other way around. Yet our current culture is moving toward more and more complexity.

After Cathy died I found notes she had written to me in her Border Patrol notebook. She wrote, "Simplicity is the key to life. People in tribal communities such as Native Americans have understood this concept for centuries."

## Intentional Communities

In Chapter Eleven, Man-Made Armageddon, I discussed the many calamities that humanity has created in the world. One of the most far-reaching problems is the looming shortage of oil. Most experts agree that we have enough oil to last until the middle of the century. But what many people fail to understand is that long before the oil runs out, the cost of oil will become so high that many of our modern conveniences will be in jeopardy. I don't believe that these predictions are an exaggeration. James Howard Kunstler wrote in *The Long Emergency* that the only intelligent thing to do is to face the problem and prepare for it.

In *Tomorrow's God*, Walsch learned that humanity's greatest weakness is dependency. We now have an opportunity to create a situation in which we are no longer dependent on distant sources of food and energy. When we do this, we will have much greater freedom and a higher quality of life. Cathy wrote in her notepad, "Not only is self-sufficiency good for the environment, its also good for the soul."

According to Hartmann in *The Last Hours of Ancient Sunlight*, for 100,000 years our ancient ancestors lived in stable, sustainable communities. These tribal communities were small and decentralized, with a democratic form of government.

In his book *The Next Evolution*, Jack Reed wrote that we have begun to see a growing trend of self-contained, local communities modeled after ancient and indigenous tribal cultures. The needs of the community will be met by the individuals who live there. Food will be grown and shared by those in the community. New energy sources such as wind and solar will take thousands of people off the economic and energy grid. Reed believes that local currency and barter systems will be used, which will truly make each group self-reliant.

According to Hartmann in *The Last Hours of Ancient Sunlight*, some intentional communities will be organized like small corporations. Everyone in the community will own the land jointly, but each individual family will own its own home on the land. Every family will share a stake in the larger community. If a family leaves, they will sell their home and their "share" back to the community.

Hartmann predicts that some people will be opposed to the idea of intentional communities because they will say that they are similar to the communal living that took place in the 1960s. But Hartmann has visited some existing intentional communities and saw no resemblance to the 1960s version.

One of the main differences is that most intentional communities have a shared purpose or mission such as helping abused children or the elderly. Hartmann said that putting a shared vision into action enhances the cohesiveness of the community.

Kunstler wrote in *The Long Emergency* that the downscaling and localizing of our society is the single most important task facing America and the rest of the world.

According to Hartmann and many others, this model of tribal living is an important part of our spiritual evolution and is key to the preservation of the human race and the planet.

## Connection with Nature

In *The Last Hours of Ancient Sunlight*, Hartmann wrote that our ancestors saw divine intelligence in everything. A Native American friend of Hartmann's told him that people mistakenly believe that Native Americans worship nature. Hartmann's friend explained that native people find ways to celebrate the earth because they see God in nature.

Hartmann wrote that as humans lost touch with the earth, our places of worship went from nature to man-made buildings. He believes that this distancing from nature was the catalyst for the decline of our civilization. This disconnect has become so strong that we have come to see the natural world and those who understood its sacredness as evil or "pagan." Our decision to separate human beings from the rest of creation caused a profound void in our spiritual understanding. We have lost touch with the divine power and beauty of the earth.

I have a very strong connection with nature that has grown increasingly stronger as I become more spiritually evolved. I find that meditation comes easily outside. By looking at the trees and flowers and listening to the birds, I am able to quiet my mind and bring my thoughts into the present moment. I speak to my sister often while outside in a natural environment, and I feel her connection to me is stronger there than anywhere else. I experience a sense of wonder and gratitude for the earth, and I see the divinity in every flower and leaf, as our ancestors did.

Paramahansa Yogananda wrote in *Autobiography of a Yogi* that science has allowed us to utilize the power of nature, and our familiarity with nature has bred contempt and lack of respect for its unseen power. Yogananda warned that humans would be well advised to put ourselves in harmony with the universal laws that govern the universe. According to Yogananda, when humanity is in communion and cooperation with nature, our command over nature's wrath will be effortless.

According to Braden in *The Isaiah Effect*, the Dead Sea Scrolls give us a glimpse into the world of the ancient Essenes. Unlike most orthodox religious traditions, they offer us a holistic and unified view of the relationship between the earth and our bodies. They spoke about a sacred union between our souls and the soul of the earth. They described how the two are intimately intertwined.

According to Braden, the Essenes believed, like many tribal traditions, that as long as we honor the thread that binds our bodies with the earth, the union will continue. When the agreement is dishonored, the union will end, our bodily temples will die, and the forces of our spirit and the spirit of the earth will return to their respective places of origin.

## Children

In March 2006, an interesting thing happened with my angel cards. When I did readings for myself I continually pulled a card that said that my life purpose involved working with children. I had never envisioned working with children before, but even when I had an angel reading with Helle, she also felt that I needed to focus on guiding children.

I was working as a part time dispatcher for the San Diego Unified School District Police Department when I learned that they were going to be hiring Community Service Officers (CSOs) to work with children at inner-city elementary schools. The job is a pseudo-law enforcement position, but mostly it resembles social work, helping troubled kids and their parents. A comment that Tom made about Cathy and me following each other into different occupations crossed my mind. At the end of her life she had worked with troubled kids. I thought that perhaps I would do the same thing.

I mentioned to one of the sergeants that I was thinking about applying for a CSO position. He immediately jumped on the idea and told me that if I could get him my application by the next day, he would personally walk it over to human resources so that I would be included in the next round of interviews being held that week. I decided that his enthusiasm was a sign that I should apply and gave him my application the next day. After a four-month background check, I did accept the position of CSO. I began to see just how badly our children need our attention right now. Many children are hurting, lost, and in need of compassion and guidance. But more important, I saw that children are full of hope and are eager to learn.

I told my sister that I wanted to go to a school where people were open to new ideas, and I hoped against all odds that I would land at a place where people had the same spiritual viewpoint that I did.

I was sent to work in City Heights, a neighborhood known for poverty and gang violence. But in the midst of all the chaos, I found a beacon of light called Central Elementary School. When I met Cindy, the vice principal, and Staci, the principal, I knew that I had found kindred spirits who were on the same quest that I was. They wanted change in the world. They specifically were working toward changing education in America, and they planned to do it one student at a time.

I felt a special connection with Cindy in particular. The first day I arrived at the school, she walked up to me and said, "You belong here." I said, "Yes, I do." It was immediately obvious to both of us that we were kindred spirits. I told Cindy about how I had lost my twin sister and that I had started the Catherine Hill Foundation to help under-privileged kids in her honor. The next day I came to work and found a butterfly sitting on the top of my computer. Cindy came into my office with a big smile on her face.

"I looked up the Catherine Hill Foundation and I found your Web site. I read the synopsis of your book *Twin Souls,* and I am so inspired by your story!" I was surprised because I hadn't even told her that I had written a book. She found the Web site and the book information on her own.

I knew Cindy and I were intended to meet. A few weeks later this became even more apparent when she came running up to me one morning before school.

"You are not going to believe what happened! Something compelled me to open one of my high school journals. Wait until you see what I wrote:

'Sometimes I think I am like a blue butterfly sitting on a fence. My wings are up straight, and all my energy is focused up or to one place. The wings are up straight, parallel to one another. Just like I am sometimes, like when I mess up and I don't do things right then all my problems are what I focus on. Maybe what I need to do is open my wings flat and let everything be open. This doesn't make much sense when it is written but I understand it. It was just a vision I had that I was a blue butterfly.'"

We both were stunned. Not only had she written about her visions of being a blue butterfly but something had compelled her to open that particular journal, which was not something she normally did.

My sister wanted to empower children. She wanted each child to see his or her own potential. And I knew that my sister had guided me to Cindy, who wanted the same thing. At Central Elementary, children aren't allowed to believe that they are limited simply because they are from a poor, inner-city neighborhood. The school's motto was "Work Hard, Be Kind, Dream Big." I had found a school where the administration, staff, and teachers understood the law of attraction and the principles of abundance.

Central had an equal balance of basic academics and creative learning, and each student was treated like an individual. I loved being there, and I loved seeing the kids thrive. I knew that I was there because to truly work toward change in the world, we must start with children.

## Undercurrent of Rage

In her book, *Archangels and Ascended Masters*, Doreen Virtue described her visit to historical sites around the world, where she conversed with many spiritual entities and highly evolved beings.

While sitting next to the ancient stone circle known as Stonehenge in southern England, Virtue was visited by the late Princess Diana. Diana told Virtue that the world's children are at a crossroads and in great need of leadership. She expressed great concern for the welfare of children and described a great undercurrent of dissatisfaction among young people that is bursting with rage. Princess Diana told Virtue that she foresaw many outbursts by youth on the horizon that would shock the world, unless an intervention occurred.

Virtue's book was published in 2003, well before the November 2005 riots in Paris during which youths torched hundreds of cars and threw Molotov Cocktails into buildings. The world was shocked as the riots continued for more than two weeks. Shortly after the French riots, Australian youths rioted in a clash between whites and the Lebanese Muslim population.

In 2006, thousands of people took to the streets in the U.S. to protest immigration reform. The majority of protesters were young people. Police officers and school administrators had to contend with hundreds of kids leaving school to join the protests. Some of the protests became violent as bottles and rocks were hurled at police.

While working as a 911 police dispatcher, I saw youth violence skyrocketing. Judging by the calls I received, it appeared that people under the age of eighteen were committing the majority of crimes.

In *Tomorrow's God*, Walsch learned that our society has had an increase in violence because we have lost respect for life and we have failed to teach children that they are part of something larger than themselves.

### Connection to Low Energy

Children are spending an increasing number of hours in front of the television screen. In *The Power of Intention*, Dr. Wayne Dyer wrote that we have harmed our kids by allowing them to connect to extremely low energy through television and video games. Dyer said that in America, kids witness 12,000 simulated murders by the time they are fourteen years old. It is absurd to think that this does not affect their respect for life. By allowing this constant stream of negative energy to invade our homes, we are allowing an atmosphere of hopelessness, violence, and disrespect.

### Outdoor Time

When I was younger, my sister, brother, and I spent many hours outdoors with other neighborhood kids, riding bikes, building forts and tree houses, inventing elaborate games of hide and seek, and playing baseball in the street. Unfortunately, this kind of creative outdoor playtime is largely a thing of the past.

In his book *Last Child in the Woods*, Richard Louv wrote that children have become increasingly disconnected to the natural world. According to Louv, exposure to nature can be a powerful therapy for ADD and other maladies. In fact, some experts believe that young people's limited exposure to nature and their addiction to electronic media may actually cause ADD, stress, depression, and other anxiety disorders.

Today kids are more likely to sit in front of a computer screen than to go hiking or swimming. What little time is spent outdoors is often confined to a playground or fenced schoolyard, and play is structured and isolated. Louv said that unlike TV, nature does not steal time—it amplifies it and gives children a sense of joy and peace.

### Lack of Silence

Another element missing from children's lives is silence. I noticed while answering 911 calls and later while making home visits as a CSO that there was a complete lack of silence in many homes. There was always someone yelling, a TV blasting, or loud music blaring in the background. Dyer wrote in *The Power of Intention* that harsh pounding music with repetitive vibration considerably lowers a person's energy level, especially when there are lyrics of pain, violence, and hatred.

One day I was out walking and I thought about the fact that no matter where I went, I could still hear some kind of human noise, whether it was cars driving by, an airplane passing overhead, or someone's stereo playing. I heard someone say, "You have developed a culture without stillness or silence." I knew this was true, and I could see the correlation between loud noise and lower energy. I suddenly felt overwhelmingly claustrophobic. I wanted to get away from the noise, but I couldn't.

People who have the ability to connect with the spiritual realm are extremely sensitive to noise. In her audio CD *Divine Guidance*, Doreen Virtue described how her ears felt like bursting when a loud alarm went off during one of her seminars. She explained that her sensitivity was due to her ability to "hear" higher frequency communication.

One of the most talented mediums I have met is Helle's angel therapist friend Lisa. Lisa told me that she is almost completely deaf in one ear. She was told by her spirit guides that this is necessary for her to be able to hear at higher frequencies and still be able to cope with everyday noise.

I was relieved to hear this because for several years I have been extremely sensitive to noise. Everyone who has worked with me knows that I cannot tolerate any high-pitched or loud sounds for even a few seconds. I have been told by several mediums that my rapidly increasing sensitivity to noise is due my ability to hear my sister and others who communicate at much higher vibrational frequencies than those in physical form.

As people evolve spiritually, they will feel the need for more stillness and silence in their lives. According to Dyer in *The Power of Intention*, silence is the cure for all ailments. Sitting in complete stillness and silence for even a few minutes will bring up our energy levels significantly.

In some cases I see children being dragged from one after-school activity or sporting event to the next without any down time to simply do nothing. In other circles I see kids in chaotic environments without a moment of quiet to even do their homework. I believe that it is critically important that children have some quiet time alone to think and to allow their imaginations to wander.

### Lack of Togetherness

Another loss that children are suffering is the lack of togetherness and family time. In *The Last Hours of Ancient Sunlight*, Hartmann wrote that in our modern world, people have sacrificed a family culture and a sense of belonging for material concerns. Cathy wrote to me in her notebook that she believed that people are driven to buy more things because of the disconnection they feel from one another and their higher selves. Cathy thought that people were working harder and longer so that they could fill up an inner spiritual void. But she believed that we could fill our spiritual void by working less and spending more time building families, friends and communities like our ancient ancestors did.

## Children Are Spiritual Beings

Walsch wrote in *Conversations with God* that we do not treat children as spiritual beings. Children are fully evolved souls, just like adults, and some children are more highly evolved than the adults in their lives. Many people have said that they believe I am good with children because I see them as souls and not just cute little kids. While working at Central Elementary School I was touched deeply when the kids looked up at me and smiled. Children are so open that when I looked at them I felt as is I was seeing their whole being.

Walsch learned that coming into a physical body is very limiting, and children have more vivid soul memories of their recent time in spirit, so it is essential to avoid restricting the child as much as possible. Children should be encouraged to explore and think about things, ask questions, and most important, children should be encouraged to remember their true spiritual nature.

## The Evolution of Humanity

P.M.H. Atwater, L.H.D., wrote in her book *Beyond the Indigo Children* that native people around the world understand clearly what is taking place in the world. This unprecedented shift has been predicted for thousands of years, and native cultures know just how big it truly is.

One of the most famous ancient prophecies is carved into a Mayan sunstone. The Mayan calendar charts an enormous passage of time from the big bang to the year 2012. Modern-day mathematicians and astronomers are floored by the accuracy of the calendar, and they are unable to figure out how it was created.

According to Atwater, one of the purposes of the calendar is to track human consciousness. It is broken down into nine stages, starting with the single-celled organisms at the time of the big bang 16 million years ago and moving all the way to the year 2011, when a great rise in human consciousness is predicted. The calendar shows that there will be a greater focus on spiritual matters, a one-world global village will be established, and the fading of boundaries and borders will occur around the world.

The Mayan calendar ends on December 21, 2012. Many people have speculated about what will happen on that date. The consensus is that it is not doomsday, as some fear, but a gateway or time-space portal that we will cross through into a new, enlightened world.

Ancient traditions have also predicted that a new race of enlightened old souls would come to help move the world toward this transformation.

According to Doreen Virtue in her Audio CD *Indigo, Crystal, and Rainbow Children*, an influx of lightworkers came into the world starting in the 1950s. Lightworkers are highly sensitive, intuitive people who feel that they have a strong connection to the other side. They have come not only to take on a personal mission, but they also have taken on a global mission and have elected to teach about love in some form.

### Indigos

According to Virtue, indigo children came into the world between the 1970s and the 1990s. The color indigo is a cross between royal blue and purple, represents the third eye chakra, and designates a very high level of spiritual enlightenment. Some say that this vibrant color can be seen in the auras of indigo children. Many believe that there are adult Indigos called "scouts" who came earlier than most to set the stage for the influx of these enlightened souls.

According to Michelle Alexander on her Web site www.indigohealings.com, indigos are known to be "system busters" and "spiritual warriors." Their group purpose is to break down all the old traditional paradigms, including our political, religious, medical, social, and educational systems. Virtue said that they are here to remove the old energy of competition, greed, and lack of integrity.

Alexander wrote that these kids are truly old souls, who have brought with them much wisdom and light. They are spiritually and psychically gifted and are talented healers. They know and see things that other people don't see, and Alexander says that they "get it" on a much deeper level.

Young indigos are often very precocious, strong-willed, and independent. They are highly intuitive, intelligent, technologically advanced, and normally have very high self-esteem. Some have even described them as acting like royalty.

According to Virtue, indigos are extremely sensitive to light and sound and can also be very emotional. They are so sensitive that they can actually feel physical pain around low energy. These young people have very little patience for rigid rules or authority, and they do not respond to discipline.

Unfortunately, parents, educators, and employers are at their wits' end with these youngsters because they are restless and have an abundance of energy. They are unable to sit still, and they are always causing trouble.

Thousands of indigos have been misdiagnosed as having Attention Deficit Disorder (ADD), Attention Deficit Hyperactivity Disorder (ADHD), and bipolar disorder. Sadly, they are often put on medication that is severely limiting and detrimental to the spirit of indigo children. Virtue calls indigo children ADHD: "attention dialed into a higher dimension."

According to Virtue, much of the restlessness in indigo children stems from their diet. Their systems cannot handle any chemicals, especially food coloring. She quoted a double-blind study conducted on indigo children that found that one cookie with food coloring had a measurable effect on hyperactivity.

According to Virtue, in *The Care and Feeding of Indigo Children*, earlier generations were given the same message to change and heal the world. They started out that way but allowed apathy and other responsibilities to distract them. Indigos will not let that happen, unless we drug them into submission. Virtue said that there are some people who want the school system to stay as it is, and they resent the changes that the indigo children represent so they label them with a variety of disorders. Virtue says that these kids are not disordered at all. They are extremely sensitive to any type of lie or lack of integrity, and they do not care whether a person is wearing a business suit or bears the title of principal—they will not hold back what they are feeling. While at school, indigos feel as though they are being forced into a world of unnaturalness and dishonesty.

According to Alexander, there has been a rise in depression, suicide, and violence among indigos. Many disclaimed their gifts and shut down their natural spiritual abilities in order to survive and fit in with their families and the rest of society. By cutting themselves off from their true essence and life purpose, they go into a downward spiral.

Virtue said in *Indigo, Crystal, and Rainbow Children* that she believes the tragedy at Columbine was an instance of indigo children not knowing how to handle their rage. Indigo children need our help in learning how to manage their anger and in discovering how to work within the system to accomplish their goals.

## Crystals and Rainbows

According to Virtue, crystal children began coming into the world at the end of the 1990s. They have very large eyes that seem able to look into our souls. Virtue says that of all the things she has learned and studied in her life, the emergence of this new group of children has given her the most hope for our future. She does not believe we would be getting these kids if we were headed in a negative direction.

According to Virtue, crystal children have pure love and magical light radiating from within them. They have open hearts, and they can immediately spot someone who does not have an open heart. Unlike the indigos, they do not have tempers and are completely forgiving.

Crystal children are even more sensitive than indigos, especially to chemicals in foods. They are naturally drawn to vegetarian foods, and they cannot tolerate over-the-counter medication.

Crystal children are highly psychic, and they communicate telepathically. Problems arise because they often do not talk until age three or four. Virtue said that they are often misdiagnosed as being autistic when they are simply evolved souls who are moving away from the spoken word, which is extremely inaccurate compared to telepathy.

Crystal children love nature and animals, and they want to be outside all the time. Virtue believes they are bringing us back to our roots in the natural world.

The newest children being born are *rainbow children*. Virtue said that because we spend so much time indoors, we are less and less able to assimilate the full spectrum of light into our bodies and therefore we do not receive enough serotonin. Virtue explained that each of our seven chakras corresponds to a color of the rainbow (red, orange, yellow, green, blue, indigo, and violet) and therefore represent what is known as rainbow energy.

Virtue believes that the rainbow children are being sent to us to bring back this important energy to our planet. These young children are little avatars who are coming here without any karma. Their only purpose is to serve others. They represent pure, unconditional love and joy. Virtue said that rainbow children are the embodiment of our divinity and are examples of how we can be.

According to Virtue, all of the new children show less electrical activity in the left brain, and they often do not succeed in the world's left-brain, linear education system. They are highly creative, right-brain thinkers who want to work independently. They do respond to music, pictures, and abstract reasoning.

Atwater suggests in *Beyond the Indigo Children* that we rethink traditional school settings completely. She even recommends that we throw out high school all together. Most young people are much more computer savvy than their teachers and can work from home or independently away from a classroom while participating in some kind of work or vocational training.

According to Atwater, the generations being born after the millennium will possess higher and higher states of human brain development and will be able to make mature decisions at a much younger age. In fact, Atwater said that all children born since the 1970s have characteristics of indigo and crystal children. She believes that changing our education system is an important step in addressing the issues that these highly evolved young people face.

## Education

Walsch wrote in *Conversations with God* that education should be about wisdom. Wisdom is knowledge applied, but we are currently ignoring wisdom in favor of the memorization of facts. We are telling children to learn about the "truth" instead of allowing them to use wisdom to come to their own truths. In *The Isaiah Effect*, Braden wrote that knowledge can be taught and passed down through written documents but that wisdom is something that must be experienced by each individual person. By asking children to memorize the information that we want them to know, we are dooming them to repeat the past.

In *Tomorrow's God*, Walsch learned that in order to transform the human race from a primitive, selfish, and violent society to a highly evolved society, we must first remove punishment from education. Criticizing or punishing a child to alter his or her behavior does not work. It only stops the behavior temporarily. We should let the child experience the natural consequences of his or her behavior and then show the child how to make amends.

While working at Central Elementary, I saw this practice in action. At first I was surprised by the fact that there didn't seem to be a lot of punishment for bad behavior. But soon I realized the wisdom of approaching problems from a different angle. When a problem arose between two students, both were instructed to write down what part he or she played in causing the incident to occur. Each student was required to take responsibility for his or her own actions. The incident was discussed so that each student could see how their behavior affected one another. The students were asked to find a way to rectify the problem. Often a child would make a beautifully decorated card for the other child who was angry or upset. The solutions were simple yet very effective because they were not about punishment but about seeing the consequences of the behavior and finding ways to make amends for the wrongdoing.

According to Hartmann in *The Last Hours of Ancient Sunlight*, this is how negative behavior is handled in tribal cultures. When someone acts in a non-beneficial way, especially a child, it is taken as a sign that the individual has not matured enough yet to see the error of his or her ways. The entire community takes on the responsibility of helping an individual correct his or her behavior, make amends, and then they take the most important step—all is forgiven.

Walsch wrote in *The New Revelations* that all of life is a lesson. We are the role models for our children. If they act insensitively or are overly materialistic, it is because they are copying our behavior. They are disrespectful to others because they see adults acting that way. Children are critical of others because they are criticized. They are violent because they see violence everywhere in their society.

Cathy worked with kids who were on the fringe of society. Some were so desperate that they had resorted to criminal activity in order to survive. But Cathy saw that each child was really a diamond in the rough. She begged other people to see how important every child is because as Cathy often said about her beloved kids, "They are our future."

### A Return to Reverence

In *The Last Hours of Ancient Sunlight*, Hartmann wrote that as a society, we have removed the sacred from our daily lives. We no longer feel the sense of wonder that our ancestors did. Native Americans teach that every moment of the day is an opportunity to see the divine and that everything is a reminder that our lives are a gift from God.

In *The Power of Intention*, Dyer wrote that we should be in a constant state of gratitude. This state of perpetual thankfulness is like a magnet for everything that is good. We should learn humility, which does not mean bowing down but simply feeling a sense of awe at the small part we play in the vastness of the infinite universe.

According to Hartmann in *The Last Hours of Ancient Sunlight*, only in recent history have humans become so concerned with our own lifetimes and nothing beyond it. We have lost our reverence for life.

In her notebook, Cathy wrote to me about society's lack of reverence: "We have become a very individualistic society where there is an every-man-for-himself attitude. People have lost ties to family and God and everything that life is really about. People don't take care of each other anymore. And we are not taking care of the environment either. We are squandering all of our natural resources. The way we treat each other and the way we treat the earth is intertwined. We must see the interconnection of all life before it is too late."

Humanity lived for thousands of years in complete harmony with all other living creatures. Crime and violence was literally nonexistent. According to Hartmann we don't have to reinvent a new way of living. We simply have to take another look at the wisdom of our ancestors.

Cathy and I believe that the solution lies in the combination of the remarkable human ingenuity that exists today, coupled with the great spiritual depth and wisdom of those who have lived before us.

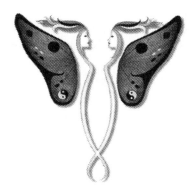

# Chapter Twenty-Four:
## Seeds of Change

In the Gospel of Thomas, Jesus said, "I have thrown fire on the world. Look! I watch it until it blazes" (Gospel of Thomas, verse 10).

Jesus was a passionate revolutionary who sought to "shake things up" on every level. He knew even in his time that nothing short of a revolt would change the powerful institutions that were keeping the rigid power structures in place.

In his book *Grassroots Spirituality*, Robert Foreman wrote that our civilization is undergoing an astounding shift. This world shift is affecting everything we do, including how we treat each other, how we conduct business, how we govern ourselves, and, Foreman says, even how we live and die.

The mainstream population has not yet grasped the size, breadth, or significance of this spiritual movement. Forman says that this is typical. For example, in the 1950s journalists were barely aware of what was taking place in black church basements around the country. And even when the marches began, few realized the true enormity of the Civil Rights movement until it was too big to ignore.

Foreman believes that the growing spiritual movement is possibly of even greater significance than the Civil Rights movement because it is reaching every corner of the globe.

## Old and New Come Together

In *The New Revelations*, Neale Donald Walsch wrote that the missing gospel that would save the world is: "We are all one," and "Ours is not a better way, ours is merely another way."

After I read that I had a dream in which I was sitting in a large ornate church. I saw, etched in the pew, traditional symbols such as a cross and the Star of David next to signs of the new age such as the sun, the moon, and the yin-and-yang symbol. When I woke up I realized the significance of the dream. It showed me that all traditions can unite. Heaven and earth can come together again. I believe that there was never meant to be a separation in the first place.

Walsch learned that going forward we will select what we believe is the best from the old traditions and expand these beliefs with new ideas and allow a bridge to be built between the old and the new. An ideal spirituality for the future is one in which we combine the knowledge of all the ancient masters with contemporary enlightened teachings. We should seek new insights from the ancient wisdom that has been passed down to us.

Cathy and I believe that humanity should strive to be like the great masters who have inspired the world's religions. In *The Power of Intention*, Dr. Wayne Dyer wrote that instead of being Buddhists we should be Buddha-like. Instead of being Muslims we should strive to be Mohammad-like, and instead of being Christians we should be Christ-like.

Our world would change in unfathomable ways if we each became more curious about other religions and cultures. Imagine the remarkable shift that would occur in

408

the world if we simply appreciated the great diversity of ideas and beliefs without insisting that our way is right and the others wrong. It is important to realize that there is no one right way up the mountain. Every master understands this truth. That is why the term *namaste* has become so popular. It means, "The God in me recognizes the God in you," or "From my spirituality to yours."

## East-West

Paramahansa Yogananda wrote in *Autobiography of a Yogi* about an encounter his mentor Sri Yukteswar had with Babaji, the great Indian saint. Babaji told Yukteswar that the East and West must establish a golden middle path where spiritual traditions and philosophies are combined. Babaji explained to Yukteswar that India would learn much from the West about material development and the West would benefit greatly from the spiritual teachings of the East.

I have noticed that in some spiritual circles it is common to denounce the West and its materialistic ways, but Yogananda saw that the combination of Eastern spiritualism and Western materialism would be an unbeatable combination.

The Buddha believed that enlightenment could not be achieved by focusing solely on worldly possessions. Nor could it be accomplished by completely withdrawing from the outer world. He knew that enlightenment could only be achieved through finding harmony between the two. Masters from both the East and West have expressed the idea that there should be a balance between the spiritual East and the material West.

Yogananda wrote in *Man's Eternal Quest* that Jesus came to be a liaison between the East and the West. Yogananda saw Jesus standing before him beseeching the world to see that even though his message traveled to the West, he was born in the East. His mission was to unite the finest principles of both.

In the West, God the Father is prominent. In the East, God the Mother is held in highest esteem. God the Father represents wisdom and intellect, and God the Mother represents compassion, forgiveness, and unconditional love. Our world desperately needs a balance of both in order to move into higher consciousness.

## West Seeks Eastern Philosophies

There is an old saying: "From the East comes light," and Westerners are beginning to see the light in Eastern teachings. Yogananda wrote in *Man's Eternal Quest* that many souls from the East have reincarnated in America to fulfill their desires for material wealth. And many souls who previously lived in America have been reborn in the India so they can benefit from the spiritual riches of the East.

The great Indian master Lahiri Mahasaya made the prediction that fifty years after his passing, an account of his life would be written because of a deep interest in Eastern philosophies that would arise in the West. Mahasaya said that yoga meditation would circle the globe and would aid in establishing a brotherhood of man based on humanity's direct perception of the one Creator.

Exactly fifty years after Mahasaya's passing in 1945, Yogananda's *Autobiography of a Yogi* was completed. The book gives an account of Lahiri Mahasaya's life along with the remarkable story of Yogananda's own life. And just as many predicted, Western business savvy is sprouting in the East and the inner spiritual practices of the East are beginning to gain a foothold in the West.

Yogananda believed that this combination of East and West would be the catalyst for the rise in human consciousness that has been predicted for thousands of years.

## Encounter with An Archangel

In December of 2005, when my dad retired from his teaching position at San Diego State University, he felt lost and unsure of his purpose.

I heard a clear voice tell me that he could become a healer. I had learned that all people could be healers as Jesus was, although some possess a special talent for the healing arts. It is simply a matter of learning how to access the inner light that is within all of us.

I gave my dad some books about healing. He seemed skeptical but took the books anyway. He began meditating on a regular basis, and I saw very dramatic changes in him. He lost most of his anxiety and became much more calm and grounded.

In March of 2006 I asked him if he would go with me to Helle and Lisa's two-day angel seminar. On the way to the seminar, my father told me that during one of his meditations, he got a message that he was a healer. He had forgotten about my prediction from several months before. I wondered if his healing abilities would somehow come out in the seminar.

When we arrived, Lisa told us that she would be in a semi-trance state for most of the weekend. I had never met Lisa before, but Helle had told me that she was an unbelievably talented medium who worked with angels and ascended masters. Helle had personally witnessed Lisa go into a trance state and channel messages from Jesus and Mother Mary. I wondered what was in store for us and who would come through to speak to us at the seminar.

My editor, Midge, also attended the seminar and was sitting next to me. We had never met in person before the seminar, but it was obvious that she and I had a strong spiritual connection, which Lisa confirmed.

We each told the group about ourselves. As I was talking, I glanced over at Helle and noticed she had tears in her eyes. After I was done, she pulled me aside and told me that while I was speaking about my mother, she saw a brilliant white light hovering behind me, and my mother had conveyed to Helle that she wanted me to know that she was very proud of me. I was deeply moved because I had not had any contact with my mother in a long time.

Finally the moment came when Lisa began the channeling. Her entire body began to shake and her skin turned red. Her head was down against her body. Suddenly her head jerked up and she began speaking in a deep, husky voice. The voice indicated that he was speaking for a group of Lisa's spirit guides. "Many miracles are unfolding at this time. A switch has been turned on for spiritual growth and expansion. Open your eyes and see beyond. All of you have gifts to share. Think outside the box. Once you are out, stay out!

"Many circles are being created! The message must get out. Create more circles. Integrate the religions. Allow yourselves to be guided by knowledge and wisdom. We are working very hard on the other side to bring great powers to you. Listen to your bodies, and don't judge what you feel. Get the message out." Lisa put her arms in a big circle. In a loud, deep voice she shouted, "We are all one!"

Lisa put her head back down on her chest for several minutes. My heart was pounding. Her guides had mentioned many things that I had been writing about in *Twin Souls*.

"What else would happen?" I wondered.

Midge and I exchanged a glance with raised eyebrows. Lisa proceeded to bring through words of wisdom for each person in the room, including one poignant message from Mother Mary to one of the participants, who was floored because she was not Catholic. Lisa explained to her later that Mother Mary is an ascended master and that she does not belong to any one religion.

Helle's living room has a large glass window overlooking her garden. It had been raining and hailing all day, but suddenly the clouds parted, and the sun burst

412

through the window. The energy in the room was so strong it was palpable. I snuck another glance at Midge, who I could tell was feeling the energy too.

Lisa looked up at my father and began speaking in another masculine voice. "You have healing hands. The ray of the thirty-third vibration is within you. You have Jesus hands. You may try many different types of machines that measure energy. It is okay to try many different things and many different healing methods. You will find what works for you. You are not alone; I am with you."

After Lisa stopped speaking, we learned that it had been Jesus who was speaking to my father. Lisa said that my father was a master healer and that his birthday, 2/22/33, indicated his ability to reach a high level of evolution.

The synchronicity was amazing because my father's father was an osteopath who was far ahead of his time. I had never met my grandfather because he died before I was born, but my father told me that he had worked with machines that measured the energy levels in people's internal organs to diagnose illness.

Later in the day, Lisa put my father into a hypnotic trance. She asked him to look down at his hands and describe what he saw.

"I see violet light coming from my hands."

I was stunned. Violet is known to be the highest spiritual color and is associated with the crown chakra at the top of the head, which is connected to the Universal Mind.

"What do you see yourself doing with your hands?"

"I see people lying on tables and I am placing my hands on them."

"And what are you doing to the people on the tables?"

"I am raising their vibrations."

"How does that feel?"

"Wonderful!" my father answered.

When my father came out of the trance, we all felt his hands. They were extraordinarily hot, as if they had been in front of a heater.

I could barely breathe. I had never pictured my father in a spiritual light before, and here he was being told by Jesus that he was a master healer.

"What could possibly be next?" I thought.

Lisa's head went back down on her chest as she breathed in and out heavily. Suddenly, her eyes flew open and her hands shot out toward me.

"I am the Archangel Michael," Lisa said in an extraordinarily deep voice. It was clear that the person speaking to me was not Lisa. Later Midge said to me incredulously, "Did you see when she opened her eyes? It was as if she wasn't there anymore." I was glad that Midge had been there to witness it.

Archangel Michael continued, "You have had many struggles. Let go of the fear; let go of the past. You are protected in every way. Your foundation is concrete. You have a very pure, clear, and true message to share. The wisdom and knowledge that you share will reach many, and they will hear at the level of their souls. The pieces of the puzzle are coming together quickly, but you must surpass your fear and have patience.

"Write without negativity but with great passion. Soon you will have two books to share. One is very deep and the other is for children. The book for children will be very, very simple. You will speak to the hearts and souls of many young people. You already have all that you need to write this simple book, and it will happen very quickly.

"I honor the colors you are wearing." I had coincidentally worn a blue and purple windbreaker—the colors that represent Archangel Michael. "We honor your strong connection to the other side. The beautiful messages that you have received will reach many who could not hear them before. In three months it will start to happen. Let go of your struggles, let go of your past, let go of the fear!"

Lisa's head went back down on her chest and she slowly came out of her trance. Everyone in the room sat transfixed. No one spoke for several minutes. I was beside myself with joy that Archangel Michael had brought me such a clear and encouraging message.

Later in the day, Lisa took us in pairs to another room to put each of us under hypnosis to see if we could access past-life memories or any other important information such as the names of our spirit guides.

Midge and I went together. I watched as Midge went immediately into a deep trance and entered her most recent past life. She discovered that she was a twin and that her twin had died at birth in that lifetime but was back with her again now as her sister.

Then it was my turn. I felt a strong surge of energy as Lisa put me under hypnosis. My eyelids were fluttering back and forth as if I were in R.E.M. sleep. Although it was an odd sensation, I was still conscious of what was going on. Midge told me later that the energy was so strong in the room that the CD playing in the background suddenly became fuzzy and began skipping.

I had a difficult time relaxing and allowing myself to go fully into a trance state, but I felt the strong presence of someone standing behind me. Lisa asked me if I saw my spirit guide and asked me to say his name.

I strained to see him in my mind's eye. I saw a very large man with a funny-looking face. It wasn't clear, but I could tell that it was not a normal-looking human face.

"What is his name?"

"Esh," was all I could come up with.

"Try again," Lisa instructed.

"Esh," I said again.

"Is it Ganesh?"

"Yes, it is Ganesh," I said, surprising myself.

"Ganesh is with you, guiding you. He will help you remove all obstacles. Trust that everything will come together."

Lisa told me later that Ganesh is an ascended master from India and one of the central figures in Hinduism. He is somewhat mystical in nature because he has the body of a man and the head of an elephant. But according to Virtue in *Archangels and Ascended Masters* he is very real and is known for trampling over any obstacles whenever called upon to do so. I was delighted when I read that Ganesh is also known for helping writers and he has the same strong protective energy as Archangel Michael.

Lisa continued the session by instructing me to look down at my hands and tell her what I saw. I saw very large man's hands and feet.

"Whose hands are they?"

"I'm not sure," I responded. My hands felt completely numb.

She questioned me further, but I still couldn't figure out whose hands they were.

"They are Archangel Michael's hands. Feel the sword in his hands. Archangel Michael is very powerful, and his sword will cut through all negativity, worry, and fear. Feel the power of Archangel Michael's sword. You have that same power within you. Do not doubt that. Take your power back."

Ganesh and Archangel Michael also advised me through Lisa that I should learn to stay in the present moment by going outside near the ocean or amongst the flowers, birds, and trees. They said that experiencing oneness with nature would always rejuvenate my power.

As I came out of the hypnosis session, I had a clear message that Archangel Michael and Ganesh were also with me to symbolize a coming together of East and West. I knew that part of my mission in writing *Twin Souls* was to show the world that there can be a balance between the two.

416

## Children's Book

I had never even thought of writing a children's book before, but three months after the seminar, I suddenly had the urge to begin writing the book that Archangel Michael had spoken about. I had a clear thought that I should take some of the concepts from *Twin Souls* and rewrite them in very simple fashion so that children could understand. I sat down and began typing. When I was done, I had written four chapters: *What Is God?, What Is Life?, What Is Death?,* and *The Great Circle.* When I read what I had written I was surprised at how profound it was and that I had completed it in less than two days.

I heard my sister say, "Contact Lena." That was a good idea. I remembered that Lena's artwork was breathtaking and she had just begun to be discovered. Her artwork was being displayed in galleries around San Diego.

I called Lena, and we set up a meeting. When I initially met with her, I was disappointed because she said that, although she wanted to illustrate the book, she didn't feel she had the time to do it along with her other artwork. I sat there wondering what to do as she left the room for a minute. When she returned, she had an odd look on her face.

"They're telling me to do it," she said.

"Who is telling you?"

"God."

Lena took the short manuscript and began reading. I felt a chill go up my spine as I watched the tears pour down her face. After she was done reading, she got up, came around the table, and wrapped her arms around me. She cried for several minutes. People in the small coffee shop looked at us with puzzled expressions.

I was stunned. I knew that the book was good and that the writing had clearly been channeled through me, but I was taken off guard by her intense reaction.

"'God is everywhere and in everything.' How could I turn down the opportunity to illustrate that? I would be honored," she said, wiping her tears away. "They are telling me that illustrating this book will heal me." Lena had been suffering with kidney failure for many years.

Amazingly, after the book was completed, Lena met a man who after hearing her story, insisted on donating his kidney to her. She underwent a successful transplant surgery and no longer had to have dialysis.

I couldn't believe it. I knew none of it was a coincidence. Lena and I came to a simple agreement with Helle as our witness, and the children's book was under way just as Archangel Michael had said. When I saw the completed manuscript of the book, which we decided to call *The Circle of Life*, it took my breath away. Something told me that although it was initially written for children, it would reach the child within us all.

**The Edge**

My encounter with Archangel Michael prompted me to remember something that I had read in *The Prophet's Way* about Thom Hartmann's mentor, Gottfried Müller, a devout Christian and highly evolved spiritual master.

Müller told Hartmann about a vivid dream he had about an experience that had occurred before he came to earth. He was in an elegant marble hall. Thousands of people were lined up in rows. A magnificent-looking man entered the hall, and Müller knew it was Archangel Michael. Everyone stood at attention, facing him.

Archangel Michael began to speak. He said that a battle would be coming to the earth. He explained that it would be fought on the most subtle spiritual levels at first, and then on an earthly level. He asked for volunteers who would be willing to go to earth to take on the battle.

Müller looked around and saw that no one was stepping forward. He was shocked because he saw so many powerful beings in the room. He saw Archangel

Michael hold up his sword and he told the people to step back if they did not want to go. Most of the people in the room stepped back. Müller thought he was the only one standing forward but then he saw some other people who had not stepped back.

Michael's face was filled with love, and he told the group that he would send them helpers. They would not be obvious to the world but they would recognize them. He told them that there would be much turmoil but also great accomplishments. He said that no matter how difficult things got, they were to remember that they were on a mission to save humanity. Then Michael told them what their most powerful weapon would be: "...to commit tiny acts of compassion." Suddenly, Müller's dream came to an end as he saw himself in the body of a newborn baby.

Müller realized that our planet is at a crossroads and that everyone who is on earth at this time is here for an important purpose.

In his book *Limitless Mind*, Russell Targ said that we are approaching an edge. The edge is a place of danger, instability, and also of great opportunity. Anything can happen at the edge because it is a point of intersection.

Targ wrote that what happens at the edge is too complex to understand, but it is a very powerful place to be because edges create unique energies. According to Hartmann in *The Prophet's Way*, people who live on the edge are agents for change. They are people who are willing to challenge old conventions. The United States was created by people on the edge who were willing to take risks to start a new society.

According to Virtue in *Healing with the Angels*, we are at the edge of a time of drastic change when we will collectively remember our spiritual gifts, intuition, and unity. Walsch wrote in *Tomorrow's God* that humanity is about to create a new form of spirituality on earth that will be our most stunning achievement.

## Cathy, We Have Critical Mass

In an e-mail dated September 24, 2002, Cathy wrote to Tom, "There are powerful universal forces working behind this spiritual movement. Have you ever noticed that when something is meant to be, it just is, against all odds? Everything just moves out of the way to let it happen. That is critical mass and it is happening right now in the world."

When I discuss *Twin Souls* with people, they often say that it sounds like a wonderful idea but they think it is too idealistic. Many have said that there are just too many people in the world who do not see the light. What they are not taking into account is the scientific principle of quantum physics called *critical mass*. My sister wrote, "Thom Hartmann explained critical mass like this: It would only take 80,000 people to start changing the world's ideas about what is acceptable and what is not. If you multiply 80,000 times 80,000 you get 6.4 billion, which is the number of people on the planet. It has something to do with wave energy multiplying itself. The complete explanation is above my pay grade."

In *Tomorrow's God* Walsch learned that critical mass occurs when only 2 to 4 percent of the population changes its beliefs. The effects of critical mass are very powerful because they are exponential. Critical mass is basically a chain reaction or a domino effect. Once the first domino falls, they all will fall, one after the other.

In *The Isaiah Effect*, Gregg Braden wrote that prophets have been saying for centuries that when one-tenth of one percent of humanity works together to create change, the consciousness of the entire world will follow suit. According to Braden, Jesus was referring to critical mass when he said, "The faith of a mustard seed moves mountains." Even a small shift in understanding will change everything.

A special meditation came to me one day while sitting in my office: I held out my hands and I visualized Cathy and many angels and guides handing me *Twin Souls, The Circle of Life,* and many other books that I would write in the future.

The cover of *Twin Souls* is a deep indigo blue. I turned my hands so that they were facing inward and all my creations turned to indigo blue energy between my hands. I looked out and I could see all around the world to other people who were holding their own contributions to the great transformation. Archangel Michael was directing us to reach our hands out and make a giant circle around the earth. We saw the earth as a small black dot below. Our indigo blue energy moved together in the center and out over the earth. All at once we let go of the energy, and it fell upon the earth, changing its color from black to brilliant blue. As we all watched, tiny twinkling lights began to go off all around the planet until the whole world was a great shining light bulb.

Each person will contribute to the transformation by changing their own views about the world. The inner will change the outer. The heart will change the head, and it will go on and on exponentially. The dominos are beginning to fall and we will have critical mass.

## Another Butterfly

On October 11, 2006 I received the news that my father, Howard Hill, had passed away suddenly from a heart attack while playing tennis. At first the shock was overwhelming. I felt so alone in the world. I realized that I only had two living family members left, my brother Mike and my beautiful thirteen-year-old half sister Katy, whom I rarely saw.

I was devastated for Katy because she and my father had been best friends. It was obvious while watching them together that they were kindred spirits. But I could see that

421

Katy was a highly evolved soul who had chosen this path, and there was nothing I could do to stop her suffering.

Unlike my initial response to my sister's death, this time I was no longer in the dark. I understood clearly that my losses were about my own spiritual growth, but they were also about reminding others that death does not exist and that we are all part of the circle of life.

A week before my father died, I purchased a reading for him with Lisa. He had experienced a great awakening, but he was still confused about his life's purpose. I did not have a chance to speak to him after the reading, so when he died I contacted Lisa to see what she and my father had spoken about.

"It doesn't surprise me that your father's soul chose to leave at this time," Lisa explained. "He had the vibrations of a master, but he was blocking them out of fear." My father had been a big fan of Dr. Wayne Dyer and had given me his book, *The Power of Intention*. So it made me laugh when Lisa said that my father saw himself as Wayne Dyer, going around lecturing on spiritual subjects to large audiences.

"He was so worried about *how* it was going to happen that he wasn't focusing on the end result and trusting the universe to bring him the answers." Lisa paused for a few minutes then said, "There has been the most beautiful butterfly flying around in my veranda the whole time you and I have been talking. It's black with yellow stripes."

After Lisa and I hung up, I kept thinking about the butterfly. Ironically, the day before I had listened to Wayne Dyer's audio CD *Inspiration,* in which he described his own encounter with a butterfly. His friend who loved monarch butterflies had passed away many years before. Dyer had just finished writing a chapter about his friend, and he decided to go out for a walk. A monarch butterfly landed on him and stayed with him for several hours. Dyer believed that the butterfly was the spirit of his long-lost friend.

Later that same day, Lisa called me back.

"Your father made his transition."

"What?"

"That exotic butterfly that I told you about stayed in my veranda all day. Something kept compelling me to remove the butterfly from the veranda and set it free. Finally I went out and picked it up and as I let it go the spirit of your father came to me. He said 'You have helped to set me free, I am home.' Your father is overjoyed to be in spirit again. Get ready to write another book. He is another powerful spirit guide for you."

Like Cathy, my father experienced a significant spiritual awakening at the end of his life. And I believe it was part of his purpose to leave the world so that he could be part of something much larger than himself. And like Cathy, he had learned that to find the higher truths he was seeking, he merely had to look within.

## The God Within

I was out walking one day and said to Cathy and my father, "I am going to have all the things on earth that you both wanted but didn't get, and I know you have been helping me to do that. But of course now you have everything and more, so I guess we will both have it all."

"On Earth as it is in Heaven," Cathy replied.

"Hmmm," I thought. "That is what this whole coming together thing is about, to make it on Earth as it is in Heaven." It seemed that whenever I thought about this idea, one of my favorite country songs would come on the radio, "When I Get Where I'm Going," by Brad Paisley and Dolly Parton: "When I get where I'm going, there'll be only happy tears. I will shed the sins and struggles I have carried all these years. And I'll leave my heart wide open. I will love and have no fear."

The good news is that we do not have to wait until we die to leave our hearts wide open and love without fear.

We simply have to remember who we are and why we are here, and we will have it all right now.

As I was finishing up this last chapter, I felt a sudden impulse to open my high school senior yearbook, something I hadn't done in years. I looked at Cathy's picture, side by side with mine. I laughed when I read our senior quotes. Mine was from a Tom Petty song: "The waiting is the hardest part." That was so appropriate for me. I have always been very impatient. I had a sudden image in my head of Kali the Hindu goddess. According to Doreen Virtue in *Archangels and Ascended Masters*, Kali's personality is one of a high-energy woman on a clear mission. Virtue said she helps people to move out of the old and into the new. She is impatient and wants people of the earth to stop dilly-dallying and move forward with single-minded passion.

Cathy's quote made me smile: "Nothing great was ever achieved without enthusiasm" by Ralph Waldo Emerson. I remembered Cathy and my mother going through a book of quotes and that was the one she chose.

A week later, I was re-reading Dyer's book *The Power of Intention*. Dyer wrote that we should live our lives with great passion. He said that the Greeks have given us one of the most beautiful words in the English language relating to passion, and that is *enthusiasm*. According to Dyer, the word enthusiasm translates to "the God within."

My heart soared. Of course, it made perfect sense. Cathy's message to the world: "Nothing great was ever achieved without the God within."

We will all feel a sense of passion and enthusiasm when we realize that we are exactly where we are meant to be. The seeds of change have been planted by all of the great teachers who have walked the earth and those who have lived before us. It is up to us to make them grow to fruition. It is time for us to bring the world to its grandest and highest state of evolution.

From the Eulogy of Catherine Mary Hill by Donald Rooker: "So I leave you with this: paraphrasing Philippians chapter 4, verse 8 in saying that...Whatever things are true, whatever things are noble, whatever things are just or pure or lovely, whatever things are good, if there is any virtue in this world and if there is anything praiseworthy in this life, meditate on these things...That is what Cathy would ask of us."

...And that is what the God within would ask of us.

# Notes

## Chapter Three Notes

1. *Twin Telepathy: The Psychic Connection* by Guy Lyon Playfair, Vega, 2003.
2. *Seth Speaks: The Eternal Validity of the Soul* by Jane Roberts and Robert F. Butts, Amber-Allen Publishing, 1994.

## Chapter Four Notes

1. *Healing Grief: Reclaiming Life After Any Loss* by James Van Praagh, New American Library, 2001.

## Chapter Five Notes

1. *Spiritual Growth: Being Your Higher Self* by Sanaya Roman, H.J. Kramer, Inc., 1998.

## Chapter Six Notes

1. *Embraced by the Light* by Betty J. Eadie, Bantam Books, 1992.
2. *Hello from Heaven: A New Field of Research—After-Death Communication—Confirms Life and Love Are Eternal* by Bill and Judy Guggenheim, Bantam Books, 1995.
3. *The Messengers: A True Story of Angelic Presence and the Return to the Age of Miracles* by Julia Ingram and G.W. Hardin, Pocket Books, 1996.
4. *In God's Truth* by Nick Bunick, Hampton Roads, 1997.
5. *Angel Numbers* by Doreen Virtue, Ph.D., and Lynnette Brown, Hay House, Inc., 2005.
6. *The Second Coming of Christ: The Resurrection of the Christ Within You* by Paramahansa Yogananda, Self-Realization Fellowship, 2004.
7. *Man's Eternal Quest: Collected Talks and Essays on Realizing God in Daily Life, Volume I* by Paramahansa Yogananda, Self-Realization Fellowship, 1982.

8. *Autobiography of a Yogi* by Paramahansa Yogananda, Self- Realization Fellowship, 1998.
9. *Conversations with God: An Uncommon Dialogue, Book One* by Neale Donald Walsch, Hampton Roads, 1995, page 1.
10. *Conversations with God: An Uncommon Dialogue, Book Three* by Neale Donald Walsh, Hampton Roads, 1998.
11. *The New Revelations: A Conversation with God* by Neale Donald Walsch, Atria Books, 2002.

### Chapter Seven Notes
1. *Journey of Souls: Case Studies of Life Between Lives* by Michael Newton, Ph.D., Llewellyn Publications, Fifth Edition Revised, Seventeenth Printing, 2004.
2. *Many Lives, Many Masters* by Brian L. Weiss, M.D., Simon & Schuster, 1988.

### Part Two — The Message Notes
1. *Homeopathy: Beyond Flat Earth Medicine: An Introduction for Students and Patients* by Timothy R. Dooley, N.D., M.D., Timing Publications, 1995.

### Chapter Eight Notes
1. *Forgotten Truth: The Common Vision of the World's Religions,* by Huston Smith, HarperSanFrancisco, 1976.
2. *Tomorrow's God: Our Greatest Spiritual Challenge* by Neale Donald Walsch, Atria Books, 2004.
3. *Conversations with God: An Uncommon Dialogue, Book One* by Neale Donald Walsch, Hampton Roads, 1995.
4. *The Second Coming of Christ: The Resurrection of the Christ Within You* by Paramahansa Yogananda, Self-Realization Fellowship, 2004.
5. *Physics of the Soul: The Quantum Book of Living, Dying, Reincarnation, and Immortality* by Amit Goswami, Ph.D., Hampton Roads, 2001.
6. *Many Lives, Many Masters* by Brian L. Weiss, M.D., Simon & Shuster, Inc., 1988.

7. *Through Time Into Healing* by Brian L. Weiss, M.D., Simon & Schuster Inc., 1992.

8. *Man's Eternal Quest* by Paramahansa Yogananda, Self-Realization Fellowship, 1982.

9. *The Power of Now: A Guide to Spiritual Enlightenment, Compact Disc Set* by Eckhart Tolle, New World Library & Namaste Publishing, 1999.

## Chapter Nine Notes

1. *Motorcycle Diaries*, Universal Studios, 2004.

2. *On the Wings of Heaven: A True Story from a Messenger of Love* by G.W. Hardin and Joseph Crane, DreamSpeaker Creations, 1999.

3. *The Second Coming of Christ: The Resurrection of the Christ Within You*, by Paramahansa Yogananda, Self-Realization Fellowship, 2004.

4. *Conversations with God: An Uncommon Dialogue, Book Two* by Neale Donald Walsch, Hampton Roads, 1997.

5. *In God's Truth* by Nick Bunick, Hampton Roads, 1997.

6. *Conversations with God: An Uncommon Dialogue, Book One* by Neale Donald Walsh, Hampton Roads, 1995.

7. *The Gospel of Thomas: Annotated & Explained* by Stevan Davies, Skylight Paths Publishing, 2002.

8. *Original Blessing: A Primer in Creation Spirituality Presented In Four Paths, Twenty-Six Themes, and Two Questions* by Matthew Fox, Bear & Company, 1983.

9. *The Prophet's Way: A Guide to Living in the Now* by Thom Hartmann, Park Street Press, 1997.

10. *A Course In Miracles*, by Helen Schucman and William Thetford, Foundation for Inner Peace, 1992, chapter 4, page 56.

11. *Tomorrow's God: Our Greatest Spiritual Challenge* by Neale Donald Walsch, Atria Books, 2004.

## Chapter Ten Notes

1. *The Second Coming of Christ: The Resurrection of the Christ Within You* by Paramahansa Yogananda, Self-Realization Fellowship, 2004 page 241.
2. *On the Wings of Heaven: A True Story from a Messenger of Love*, by G.W. Hardin with Joseph Crane, DreamSpeaker Creations, 1999, page 55.
3. *Conversations with God an uncommon dialogue, Book One* by Neale Donald Walsh, Hampton Roads, 1995.
4. *The Power of Intention: Learning to Co-Create Your World Your Way* by Dr. Wayne Dyer, Hay House, Inc., 2004.

## Chapter Eleven Notes

1. *The Last Hours of Ancient Sunlight: The Fate of the World and What We Can Do Before It's Too Late* by Thom Hartmann, Three Rivers Press, 1999.
2. *The Prophet's Way: A Guide to Living in the Now* by Thom Hartmann, Park Street Press, 1997.
3. *The Elder Brothers* by Alan Ereira, Knopf, 1992.
4. *The Voice of the Great Spirit: Prophesies of the Hopi Indians* by Rudolph Kaiser, Shambhala Publications, Inc., 1991.
5. *World War III* by Michael Tobias, Bear & Company Publishing, 1994.
6. *Conversations with God: An Uncommon Dialogue, Book One* by Neale Donald Walsch, Hampton Roads, 1995.
7. *The Long Emergency: Surviving the Converging Catastrophes of the Twenty-First Century* by James Howard Kunstler, Atlantic Monthly Press, 2005.
8. *Conversations with God: An Uncommon Dialogue, Book Two* by Neale Donald Walsch, Hampton Roads, 1997.
9. *A Course In Miracles* by Helen Schucman and William Thetford, Foundation for Inner Peace, 1992.
10. *Science News*, September 1998.
11. *Embraced by the Light* by Betty J. Eadie, Gold Leaf Press, 1992.

12. *The Secret of the Power of Intention* by Dr. Wayne Dyer, Hay House, 2004.

## Chapter Twelve Notes

1. *In God's Truth* by Nick Bunick, Hampton Roads, 1998.
2. *The Second Coming of Christ: The Resurrection of the Christ Within You* by Paramahansa Yogananda, Self-Realization Fellowship, 2004.
3. *The Lost Teachings of Jesus, Volume One* by Mark L. Prophet and Elizabeth Claire Prophet, Summit University Press, 1986.
4. *Beyond Belief: The Secret Gospel of Thomas* by Elaine Pagels, Random House, 2003.
5. *A History of God: The 4000-Year Quest of Judaism, Christianity, and Islam* by Karen Armstrong, Alfred A. Knopf, 1993.
6. *Mind Over Matter: Conversations with the Cosmos* by K.C. Cole, Harcourt Press, 2003.
7. *The Masters and the Spiritual Path* by Mark L. Prophet and Elizabeth Claire Prophet, Summit University Press, 2001.
8. *Autobiography of a Yogi* by Paramahansa Yogananda, Self-Realization Fellowship, 1998.
9. *The Messengers: A True Story of Angelic Presence and the Return to the Age of Miracles* by Julia Ingram and G.W. Hardin, Pocket Books, 1996.
10. *A Course in Miracles* by Helen Schucman and William Thetford, Foundation for Inner Peace, 1992.
11. *Conversations with God: An Uncommon Dialogue, Book One* by Neale Donald Walsch, Hampton Roads, 1995, pages 95.
12. *The Gospel of Thomas: Annotated & Explained* by Stevan Davies, Skylight Paths Publishing, 2002.
13. *The Power of Now: A Guide to Spiritual Enlightenment* by Eckhart Tolle, Namaste Publishing, 1999.

14. *The Gnostic Gospels of Jesus: The Definitive Collection of Mystical Gospels and Secret Books about Jesus of Nazareth,* by Marvin Meyer, HarperCollins, 2005.

15. *Many Lives, Many Masters* by Brian L. Weiss, M.D., Simon & Schuster, 1988.

16. *The New Revelations: A Conversation with God* by Neale Donald Walsch, Atria Books, 2002.

17. "A Town at War," *People* Magazine, October 31, 2005.

18. *The Seat of the Soul* by Gary Zukav, Fireside, 1989.

### Chapter Thirteen Notes

1. *The Lost Years of Jesus: Documentary Evidence of Jesus' 17-year Journey to the East* by Elizabeth Clare Prophet, Summit University Press, 1984.

2. *The Second Coming of Christ: The Resurrection of the Christ Within You* by Paramahansa Yogananda, Self-Realization Fellowship, 2004.

3. *The Lost Teachings of Jesus, Volume One,* by Mark L. Prophet and Elizabeth Claire Prophet, Summit University Press, 1986.

4. *A Course in Miracles* by Helen Schucman and William Thetford, Foundation for Inner Peace, 1992.

5. *Autobiography of a Yogi* by Paramahansa Yogananda, Self-Realization Fellowship, 1998.

6. *The Gospel of Thomas: Annotated & Explained* by Stevan Davies, Skylight Paths Publishing, 2002.

7. *The Masters and the Spiritual Path* by Mark L. Prophet and Elizabeth Clare Prophet, Summit University Press, 2001.

8. *Tomorrow's God: Our Greatest Spiritual Challenge* by Neale Donald Walsch, Atria Books, 2004.

### Chapter Fourteen Notes

1. *The Masters and the Spiritual Path* by Mark L. Prophet and Elizabeth Clare Prophet, Summit University Press, 2001.

2. *The Second Coming of Christ: The Resurrection of the Christ Within You* by Paramahansa Yogananda, Self-Realization Fellowship, 2004.

3. *Tomorrow's God* by Neale Donald Walsch, Atria Books, 2004.

4. *On the Wings of Heaven: A True Story from a Messenger of Love* by G.W. Hardin and Joseph Crane, DreamSpeaker Creations, Inc., 1999.

5. *Conversations with God: An Uncommon Dialogue, Book One* by Neale Donald Walsch, Hampton Roads, 1995.

6. *In God's Truth* by Nick Bunick, Hampton Roads, 1998.

7. *The Lost Teachings of Jesus* by Mark L. Prophet and Elizabeth Clare Prophet, Summit University Press, 1986.

8. *Archangels and Ascended Masters: A Guide to Working and Healing with Divinities and Deities* by Doreen Virtue, Ph.D., Hay House, Inc., 2003, page 133.

9. *Autobiography of a Yogi* by Paramahansa Yogananda, Self-Realization Fellowship, 1998.

## Chapter Fifteen Notes

1. *Spiritual Growth: Being Your Higher Self* by Sanaya Roman, H. J. Kramer, Inc., 1989.

2. *Conversations with God: An Uncommon Dialogue, Book One* by Neale Donald Walsch, Hampton Roads, 1995.

3. *Autobiography of a Yogi* by Paramahansa Yogananda, Self-Realization Fellowship, 1998.

4. *Tomorrow's God* by Neale Donald Walsch, Atria Books, 2004.

5. *Journey of Souls: Case Studies of Life Between Lives,* by Michael Newton, Ph.D., Llewellyn Publications, Fifth Revised Edition, Seventeenth Printing, 2004.

6. *Divine Guidance: How to Have a Dialogue with God and Your Guardian Angels* by Doreen Virtue, Ph.D., St. Martin's Press, 1998.

7. *Heaven and Earth: Making the Psychic Connection* by James Van Praagh, Simon & Schuster, Inc., 2001.

8. *In God's Truth* by Nick Bunick, Hampton Roads, 1998.
9. *Conversations with God: An Uncommon Dialogue, Book Three* by Neale Donald Walsch, Hampton Roads, 1998.
10. *The Second Coming of Christ: The Resurrection of the Christ Within You* by Paramahansa Yogananda, Self-Realization Fellowship, 2004.

## Chapter Sixteen Notes

1. *Ask and It Is Given: Learning to Manifest Your Desires* by Esther and Jerry Hicks, Hay House, Inc., 2004.
2. *Heaven and Earth: Making the Psychic Connection* by James Van Praagh, Simon & Schuster, Inc., 2001.
3. *Divine Guidance: How to Have a Dialogue with God and Your Guardian Angels* by Doreen Virtue, Ph.D., St. Martin's Press, 1998.
4. *Journey of Souls: Case Studies of Life Between Lives* by Michael Newton, Ph.D., Llewellen Publishing, Fifth Revised Edition, Seventeenth Printing, 2004.
5. *Spiritual Growth: Being Your Higher Self* by Sanaya Roman, H. J. Kramer, Inc., 1989.
6. *The Messengers: A True Story of Angelic Presence and the Return to the Age of Miracles* by Julia Ingram and G.W. Hardin, Pocket Books, 1996.
7. *The Second Coming of Christ: The Resurrection of the Christ Within You* by Paramahansa Yogananda, Self-Realization Fellowship, 2004, page xxxii.
8. *The Shorter Oxford Dictionary*, Oxford University Press, 1975.
9. *The Physics of Angels: Exploring the Realm Where Science and Spirit Meet* by Mathew Fox and Rupert Sheldrake, HarperCollins, 1996.
10. *In God's Truth* by Nick Bunick, Hampton Roads, 1998.
11. *Healing with the Angels: How the Angels Can Assist You in Every Area of Your Life* by Doreen Virtue, Ph.D., Hay House, Inc., Twenty-third Printing, 2005.

12. *Archangels and Ascended Masters: A Guide to Working and Healing with Divinities and Deities* by Doreen Virtue, Ph.D., Hay House, Inc., 2003.

13. *A Reader's Journal: The Archangel Michael, His Mission and Ours* by Rudolf Steiner, Anthroposophic Press, 1994.

14. *Messages from Your Angels Oracle Cards* by Doreen Virtue, Ph.D., Hay House, Inc., 2002.

15. *Angel Numbers* by Doreen Virtue, Ph.D., and Lynnette Brown, Hay House, Inc., 2005.

16. *The Spontaneous Fulfillment of Desire: Harnessing the Infinite Power of Coincidence,* by Deepak Chopra, Three Rivers Press, 2003.

**Chapter Seventeen Notes**

1. *Tomorrow's God: Our Greatest Spiritual Challenge* by Neale Donald Walsch, Atria Books, 2004.

2. *Divine Guidance: How to Have a Dialogue with God and Your Guardian Angels* by Doreen Virtue, Ph.D., St. Martin's Press, 1998.

3. *What God Wants: A Compelling Answer to Humanity's Biggest Question* by Neale Donald Walsch, Atria Books, 2005.

4. *The Messengers: A True Story of Angelic Presence and the Return to the Age of Miracles* by Julia Ingram and G.W. Hardin, Pocket Books, 1996.

5. *The Isaiah Effect: Decoding the Lost Science of Prayer and Prophecy* by Gregg Braden, Three Rivers Press, 2002.

6. *The New Revelations: A Conversation with God* by Neale Donald Walsch, Atria Books, 2002.

7. *Conversations with God: An Uncommon Dialogue, Book One* by Neale Donald Walsch, Hampton Roads, 1995.

8. *The Purpose-Driven Life: What on Earth Am I Here For?* by Rick Warren, Zondervan, 2002.

9. *The Second Coming of Christ: The Resurrection of the Christ Within You* by Paramahansa Yogananda, Self-Realization Fellowship, 2004, page 784.

10. *Edgar Cayce on Religion and Psychic Experience* by Harmon H. Bro, Ph.D., Association for Research and Enlightenment, Inc., 1970.
11. *The Last Hours of Ancient Sunlight: The Fate of the World and What We Can Do before It Is Too Late* by Thom Hartmann, Three Rivers Press, 1999.
12. *A Course in Miracles* by Helen Schucman and William Thetford, Foundation for Inner Peace, 1992.
13. *Conversations with God: An Uncommon Dialogue, Book Three* by Neale Donald Walsch, Hampton Roads, 1998.
14. *The Gospel: Explained by the Spiritist Doctrine* by Alan Kardec, Alan Kardec Educational Society, Second Edition Revised, 2003, pages 152, 182.

## Chapter Eighteen Notes

1. *Journey of Souls: Case Studies of Life between Lives* by Michael Newton, Ph.D., Llewellyn Publications, Fifth Revised Edition, Seventeenth Printing, 2004.
2. *Destiny of Souls: New Case Studies of Life between Lives* by Michael Newton, Ph.D., Llewellyn Publications, First Edition, Fourth Printing, 2002.
3. *In God's Truth* by Nick Bunick, Hampton Roads, 1998.
4. *The Seat of the Soul* by Gary Zukav, A Fireside Book, Simon & Schuster, 1989.
5. *Conversations with God: An Uncommon Dialogue, Book two* by Neale Donald Walsch, Hampton Roads, 1997.
6. *Conversations with God: An Uncommon Dialogue, Book Three* by Neale Donald Walsch, Hampton Roads, 1998.
7. *Many Lives, Many Masters* by Brian Weiss, M.D., Simon & Schuster, Inc., 1998.
8. *Angel Medicine: How to Heal the Body Mind with the Angels* by Doreen Virtue, Hay House, Inc., Inc., 2004.
9. *Angel Numbers* by Doreen Virtue, Ph.D., and Lynnette Brown, Hay House, Inc., 2005, pages 185.
10. *Tomorrow's God: Our Greatest Spiritual Challenge* by Neale Donald Walsch, Atria Books, 2004.

## Chapter Nineteen Notes

1. *Journey of Souls: Case Studies of Life Between Lives* by Michael Newton, Ph.D., Llewellyn Publications, Fifth Revised Edition, Seventeenth Printing, 2004, pages 30.

2. *The New Revelations: A Conversation with God* by Neale Donald Walsch, Atria Books, 2002.

3. *The Gospel: Explained by the Spiritist Doctrine* by Alan Kardec, Alan Kardec Educational Society, Second Edition Revised, 2003.

4. *Home with God: In A Life That Never Ends* by Neale Donald Walsch, Atria Books, 2006.

5. *Heaven and Earth: Making the Psychic Connection* by James Van Praagh, Pocket Books, Simon & Schuster Inc., 2001.

6. *Destiny of Souls: New Case Studies of Life between Lives,* by Michael Newton, Ph.D., Llewellyn Publications, First Edition, Fourth Printing, 2002.

7. *The Second Coming of Christ: The Resurrection of the Christ Within You* by Paramahansa Yogananda, Self-Realization Fellowship, 2004.

8. *Conversations with God: An Uncommon Dialogue, Book Two* by Neale Donald Walsh, Hampton Roads, 1997.

9. *Through Time Into Healing* by Brian L. Weiss M.D., A Fireside Book, Simon & Schuster, 1992.

10. *Spirited Away,* Reader's Digest, February 2006.

11. *Life After Life: The Investigation of a Phenomenon—Survival of Bodily Death* by Raymond M. Moody, Foreword written by Elizabeth Kübler-Ross, Harper San Francisco, second edition, 2001.

12. *Reaching to Heaven: A Spiritual Journey Through Life and Death* by James Van Praagh, A Signet Book, New American Library, Penguin Putnam, Inc., 1999.

13. *Conversations with God: An Uncommon Dialogue, Book One* by Neale Donald Walsh, Hampton Roads, 1995.

## Chapter Twenty Notes

1. *The Isaiah Effect: Decoding the Lost Science of Prayer and Prophecy* by Gregg Braden, Three Rivers Press, 2000, page 132.

2. *The Power of Intention: Learning to Co-Create Your World Your Way* by Dr. Wayne W. Dyer, Hay House, Inc., 2004.

3. *The Seat of the Soul* by Gary Zukav, Fireside, 1989.

4. *Journey of Souls: Case Studies of Life Between Lives*, Llewellyn Publications, Fifth Revised Edition, Seventeenth Printing, 2004.

5. *Embraced by the Light* by Betty J. Eadie, Bantam Books, 1992.

6. *Power vs. Force: The Hidden Determinants of Human Behavior* by David R. Hawkins, M.D., Ph.D., Hay House, Inc., 1995.

7. *Conversations with God: An Uncommon Dialogue, Book One* by Neale Donald Walsch, Hampton Roads, 1995.

8. *Ask and It Is Given: Learning to Manifest Your Desires* by Jerry and Esther Hicks, Hay House, Inc., 2004, pages xxvi, 25.

9. *Conversations with God: An Uncommon Dialogue, Book Two*, by Neale Donald Walsch, Hampton Roads, 1997.

10. *Rudy*, TriStar Pictures, 1993.

11. *Healing with the Angels: How the Angels Can Assist You in Everyday Life* by Doreen Virtue, Ph.D., Hay House, Inc., 1999.

12. *The Abundance Book* by John Randolph Price, Hay House, Inc., 1987.

13. *The Secret* by Rhonda Byrne, Atria Books, 2006.

14. *Quantum Success: The Astounding Science of Wealth and Happiness* by Sandra Anne Taylor, Hay House Inc., 2006.

15. *The Eye of the I: From Which Nothing Is Hidden* by David R. Hawkins, M.D., Ph.D., Veritas Publishing, 2001.

## Chapter Twenty-One Notes

1. *The Second Coming of Christ: The Resurrection of the Christ within You* by Paramahansa Yogananda, Self-Realization Fellowship, 2004.
2. *What the Bleep Do We Know!? Discovering The Endless Possibilities for Altering Your Everyday Reality* by William Arntz, Betsy Chasse, and Mark Vincente, Health Communications, Inc., 2005.
3. *Gentile Bridges: Conversations with the Dalai Lama on the Sciences of the Mind* by Jeremy W. Hayward, Ph.D., and Francisco J. Varela, Ph.D., Shambahala Publications, Inc., 1992.
4. *The Field: The Quest for the Secret Force of the Universe* by Lynne McTaggart, HarperCollins, 2002.
5. *Limitless Mind: A Guide to Remote Viewing and Transforming of Consciousness* by Russell Targ, Forward by Jean Houston, New World Library, 2004.
6. *Tomorrow's God: Our Greatest Spiritual Challenge* by Neale Donald Walsch, Atria Books, 2004.
7. *The Self-Aware Universe: How Consciousness Creates the Material World* by Amit Goswani, Ph.D., with Richard E. Reed and Maggie Goswani, Forward by Alan Wolf, Penguin Putnam, Inc., 1995.
8. *The New Revelations: A Conversation with God* by Neale Donald Walsch, Atria Books, 2002.
9. *The Dancing Wu Li Masters: An Overview of the New Physics* by Gary Zukav, Bantam Books, 1979.
10. *The Power of Intention: Learning to Co-Create Your World Your Way* by Dr. Wayne W. Dyer, Hay House, Inc., 2004.
11. *The New Physics and Cosmology: Dialogues with the Dalai Lama,* edited by Arthur Zajonc, Oxford University Press, 2004.
12. *The Quantum Self: Human Nature and Consciousness Defined by the New Physics* by Danah Zohar, Quill/William Morrow, 1990.

13. *Twin Telepathy: The Psychic Connection* by Guy Lyon Playfair, Vega, 2003.
14. *The Undivided Universe* by David Bohm and B. Hiley, Routledge, 1993.
15. *The Isaiah Effect: Decoding the Lost Science of Prayer and Prophecy* by Gregg Braden, Three Rivers Press, 2000.
16. *The Spontaneous Fulfillment of Desire: Harnessing the Infinite Power of Coincidence* by Deepak Chopra, Three Rivers Press, 2003.
17. "The Most Secret Agent," *Readers Digest*, March 2006.
18. *Getting in the Gap: Making Conscious Contact with God Through Meditation* by Dr. Wayne W. Dyer, Hay House, Inc., 2003.
19. *The Prophet's Way: A Guide to Living in the Now* by Thom Hartmann, Park Street Press, 1997.
20. *The Hidden Messages in Water* by Masuru Emoto and David A. Thayne, Beyond Words Publishing, Inc., 2004.
21. *Original Blessing: A Primer in Creation Spirituality Presented in Four Paths, Twenty-Six Themes, and Two Questions* by Matthew Fox, Bear & Company, 1983.
22. www.yogananda-srf.org

## Chapter Twenty-Two Notes

1. *Healing the Soul of America: Reclaiming Our Voices as Spiritual Citizens* by Marianne Williamson, Touchstone, 1997.
2. *Conversations with God: An Uncommon Dialogue, Book Two* by Neale Donald Walsch, Hampton Roads, 1997.
3. *Tomorrow's God: Our Greatest Spiritual Challenge* by Neale Donald Walsch, Atria Books, 2004.
4. *The Secret* by Rhonda Byrne, Atria Books, 2006.
5. *The Prophet's Way: A Guide to Living in the Now* by Thom Hartmann, Park Street Press, 1997, 2004.
6. *Conversations with God: An Uncommon Dialogue, Book Three* by Neale Donald Walsch, Hampton Roads, 1998.

7.  *Peace Is the Way* by Deepak Chopra, Harmony Books, 2005.
8.  *On Killing: The Psychological Cost of Learning to Kill in War and Society* by Dave Grossman, Lt. Col (RET), Self-Published by Dave Grossman, 1995, 1996.
9.  *The Isaiah Effect: Decoding the Lost Science of Prayer and Prophecy* by Gregg Braden, Three Rivers Press, 2000.
10. *The Seat of the Soul* by Gary Zukav, Fireside, 1989.
11. *The Power of Intention: Learning to Co-Create Your World Your Way* by Dr. Wayne Dyer, Hay House, 2004.
12. *What Would Jefferson Do? A Return to Democracy* by Thom Hartmann, Three Rivers Press, 2004.
13. *Man's Eternal Quest: Collected Talks and Essays on Realizing God in Daily Life, Volume One*, by Paramahansa Yogananda, Self-Realization Fellowship, 1982, page 10.

### Chapter Twenty-Three Notes

1.  *The Prophet's Way: A Guide to Living in the Now* by Thom Hartmann, Park Street Press, 1997, 2004.
2.  *The Isaiah Effect: Decoding the Lost Science of Prayer and Prophecy* by Gregg Braden, Three Rivers Press, 2000.
3.  *The Last Hours of Ancient Sunlight: The Fate of the World and What We Can Do Before It's too Late* by Thom Hartmann, Three Rivers Press, 1999.
4.  *Conversations with God: An Uncommon Dialogue, Book Three* by Neale Donald Walsch, Hampton Roads, 1998.
5.  *The Long Emergency: Surviving the Converging Catastrophes of the Twenty-First Century* by James Howard Kunstler, Atlantic Monthly Press, 2005.
6.  *Tomorrow's God: Our Greatest Spiritual Challenge* by Neale Donald Walsch, Atria Books, 2004.
7.  *The Next Evolution: A Blueprint for Transforming the Planet* by Jack Reed, Community Planet Foundation, 2001.
8.  *Autobiography of a Yogi* by Paramahansa Yogananda, Self-Realization Fellowship, 1998, page 412.

9. *Archangels and Ascended Masters: A Guide to Working and Healing with Divinities and Deities* by Doreen Virtue, Ph.D., Hay House, Inc., 2003.

10. *The Power of Intention: Learning to Co-Create Your World Your Way* by Dr. Wayne Dyer, Hay House, Inc., 2004.

11. *Last Child in the Woods: Saving Our Children from Nature-Deficit Disorder* by Richard Louv, Algonquin Books, 2005.

12. *Divine Guidance: How to Have a Dialogue with God and Your Guardian Angels* by Doreen Virtue, Ph.D., St. Martin's Press, 1998.

13. *Conversations with God: An Uncommon Dialogue, Book Two* by Neale Donald Walsch, Hampton Roads, 1997, page 117.

14. *Beyond the Indigo Children: The New Children and the Coming of the Fifth World* by P.M.H. Atwater, L.H.D., Bear & Company, 2005.

15. *Indigo, Crystal, and Rainbow Children: A Guide to the New Generation of Highly Sensitive Young People* by Doreen Virtue, Ph.D., Hay House, Inc., 2005.

16. www.indigohealings.com

17. *The Care and Feeding of Indigo Children* by Doreen Virtue, Ph.D., Hay House, Inc., 2001.

18. *The New Revelations: A Conversation with God* by Neale Donald Walsch, Atria Books, 2002, page 210.

## Chapter Twenty-Four Notes

1. *Grassroots Spirituality: What It Is, Why It Is Here, Where It Is Going* by Robert Foreman, Imprint Academic, 2004.

2. *The New Revelations: A Conversation with God* by Neale Donald Walsch, Atria Books, 2002, page 210.

3. *The Power of Intention: Learning to Co-Create Your World Your Way* by Dr. Wayne Dyer, Hay House, Inc., 2004.

4. *Autobiography of a Yogi* by Paramahansa Yogananda, Self-Realization Fellowship, 1998.

5. *Man's Eternal Quest: Collected Talks and Essays on Realizing God in Daily Life, Volume I*, by Paramahansa Yogananda, Self-Realization Fellowship, 1982.

6. *Archangels and Ascended Masters: A Guide to Working and Healing with Divinities and Deities* by Doreen Virtue, Ph.D., Hay House, Inc., 2003.

7. *The Prophet's Way: A Guide to Living in the Now* by Thom Hartmann, Park Street Press, 2004.

8. *Limitless Mind: A Guide to Remote Viewing and Transforming of Consciousness* by Russell Targ, Forward by Jean Houston, New World Library, 2004.

9. *Healing with the Angels: How the Angels Can Assist You in Every Area of Your Life* by Doreen Virtue, Ph.D., Hay House, Inc., 1999.

10. *Tomorrow's God: Our Greatest Spiritual Challenge* by Neale Donald Walsch, Atria Books, 2004.

11. *The Isaiah Effect: Decoding the Lost Science of Prayer and Prophecy* by Gregg Braden, Three Rivers Press, 2000.

12. *Inspiration: Your Ultimate Calling* by Dr. Wayne Dyer, Audiobook, Hay House, Inc., 2006.

13. *"When I Get Where I'm Going"* by Brad Paisley and Dolly Parton, Time Well Wasted, Arista Nashville, 2005.

14. *"The Waiting Is the Hardest Part"* by Tom Petty & The Heartbreakers, Tom Petty & The Heartbreakers Greatest Hits, MCA Records, 1993.

15. The Eulogy of Catherine Mary Hill by Donald Rooker

# About the Author

Elizabeth Anne Hill is the founder and president of the Catherine Hill Foundation, a nonprofit organization that raises funds and awareness for at-risk, underprivileged, and homeless children in San Diego and nationwide.

Hill, who has a bachelor's degree with distinction in applied communication from San Diego State University, has worked as a Reserve Deputy for the San Diego County Sheriff's Department, a 911 Police Dispatcher for the San Diego Police Department, and a Community Service Officer with the San Diego Unified School District Police Department.

As a San Diego Hospice and Palliative Care Patient Volunteer, Hill assisted critically ill patients and their family members during the last six months of life.

She hosts her own Internet radio talk show called *Gateway 4 the Golden Age* at www.contacttalkradio.com.

Hill has written two children's books, *The Circle of Life* and *The Gift,* and is working on the third in the spiritual series for young people. Also coming soon, a follow-up book to *Twin Souls,* written after the death of her father Howard Hill, called *Soul Searching: A Story of Endings and Beginnings.* For more information about Elizabeth and her books, please visit www.gateway4thegoldenage.com.

For more information about the Catherine Hill Foundation, please visit www.catherinehillfoundation.org.